GCSE WORLD HISTORY

LONGMAN REVISE GUIDES

SERIES EDITORS:
Geoff Black and Stuart Wall

TITLES AVAILABLE:
Biology*
Business Studies*
Chemistry*
Economics*
English*
English Literature*
French
Geography
German
Information Systems*
Mathematics*
Mathematics: Higher Level*
Music
Physics*
Psychology
Religious Studies*
Science*
Sociology
Spanish
Technology*
World History

* New Editions For Key Stage 4

GCSE WORLD HISTORY

Ed Rayner and Ron Stapley

LONGMAN REVISE GUIDES

Longman

Addison Wesley Longman Limited,
Edinburgh Gate, Harlow,
Essex CM20 2JE, England
and Associated Companies throughout the world.

© Longman Group UK Limited 1988

First published 1988
Tenth impression 1996

British Library Cataloguing in publication Data

Rayner, Ed
   World History.- (Longman GCSE revise guides).
   1. History - Study and teaching 9Secondary)-
   Great Britian. 2.General Certificate of Secondary
   Education - Study guides
   I. Title II. Stapley, Ronald
   907' .6D 16.4.G7

ISBN 0-582-01578-2

Set in 10/12 Century Book Roman

Produced by Longman Singapore Publishers Pte Ltd
Printed in Singapore

CONTENTS

EDITORS' PREFACE

Longman Revise Guides are written by experienced examiners and teachers, and aim to give you the best possible foundation for success in examinations and other modes of assessment. Much has been said in recent years about declining standards and disappointing examination results. While this may be somewhat exaggerated, examiners are well aware that the performance of many candidates falls well short of their potential. The books encourage thorough study and a full understanding of the concepts involved and should be seen as course companions and study guides to be used throughout the year. Examiners are in no doubt that a structured approach in preparing for examinations and in presenting coursework can, together with hard work and diligent application, substantially improve performance.

The largely self-contained nature of each chapter gives the book a useful degree of flexibility. After starting with Chapter 1, all other chapters can be read selectively, in any order appropriate to the stage you have reached in your course. We believe that this book, and the series as a whole, will help you establish a solid platform of basic knowledge and examination technique on which to build.

Geoff Black & Stuart Wall

ACKNOWLEDGEMENTS

We are indebted to the following Examination Groups for permission to reproduce past examination questions. Whilst permission has been granted to reproduce their questions, the answers, or hints on answers are solely the responsibility of the Authors and have not been provided or approved by the Group.

University of London Examinations and Assessment Council (ULEAC)
Midland Examining Group (MEG)
Northern Examinations and Assessment Board (NEAB)
Northern Ireland Council for Curriculum, Examinations and Assessment (NICCEA)
Southern Examining Group (SEG), including the Associated Examining Board (AEB)
Welsh Joint Examination Committee (WJEC)

The illustration on p.44 is based on a map which first appeared in *A Sketchmap History of the First World War and After* by Richards, Goodson and Morris. We are indebted to Thomas Nelson and Sons Limited for allowing us to use this illustration.

Ed Rayner and Ron Stapley

THE
GCSE
IN
HISTORY

**THE ACQUIRING OF
    HISTORICAL
    KNOWLEDGE
HISTORICAL SOURCES
HISTORICAL
    INTERPRETATION
EMPATHY
COURSEWORK
ASSESSMENT
HOW TO USE
    CHAPTERS 2 TO 16
ENGLISH**

G E T T I N G   S T A R T E D

The aim of this book is to help those studying twentieth century world history for the General Certificate of Secondary Education. No book can provide you with instant success. For success you will need to devote several hours a week to concentrated study throughout the course. This book will help you to study to the best advantage, but it cannot engage in discussion with you; therefore it is important to follow the guidance of your teacher and to exchange ideas with your fellow students.

If you are a private candidate studying for the examination without the benefit of contact with fellow students – even without a teacher – you will find things even more difficult. You will have no one to measure yourself against: you will have to set your own pace and you will have only books to turn to for guidance. We have therefore written this book in the hope that it will be useful to you in your self-imposed task.

GCSE AIMS AND REQUIREMENTS

The introduction of the GCSE in l988 marked a major change in the examination system, although to some extent it reflected new approaches developed during the previous ten to fifteen years. The main features of the new system are contained in the requirements laid down by the Secondary Examinations and Assessment Council (SEAC). For history the SEAC has listed a number of nationally-agreed aims to which all syllabuses must conform. History syllabuses are required to:

➤ stimulate interest in and enthusiasm for the past;
➤ promote knowledge and understanding of the past and its links with the present;
➤ link this knowledge to the historical evidence upon which it is based;
➤ develop skill in locating, handling and understanding historical evidence and its limitations;
➤ develop understanding of cause and consequence, continuity and change, similarity and difference;
➤ appreciate the development through time of social and cultural values;
➤ provide a sound basis for further study and the pursuit of personal interest.

These aims, in fact, embody what has been the practice of the best history teachers for many years. To achieve these aims you, the student, will need to be able to develop a number of historical skills deriving from the aims. Thus the SEAC says that all GCSE candidates in history will be required:

(a) to recall a substantial amount of historical knowledge and to write about it clearly;
(b) to understand and make use of the ideas of cause and consequence, continuity and change, similarity and difference;
(c) to look at events and problems from the past in the way that those living at the time would have looked at them;
(d) to show skill in studying historical evidence by understanding and extracting information from it; interpreting and assessing it; distinguishing between fact, opinion and judgement; pointing out deficiencies in it as evidence, e.g. gaps and inconsistencies, and detecting bias; and by comparing various types of evidence and forming conclusions based upon this comparison.

How candidates can develop these skills effectively will be discussed later in this chapter, and, in relation to specific topics, in subsequent chapters. But before you can develop skills, a syllabus has to be chosen, and this is likely to be done by your teacher or your school rather than by you. Each of the boards has one or more syllabuses relating to the twentieth century, as shown in the accompanying list (Table A on page 3). This table shows the wide variety of syllabuses which are offered by the boards responsible for the GCSE history examination.

Two papers are normally required, in which you will be tested in ways that vary between the boards; but all the boards use short-answer questions, in which the required answers may be no longer than a single sentence, and essay questions, in which extended writing of several paragraphs is required. Essay questions are usually structured, i.e. divided up into two or more subsections. The SEG specifies an empathy essay, i.e. an essay requiring you to see the past as those living in it saw it. All boards require you to answer evidence-based questions, and all boards require coursework, although the percentage of the total marks allocated to coursework varies between them. Some boards accept a Paper 3 instead of own coursework from external candidates, i.e. those studying on their own and not attending any kind of educational institution. All boards have special topics with candidate choice, and do not expect you to have covered the whole of the syllabus. These special topics are called sections (ULEAC), themes (NEAB) or topics (MEG and SEG). MEG has a compulsory core section, and SEG has compulsory themes. The grid (Table B on page 4) shows how the most important twentieth-century topics are distributed between the boards.

Table of GCSE syllabuses: Table A		
ULEAC	A	Modern world history
	B	British and European history from the mid-nineteenth century
	C	British economic and social history
	D	Schools Council History Project
	Mature:	Either
		Syllabus A: World Powers in the Twentieth Century
		or:
		Industrial Society in Britain
MEG		Modern world (1914 to the present)
		British and European history (syllabus F: 1867 to the present)
		British social and economic history
		Schools Council History Project
NEAB	A	Schools Council History Project
	B	Modern world history
	C	British social and economic history since 1750
	Mature:	chiefly local history and fieldwork
SEG	1	British social and economic history since 1750
	2	World powers from 1917
	3	British history, 1485–1714
	4	British history, 1815–1983
	5	Aspects of British, European and World History, 1862–1974
	6	History of medicine
NICCEA		Modular*
WJEC		Modular*
	Mature:	Social and Industrial History of England and Wales 1760–1875

* A modular syllabus arrangement is one that is composed of 'modules' i.e. components, selections from which have to be studied for the GCSE examination. In the case of the WJEC, one of these modules has as its subject a modern world study (examined through coursework), and offers a choice between the Arab-Israeli conflict, the rise of communist China, modern Japan, superpower rivalry since 1945 and British decolonization in India and Africa.

PREPARING FOR THE EXAMINATION

Good preparation is absolutely essential to examination technique. Your preparation must be thorough in coverage, sound in depth and detail, and secure in accuracy. As the examination is skills based, the emphasis will be on analysis and judgement. But it would be a mistake to think that you can discuss and analyse history without knowing any. First you must learn what happened, and only then can you begin to tackle the basic questions of how and why it happened. No actor or musician would dare perform in public without adequate rehearsal; similarly no student can perform well in a public examination without adequate preparation. The commonest cause of examination nerves is going into the examination room knowing that you are ill-equipped to tackle the examination paper. To assist in your preparation, each of the SEAC requirements demanded of GCSE history candidates, as listed earlier in this chapter, will now be dealt with in turn.

GCSE Examination topics: Table B

Topic	ULEAC		MEG			NEAB		SEG		NICCEA	WJEC
	SCHP	Syll. A	Mod. World	Syll. F	SCHP	A	B	2	5		
First World War	❑		✓	✓			✓		✓		
Int. Relations, 1919–39	❑	✓	✓	✓	✓*	✓	✓		✓	✓*	
Int. Relations after 1945	❑	✓	✓		✓		✓	✓	✓	✓	✓
Lenin	❑	✓	✓				✓	✓	✓	✓	✓
Stalin	❑	✓	✓				✓	✓	✓	✓	✓
Hitler & Germany	❑	✓	✓	✓			✓	✓	✓	✓	✓
Mussolini	❑	✓	✓								
USA & the New Deal	❑	✓	✓				✓	✓	✓	✓	
Second World War	❑	✓	✓	✓			✓	✓	✓		
USA after 1945	❑	✓						✓	✓	✓	
Southern Africa & race	❑	✓	✓		✓		✓		✓		
China to 1949	❑	✓	✓				✓	✓		✓	✓
China after 1949	❑	✓	✓	✓		✓	✓	✓		✓	✓
Japan	❑	✓	✓	✓	✓						✓
Arab–Israel Conflict	❑	✓	✓	✓	✓	✓	✓	✓	✓	✓	✓
India	❑	✓	✓						✓		✓
South-east Asia	❑	✓	✓								
Cuba & Latin America	❑	✓	✓		✓				✓		
Decolonisation	❑	✓	✓				✓	✓	✓		✓
Western European Unity	❑	✓	✓	✓	✓	✓	✓				

* Ireland   ❑ Coursework

---

1 ▸ THE ACQUIRING OF HISTORICAL KNOWLEDGE

"Note-taking and knowledge."

When you embark upon your course, you will need a good textbook, a strong file for your notes, access to a good library and a firm commitment to study. If your teacher gives you class notes, try to learn them as soon as possible afterwards whilst the teacher's explanation is fresh in your mind. Supplement the teacher's notes with additional material from your reading. If, as is more probable, you make your own notes under guidance, develop a good note-taking technique: use headings, subheadings and abbreviations. Make sure that you list all the main points rather than developing only one or two of them in unnecessary detail. Memorable events should be listed rather than described; for example, in dealing with the circumstances of the March 1933 election in Germany, a preliminary description of the Reichstag fire would hardly be needed; an entry such as 'Reichstag fire (van der Lubbe, Nazi involvement ??)' should recall for you the salient facts, just as the question marks should remind you of the controversy concerning the extent both of van der Lubbe's and of the Nazis' involvement in the fire. If, when you revise, such a note makes no sense, then you should refresh your memory of it by looking it up in the textbook. But if you have developed a good note-taking technique, the incomprehensible note should be comparatively rare. Your notes will be the main source for the factual knowledge required in the examination. In the final run-up to the examination, you will rely heavily on your notes. Only the genius can afford to dispense with note-taking and note-learning.

You should also take care not to generate too much in the way of note material, especially not multiple accounts of the same event as presented by a number of textbooks. Remember that the more care you take in the making of your notes, the more time and trouble you will save yourself when you come to use them. If they are pencilled in an illegible scrawl they will be a distraction and an annoyance. Likewise it is no good supposing that by carrying your notes about with you tucked under your arm, you will somehow absorb them. You will have to try to learn them. Each time you go through them, you make subsequent revisions quicker and easier, until at your final revision you can get through them very rapidly indeed.

Once you have acquired a mastery of the facts, logic and reasoning can often help to prevent the making of unnecessary errors. If, for instance, you were half-convinced that the Second World War began at the time of the Munich crisis, a recollection that the first hostilities occurred in Poland might cause you to think again and to reason out that in that case the war could not have started over a crisis in Czechoslovakia.

When you have mastered a considerable body of factual historical information you will be able to develop all the historical skills required. Without historical knowledge, it would be like trying to make bricks without straw.

2 > HISTORICAL SOURCES

All the GCSE history syllabuses require study of historical sources, and the examinations include set questions based upon source material. The sources used are most often written ones: newspapers, letters, reports, diaries, etc. But there are also maps and cartoons and, from the late nineteenth century onwards, an increasingly plentiful supply of photographs. Sources that originate from the time of the event or issue with which they are linked are referred to as **_primary sources_**; often the writer will have been an eyewitness of the event he describes. Sources written at a significantly later date – and this is true of all history textbooks – are based upon these primary sources, but because they are at one remove from reality they are referred to as **_secondary sources_**. Sometimes the classification is not quite so clear-cut. For example, newspapers are contemporary secondary sources, since they are based on reports by those who may not have been eyewitnesses. All the same, they are often regarded as primary, since they do not have the benefit of hindsight and give the contemporary view of the event as it happened.

In all sourcework careful study of the source is essential: you will need to understand exactly what a written source means, and you will need to grasp the message of a cartoon. The basic skill required is to select evidence from sources, and this usually means finding the relevant evidence and expressing it accurately in your own words. Examples of this are to be found in worked evidence questions in this book.

Students will also have to compare evidence sources for reliability; remember that what a source omits can be as important for judging reliability as what a source includes. For example, if two sources deal with a riot, it will be very significant if one source states that the police were provoked by taunts and stonethrowing, whilst the other refers to the taunts and omits the stonethrowing. If there was stonethrowing, it looks from the omission as if the second source is trying to show the police action in a bad light by deliberately playing down the provocation. Or perhaps the first source invented the stonethrowing in order to bolster the excuse for police intervention.

You will also be required to recognize and identify bias or prejudice in sources: this requires practice, and can often lead to any expression of opinion being castigated as bias, but real bias should not be difficult to recognize in obvious cases. Bias arises from the deliberate or unconscious expression of some view of the author without any attempt to justify its use in the extract by reasoned argument. Take the following extract:

> The Conservatives in Britain in the years after the Second World War were concerned only to promote big business; they were not interested in the needs of the mass of the people. They paid lip-service to democracy but they did not really believe in it. Conservative politicians were cynical and unscrupulous, and their policies from 1951 to 1964 were a disaster.

This, you may think, reads like party propaganda from the conservatives' opponents. Historians should note the lack of any attempt to qualify the most sweeping of generalized condemnations; they could hardly regard this as an objective comment. If you believe the passage to be essentially true in all its details, you must none the less admit that it offers no evidence for the opinions it puts forward, relying on assertion instead of argument. Its very extremism tends to destroy the credibility of the passage.

However, bias that is more subtle can be more effective. Consider this extract:

The settlement of 1919 saddled Germany with a crippling reparations bill of £6,600,000,000, rendered her incapable of self-defence by depriving her of her air force and an effective navy and restricting her army to 100,000 men, and denied her subjects the right of self-determination, as when Alsace-Lorraine was given to France.

Here there are a number of facts: the reparations bill was £6,600,000,000, Germany did lose her air force, her army was restricted to 100,000 men, and Alsace-Lorraine was given to France. But the rest of the passage is full of opinions for none of which there is any evidence and all of which are debatable. Was the reparations bill really crippling? Was Germany's navy not effective? The implication that her subjects were denied self-determination was certainly true of Alsace-Lorraine, but it was not true of those German territories (e.g. north Schleswig) where plebiscites were in fact held. You may be asked to distinguish between fact and opinion in a passage like this, or to look for bias in it. When documents have a bias, or show bias, they are said to be biased. 'To be biased' is the equivalent verb. Students often get this wrong. The same is true of the word 'prejudice': things show prejudice or are prejudiced. Once you are able to detect bias or prejudice, you will be able to point out how it is achieved; by the choice of words or the use of insinuation, or by statements that go only part of the way towards the truth.

Evidence questions usually require the studying of more than once source. Single sources do not provide opportunities for the comparison of sources. In the cases where single sources are used, they may be used as a trigger for factual recall, and then the amount of specific evidence questioning is limited. Where sources are to be used as evidence rather than stimulus, they are usually followed by a series of subquestions which begin by identifying the evidence contained in the sources, and continue with more searching subquestions dealing with comparison of the content and the value of the sources and their reliability, and possibly leading on to an assessment of bias where it occurs.

3 ▶ HISTORICAL INTERPRETATION

GCSE requires you to demonstrate your skills.

Once you have acquired a basic mastery of what happened (i.e. the facts) you should be in a position to consider causes and consequences. Here you begin to move away from the facts into an area where ideas and arguments differ; and although you may well have lists of causes in your notes, the best way to develop the analytical skills required in this section is through the prepared essay, where arguments based on the evidence can be brought together and presented in as convincing a manner as possible. Effective essay writing will lead naturally to effective coursework, which for most boards takes the form of extended prepared essays.

CAUSE AND CONSEQUENCE

Essay writing gives scope not only for differing opinions but also for different emphasis. In a question, for example, on the causes of the Second World War, some students will argue strongly that Hitler's aggressive policies were the main cause; others will shift a substantial portion of the blame on to the western powers, their policies of appeasement and their suspicion of Russia. Excellent answers, of course, should refer to both sorts of causes, attempting to strike a balance between them; but answers of similar merit may well be different in emphasis and approach.

If you do make a list of causes to learn like facts, you should make sure that you understand them sufficiently to handle them flexibly in reply to an examination question. If you were asked to discuss the view that Hitler cannot be held solely responsible for the outbreak of the Second World War, you would find a list of memorized causes no more than a starting point for developing an effective answer to the question. You would need to analyse the relative importance of the various causes of the war if you were to make a worthwhile judgement on Hitler's responsibility for it. In this respect, history is not a science. Scientific causes conform to stated and proven physical laws, but historians' causes do not. They represent instead an analysis and an assessment based on experience. Even at GCSE level it is absurd to claim (as one candidate did) that there were seventeen causes of the Russian Revolution of March 1917; someone else might produce only eight, but those nevertheless might be more convincing than the seventeen.

Consequences, too, can be very much a matter of dispute. Some consequences may well be more important than others, and, as with causes, it is important to distinguish between those that were short term and those that were long term. A short-term consequence of the dropping of atomic bombs on Hiroshima and Nagasaki in August 1945 was undoubtedly the decision of Japan to surrender. Long-term consequences might well include the ongoing threat of a world-wide nuclear war. CND (the Campaign for Nuclear Disarmament) is an indirect consequence of that episode. The perception of these consequences depends on the historian's point of view, according to his time and place; they change as his perception changes and have no final validity. Remember, therefore, that no historical verdict is ever final, and that many of those you presently accept will be revised before you are much older. George Orwell, in his novel, Nineteen Eighty-Four, found it quite unforgivable that in the future history might be rewritten so as to bear a particular interpretation; it should be said that history is **always** being rewritten from one point of view or another. In the same way, in GCSE, the answer to the question 'Explain the importance of the German problem in international relations after 1945' must vary according to the viewpoint of the historian, and would certainly be answered differently by spokesmen from the east and the west.

CONTINUITY AND CHANGE

Historians are always interested in the ideas of change and continuity. Revolutions, such as those of 1917 in Russia, are episodes of concentrated change and are easy to identify, but change is often slower and less noticeable. Thus, social change is generally undramatic, but fairly continuous. Some might consider that the twentieth century changes in education, living standards (at least in the developed world), health and so on have been almost a revolution in themselves. These differing views about revolution show that the idea of revolution to a historian is not capable of a clear-cut definition. Like causation, it is a matter of opinion and argument.

While there is change, there is also **continuity**, and a historian will want to trace this continuity. Most modern problems have their origins in the past, and as students of the twentieth-century you will have become very much aware of this in your work. The origins of the Israel/Palestine question, as well as the problems of Northern Ireland, are deeply rooted in the past; you will be able to name many more examples. Moreover, continuity is not merely a characteristic of problem areas and trouble spots. It is true that revolution has brought fundamental alterations in Russia, but continuity rather than change is arguably more characteristic of western Europe since the First World War.

SIMILARITY AND DIFFERENCE

You will notice that the last sentence contains a comparison and emphasizes differences in the rate of change between Russia and western Europe. In GCSE, you will be expected frequently to make such comparisons – to show, for example, the similarities and differences between the aims of the victorious powers at the Peace Conference of 1919, or maybe make a comparison of the strengths and weaknesses of two opposing major powers.

BALANCED JUDGEMENTS

The ability to deal competently with all these aspects of historical interpretation is a skill which will be tested in the examination. It is important, therefore, not to see history as a sequence of isolated facts to be memorized parrot fashion. Once you move from the facts to discussion and argument it is important to make qualified and balanced judgements and not sweeping generalizations. Choose your words with care. A statement such as 'Chiang Kai-shek and his nationalists brought nothing but disaster to China' is as one-sided as the biased evidence earlier in this chapter. At least the elimination of the warlords ought to be considered on the credit side for the nationalists; and you may have the rather uneasy feeling that history tends to be on the side of the winners, so that anything of benefit that Chiang was able to do gets submerged under the more successful Mao Tse-tung (Mao Zedong). You will undoubtedly find things to say in the Nationalists' favour, even if your final verdict is one of qualified disapproval. Thus, such words as 'always', 'never' and 'entirely' are words you ought to be wary of. Things are never as clear as they look, and simple statements such as 'Hitler and Mussolini always had the same aims' or 'Russia was entirely responsible for the allied victory in 1945' show shallowness in historical thinking. You must train yourself to make more informed judgements than these.

4 ▷ EMPATHY

> 66 Empathy means a feeling for the past. 99

It has already been explained that one historical skill required of you is to see past events and problems as they appeared to people living at the time.

This skill is now generally tested in course-work rather than in the examination. Where it survives you will be asked to look at events as if they were just occurring, and your judgments will be those of contemporaries rather than historians. This means that you will need to be well-informed, because if you try to write about historical events using only your power of imagination you will display ignorance rather than empathy. However, if you merely give a factual account of events you will almost certainly be unable to capture the flavour of the period and empathy will be beyond you. Some credit will be given for accurate narrative, but only at the lowest Level. To achieve the highest Level you will be expected to show not only how people's views differed as between different groups, but particularly how differences of opinion occurred within groups. Thus, for example, while some communists might regard Hitler's coming to power in January 1933 as a disaster, other communists might regard Hitler's chances of holding on to power as so slim that the communists must benefit from his expected failure. Similarly not all American women in the 1960s supported Women's Rights Movements, nor could all British Conservatives in the 1980s be labelled as Thatcherites.

The question will determine the form of your answer; most will be open-ended, asking how 'people' reacted to specific events. But there may still be examples of role-play where you have to imagine yourself in an historical situation and possibly write as a victim or opponent of a régime, or as a journalist or observer. In any case to answer any empathy question properly you are going to need information, colour and a sympathetic feel for the past. Without information you will be unable to create an effective historical context, and your answer might well be equally applicable to several historical situations; thus your answer on how the Germans viewed Hitler's rise to power might equally apply to how Italians saw Mussolini or even how the Romans viewed the Emperor Augustus. So your historical context has to be clear, accurate and authentic. Don't spoil it with anachronisms i.e. pushing modern developments too far back in time, e.g. 'Hitler's television appearances convinced many Germans that Hitler was right' or 'Many Germans worried how Hitler would handle the problem of nuclear weapons.' Errors such as these reduce the credibility of the rest of the answer.

The examiners will be looking for a real understanding of the past and a sensible evaluation of how people regarded events as they happened. At the lowest Level you will be expected to recognise that people of the past had views of their own, as do those of the present. At the next Level you should recognise that people of the past often differed between themselves in their opinions e.g. soldiers might think differently from teachers, or industrialists from civil servants. At the highest Level you will recognise that there were differences even within groups: that not all industrialists thought the same for example about Hitler, or that not all teachers in the Italy of the 1930s had identical opinions about Mussolini. An important element of the highest Level is that opinions can change over time, so that individuals might have a very different view of things after the passage of, say, twenty years. Practice in this type of question is essential. The following example should give you an idea of what you need to do.

What would have been the feelings of the German people on the outbreak of war against France and Britain in September 1939?

The first answer knows all about empathy in theory.

Of course not all Germans would welcome war. Some would be afraid, others would see it as a possible danger to the régime, and a few might regard all war as evil. While there was a chance of success some might support it, but others might fear defeat. Some might be worried about heavy civilian and military casualties, while others would expect Germany's superiority to make large numbers of casualties unlikely. Religious people might worry about the morality of war, but most believed that just causes were unnecessary and that 'might is right'.

There is *some* merit here: certainly the candidate is aware of the need to show diverse opinions, and is confident, no doubt, of achieving Level 3. But the answer is very brief – for 25 marks it should approach an ordinary examination essay in length. And its empathy, despite some high-flown language and common sense, is very generalised. It has no context of time or place: there is nothing to indicate that it really is Germany which is being considered, and the generalisations could as well apply to 1914 as to 1939, or indeed to almost any war, ancient or modern. It is, in fact, merely a Level One answer. Now consider another effort.

Few people welcome war for its own sake. Germans who admired Hitler might well accept his judgment, but nevertheless would have some misgivings about cost, casualties and suffering. Those with long memories might well fear a re-run of the First World War with its enormous casualties, and its 'starving winter', but for others the new war would provide an opportunity for revenge for the humiliations of the First. And the welcome for war would not be confined to staunch Nazis; for some, patriotism would smother doubts about the Nazis, and Hitler would be regarded as the instrument of Germany's revenge for the 'Diktat' of 1919.

In a totalitarian state as Germany was in 1939 public disagreement with the war would not be tolerated. Thus although some of Hitler's most senior officers had private reservations about Germany's ability to fight and win a prolonged war, they took care not to say so in public, and most of Hitler's generals and commanders blindly followed his lead and encouraged his aggression. Perhaps some were shocked that cheap victories through diplomatic bluff had given way to war, but they prepared to make the best of it. So did the industrialists and businessmen. Some, particularly those in the armaments industry like the Krupps, saw war as the opportunity to expand their businesses and their influence, and others saw occupied territories as captive markets, but not all would welcome a war which, like all wars, would disrupt trade, and might for the first time lead to a destructive aerial war which could flatten factories and warehouses.

It might be expected that Hitler's opponents would welcome a war as the best chance of removing him. But Hitler's political position was likely to be strengthened by war, particularly a successful one, and those close to him were paralysed into doing nothing. Communists were confused by the Molotov-Ribbentrop Pact; some hoped that a disastrous war would weaken Hitler and liberate them from the concentration camps, while others hoped that the war and Hitler's friendship with Stalin would mean the end of his persecution of them. Similarly the Jews might have been alarmed by a war which would give Hitler an excuse to harass them further, but the needs of war might bring Hitler to need some influential Jews with business expertise, and a single-minded concentration on the war could mean that the policies begun with the Nuremburg Laws and the Crystal Night might be halted. Religious leaders too would be divided; there were those who felt that the nation would turn more strongly to religion in war and that therefore Hitler would tone down his persecution of independently-minded churches and their leaders, but some felt that war would give Hitler the excuse, opportunity and political strength to confront the churches more effectively.

The suddenness and unexpectedness of the war did not lead to the wild and foolish celebrations of 1914; in Berlin news of the war was greeted in stunned silence. There was a mood of resigned acceptance, but beneath it was a wide range of opinion from the fevered enthusiasm of Hitler's devotees, to the gloomy pessimism of those who had believed almost to the last that war over Poland would be avoided.

This answer is longer, and it has a number of points of historical reference: the 'Diktat, Krupps, Molotov-Ribbentrop Pact, concentration camps, Nuremburg Laws, Crystal Night, and so on. At least no-one could doubt that this is about Germany and the outbreak of war in 1939, although you may well be able to think of useful points which have not been included. You should always have a suitable list of relevant historical references to identify your empathy essay in place and time. Note that in both answers the candidate has tried to show divisions of opinion within groups, but whereas in the first answer it was a sterile generalised exercise, in the second the candidate explores in some relevant depth the likely diversity of opinion.

Role-play exercise such as 'Imagine you were ...' provide difficulties for those wishing to demonstrate the highest Level of empathy through diversity of opinion. But these difficulties are not insuperable provided you remember to introduce in your essay other people of varying views. More likely are questions beginning 'What would have been the feelings (or experiences) of ...' such as the one above. In twentieth-century work you could be given a picture or photograph and be asked to think yourself into the situation of those shown in it. For example a photograph showing refugees, or riot victims, may be accompanied by a request to explain their reactions to their experiences, and here information and colour will be required. Such a request should not be hard to follow if you are well-informed, understand the circumstances of the photograph and can bring to your answer a combination of **historical knowledge** and **historical imagination**, the last two being key requirements in all empathetic work. But to use a photograph properly you have to study it carefully and make use of the details in it. A quick glance is simply not enough.

5 > COURSEWORK

All worthwhile history courses involve coursework: the writing of notes and essays, the preparation of projects, and so on. But for the GCSE, certain items of coursework will be required as part of the examination, and will carry a minimum of 20 per cent of the mark allocation for the whole examination. In practice, 30 per cent of the marks are allocated to coursework by the majority of boards.

As your teacher will have chosen the syllabus and will be monitoring and assessing your coursework, you will need to rely heavily on your teacher's guidance in choosing and planning the work that you are going to do. (For external candidates who have no teacher, there is at least one board (LEAG) which sets a Paper 3 (for external candidates) instead of the coursework requirement. This paper tests the same things as would have been tested in coursework). The coursework required will normally be in written form, but this may be supplemented by drawings, photographs or even tape recordings. Maps, diaries, letters and extracts from imaginary newspapers could be asked for, or ordinary essay work might be acceptable. But most written work will need to be at least 1,200 words long and in some cases 2,000 words or even more, so that it will normally take the form of an extended essay or a project investigating some historical issue or problem. It is not intended to offer you the opportunity to write a rather lengthy narrative.

At least two pieces of coursework are asked for by most boards – sometimes three or four. The problems to be looked at in the coursework may be chosen from a specific list, but for some boards the teacher or the student selects their own coursework titles from a broad subject area. In this case you should have a specific problem to investigate, e.g. 'The effect of the Abyssinian crisis on international relations, 1935–6'; rather than just 'Abyssinia, 1935–6', which could well lead to narrative rather than problem analysis. Your choice will in part be determined by what interests you, but be particularly careful, if you have a local history option, not to become involved in the over-specialized and not to descend to the trivial. 'The history of Bloggsville Football Club, 1887–1987' may well end up with more football in it than history, and candidates may be disappointed to realize that several pages of photographs of successive Bloggsville teams will not impress the examiners. It may well be that a study of unemployment in Bloggsville, 1919–39, or even the contribution to the town's development made by the local brickworks would be a better subject to choose. It should be noted that it is not so much the subject matter of a project that makes it unsuitable as the manner in which it is investigated; in other words, the development of a local football club is a quite legitimate area of study, provided that it is studied in a historical way and the result is not just a scrapbook. Certainly local issues will give you a variety of primary sources to choose from; major national and international issues will necessarily be researched from secondary sources.

Remember to discuss your choice of topic with your teacher, together with the sources you propose to consult. But do not expect precise guidance on what to write or how to write it; the coursework will have to be certified as your own work, and not that of anyone else – particularly not your teacher. It follows, too, that coursework should not be lifted in chunks straight from your sources. There is little value in copying out paragraphs from a variety of books, stitching them together with a few phrases of introduction and then pretending that the work is all your own. You will be expected to show skills of arrangement, analysis, assessment and argument, and you cannot do this if you simply copy what others have written. So your various pieces of coursework will need to be well planned in advance; they will need to be of approximately the length asked for (too wide a variation could cost you marks); above all, they will need to identify and investigate a clear historical problem and offer conclusions.

Depending on the nature of the coursework set, a useful coursework method would be:

1. Choose and discuss the title.
2. Collect a list of resources.
3. Unless the theme is too specialized, read up the subject matter in your textbook(s) and make notes, so that you have a general idea of the topic.
4. In the light of the material studied, refine and modify your title so that you can be sure that your information will enable you to deal adequately with it.
5. Start tracking your selected subject in the sources; make notes and cross-references, and select a limited number of useful short extracts for quotation (if this is appropriate).
6. Select suitable visual and statistical material, if available and if relevant.
7. Read through the collected material, plan its arrangement (including visual, etc.) so as best to assist the development of your argument, and check that your conclusions are sensible.
8. Prepare a synopsis, write your first rough draft and develop your final polished version from it.

Don't neglect or postpone your coursework.

Remember that the work should be neatly presented, with a table of contents, and that it should be written in as effective a style as you can manage. As your coursework carries a considerable proportion of the marks, you must expect to spend a lot of time on it. Remember that inadequately prepared or hastily written coursework could well cost you a grade or even two grades in the final assessment.

6   ASSESSMENT

As your grade will depend on what the examiners think of your examination work and what your teacher thinks of your coursework, it is useful for you to have a clear idea of what these people expect of you.

Any written answer developed beyond a word or so will be rewarded at different *levels* according to the skills content of the answer. Let us take an example. It is from a specimen paper issued by SEG.

From 1928 major changes in industry and agriculture took place in the Soviet Union.
(a) Why were these changes introduced?
(b) How successful were these changes in the years up to 1941?
(c) How were the ordinary people of the Soviet Union affected by these changes?

This is a three-part essay marked out of 30. Let us take the middle part. Here you are obviously being asked to exercise the skills of historical analysis and judgement and not merely to give an account of the changes, assuming that the degree of their success is self-evident. If all you can do is to give a narrative account of the changes, the mark scheme assesses you at Level 1.

Level 1: Narrative answers largely describe the Five Year Plan and collectivization. 1 mark to 4 marks.

So no matter how good your description, 4 is the maximum here. If you can manage to include some kind of assessment, however, you rise to Level 2.

Level 2: Answers include a judgement supported by generalized statements such as 'Production levels rose; therefore there was success'. 5 marks to 8 marks.

Level 3: You need to provide an answer which includes 'judgement based on more specific knowledge, and additionally drawing distinctions between different branches of the economy, recognizing that results and thus success were uneven'. This level scores 9 to 12 marks.

All marking, including that of coursework, is to be done using these levels of achievement, within which marks will vary according to the amount of historical content. Your grade will be determined by the level you have reached in:

(a) acquiring historical knowledge and being able to communicate it;

(b) finding and making use of historical evidence, and

(c) developing and making use of powers of historical reasoning (i.e. using knowledge and evidence to analyse and make judgements about historical problems).

Demonstrated ability in all these will earn you a high grade.

But even if you are well equipped with historical skills, marks can be lost through carelessness; and if your skills are not as strong as they might be marks could be saved by careful attention during the examination to the following points:

> 💬 **Don't forget these important points in your work.** 💬

1. Make sure that you know what you have to do: how many questions you have to answer, which parts are compulsory and which are the areas covering the sections for which you have been specifically prepared.

2. Read the questions, and the source material, carefully; make sure that you have properly understood the question before attempting it, that you know how many parts it contains if it is structured and what is required in each part.

3. If the marks for a part question are given on the examination paper, use that as a guide for how much you should write; if only 1 mark is on offer, a one-word, or one phrase, answer (at most a sentence) will be adequate. Anything more would be a waste of time. But if 8 marks are offered, you would need to make a number of points, and should develop the answer into a useful paragraph to have any chance of reaching the maximum.

4. Plan your time carefully; do not waste time on one question so that you run out of time on another. Make sure that you answer all the questions required within the examination time limit.

5. If you must make plans for the longer answers, make them brief, merely listing the points you intend to develop in your answer. If a plan is as long as the answer it is prepared for, you will find either that your answers are too brief or that you run out of time before you have finished. Answers which merely turn out to be a fair copy of the plan are an instance of culpable repetitiveness.

6. Remember that it is unlikely that questions will call for a lengthy narrative; skills other than merely recalling historical information are almost certain to be required, and the more skills you manage effectively to demonstrate, the higher your grade is likely to be.

One final word of warning: do not be hoodwinked by such phrases as 'merely recalling historical information' into thinking that this is the least important attribute for a student of GCSE history. No one should attempt to dismiss 'historical information' too lightly. It is the essential material on which all the historical skills are practised.

This book is not intended as a substitute for a textbook. You should use it to supplement the work done, either in class under teacher guidance or through your own reading of books. It will help you develop your skill in writing by practising the questions – of whatever type – and will provide you with a useful basis for revising for the GCSE examination itself.

Each chapter is arranged in a similar way. The section 'Historical Developments' gives you a brief summary of the main narrative points of the topic to be studied, and also tackles issues of cause and consequence. You should explore and develop the points given here in conjunction with notes and textbooks. The section 'Ideas and principles' will deal with ideas, problems and vocabulary associated with the topic. 'Applied materials' will list useful sources, from which you should be able to make a selection according to what is available in your school or public library.

'Examination questions' gives a selection of questions of different types, the answers to some of which are discussed in outline. From time to time we present a 'Tutor's answer', to give you an idea of what a complete answer should look like. The chapters provide brief suggestions for further work if you feel that you need more practice in mastering the material and further developing the necessary skills. Each chapter ends with a student's answer to a typical question. Examiner comments are made on the answer to give you an idea of what the examiner is looking for.

8 ENGLISH

From 1992 candidates may earn an additional 5% in their *examination work* for their English skills. For these additional marks account will be taken of spelling, punctuation, correct use of grammar and appropriate use of vocabulary. In practice only candidates with very weak English will fail to score, but the English marks could be vital for those at or around the grade boundaries.

THE
FIRST
WORLD WAR

**THE COMING OF THE
    WAR.
THE BEGINNING OF
    THE WAR
THE WAR FRONTS
THE NEW TECHNOLOGY**

GETTING STARTED

Historians have long been anxious to establish what caused the
First World War. This is partly because people felt that the horrors of the war were so ghastly that every effort should be made
to prevent such a catastrophe happening again and that if only
the causes could be known they could be prevented in future. It
is also partly because Clause 231 of the Versailles Treaty at the
end of the war, which pronounced Germany guilty of causing it,
came to be widely regarded as unjust and led historians to point
out other guilty parties. Another reason was the unexpectedness
of the war. The final crisis came so abruptly in the summer of
1914 that the outbreak was a great shock to nations which had
witnessed no major conflict for more than a century. Though
there had been crises before, diplomacy had always resolved
them; but suddenly a conflict broke out whose results were
made all the more appalling by the vast technological progress
made by most modern industrial states. What brought about
this struggle?

HISTORICAL DEVELOPMENTS

1 > THE COMING OF THE WAR

NATIONALISM

First, there was nationalism. This was the struggle of people of the same language group to form independent states, and it had been the main motive force of European history in the preceding century. Italy and Germany had both made their appearance on the map, unbalancing the delicate equilibrium existing there. In particular, the growth of German power in the years before the war seemed specially menacing to Britain, whose world position had not so far been seriously rivalled. At the same time many other features of the map of Europe at this time were quite unfamiliar. Poland did not exist. Other nation groups, like Danish and Czech ones, for example, still lived partly or completely under alien rule. Instead of modern nation states the map was dominated by four autocratic empires: Russia, Turkey, Germany and Austria-Hungary. This latter was a disintegrating patchwork of some fifteen nations under the rule of the Emperor Franz Josef. Indeed, the final crisis leading to the war was a quarrel between this empire and its ambitious neighbour, Serbia.

ECONOMIC RIVALRY

Secondly, there was economic rivalry. Both Britain and Germany were expanding industrial nations, the former well established, the latter speedily emerging as its major competitor. Germany's recent industrialization, and the rapid advance of its coal, steel, ship-building and chemical industries, seemed likely to lead to the expulsion of Britain from its export markets, and perhaps even to Germany rivalling British sales in its own market, unprotected by tariffs. Certainly fear was one emotion which Britain felt; but both governments seemed to be aware that their trade rivalry might easily turn into armed conflict.

COLONIAL RIVALRY

Linked with this, there was also colonial rivalry. Britain and France already had extensive overseas empires, and even small powers such as Belgium and Portugal held colonial territories. Germany was a newcomer to the scene, but a successful one. The Germans were driven partly by the prevailing economic wisdom that colonies were needed to provide industrial states with raw materials and markets, and partly by the desire for prestige – as Kaiser Wilhelm put it, a 'place in the sun'. And whatever their direct involvement in any area, the Germans always seemed ready to exploit colonial quarrels, say in Egypt or Morocco, in order to gain some advantage over their rivals.

COMPETITION IN ARMAMENTS

Competition in armaments was bound to be the result. Industrial resources and technological know-how were increasingly being turned to warlike purposes. European nations, with the exception of Britain, had adopted conscription to enlarge their armies, and the three largest armies were those of France and Germany, with nearly 600,000 men each, and Russia, with nearly 900,000. Naval rivalries also swiftly developed, especially between Britain and Germany. The Germans began to launch warships with bigger guns, more penetrating shells and thicker steel plate to protect them from attack; Britain responded with a series of mammoth Dreadnoughts, and introduced a 'two-power' naval standard. Of course, the arms race cannot be said to be itself a cause of war, any more than red spots on the skin can be said to be the cause of measles, but it certainly meant that when the conflict arrived it would be a particularly devastating one.

THE ALLIANCE SYSTEM

Don't mistake symptoms for causes.

The alliance system was also a symptom rather than a cause of conflict. Germany, Austria and Italy formed the Triple Alliance, whilst France and Russia formed the Dual Alliance; though Britain was not committed to either of them, it had links with both the members of the Dual Alliance, with whom it was linked in the form of a Triple Entente. What began as a quarrel between Austria and Serbia soon spread, with Germany supporting Austria and Russia supporting Serbia; this in turn led to a German declaration of war on Russia and then on France, and finally, on the German invasion of Belgium, to a British declaration of war on Germany. The alliance system was like a rope, linking together the members of a climbing team to guarantee their safety, but one which, when a climber fell, dragged the whole team to destruction. The existence of the system meant that when war came it could not be localized, but would necessarily develop into a wider war.

THE NATIONALIST POPULAR PRESS

The rival newspapers of the nationalist popular press were also the battleground of a phantom war of words before the real war broke out. Improved technical processes now meant that it was possible to run off millions of copies from the 'gutter press', which exploited and often inflamed the prejudices of a half-educated public. Of course, newspaper bosses had no responsibility for the conduct of affairs; they were interested only in selling their wares, and often their biased reporting made bad affairs worse. No sane government wanted war, but where a relatively free press existed governments sometimes found difficulty in allaying their people's fears.

RESPONSIBILITY FOR THE WAR

European socialists were not only looking at newspaper tycoons when they blamed the capitalist system for being responsible for the conflict; they believed it was capitalism itself which was to blame. Within each country they saw a conspiracy between capitalist bosses to underpay and exploit their workers in the interest of their profits; whilst in colonial empires they saw an even more widespread conspiracy between the colonialists to exploit the native people for the benefit of the colonialists. Rival capitalist states, too, were engaged in a cannibalistic struggle between themselves; whilst struggling for markets and materials in an ever-shrinking world they were investing much of their treasure in armaments and pouring out the blood of their young men in order to preserve their dividends. Marxists regarded imperialism, capitalism and war as being inseparably joined as different aspects of the same evil.

Whatever the underlying truth of this analysis, no government in practice ever admitted it. But the element of national selfishness was undoubtedly present. France feared German expansion and sought revenge for earlier humiliation. Britain pursued a selfish policy, using the friendship of others but unwilling to pledge firm support in return. Russian and Austrian policies were expansionist and their designs were diametrically opposed in the Balkans, both powers behaving recklessly in view of their internal decay. Italy hesitated in order to be sure of jumping on the winning bandwagon. In this context it seems harsh to lay the entire blame for the war on Germany. The Kaiser's strategic aims were largely defensive. He felt he had to preserve the existence of his only reliable ally, Austria; he needed to break free of the encircling powers of the Triple Entente; he dreaded a war on two fronts; and he wanted to resist the military pressure of the French and the commercial competition of the British. Granted the likelihood of eventual war, he felt he had to prepare for it by creating a mighty army and navy and vesting great authority in the soldiers of his general staff. In the end it was not the Kaiser or the Chancellor who had the final word; it was the chief of the general staff, von Moltke. But to the extent that the Kaiser decided to settle his problems militarily instead of by diplomacy, it could be said that it was Germany that touched off the war.

2 ▶ THE BEGINNING OF THE WAR

The immediate cause of Britain's entry into the war was the German invasion of Belgium at the beginning of August 1914. The assassination of the Austrian Archduke Franz Ferdinand at Sarajevo at the end of June had led to a 'loaded pause' of almost exactly a month, during which the Austrian government had been busy se-

❝ You need to start with the assassination of the Archduke...and the invasion of Belgium ❞

curing the support of Germany before sending at the end of July a ferocious ultimatum to Serbia, the acceptance of which would have virtually ended any pretence of independence on the part of its government. Its very submissive response was treated as a rejection by Austria, bent on a preventive war, and by the end of the month the Germans and the Austrians were at war with the Serbs, the Russians and the French. It seems likely that Britain would have gone to war even if the German armies had not put into operation the Schlieffen Plan, made some years earlier by the German chief of staff and based on the assumption that the most efficient way of defeating France was by sweeping through Belgium; but as things stood, by violating the Treaty of London, made in 1839 to preserve Belgian neutrality, the Germans provided Britain with a ready excuse for war.

Working to a detailed timetable, German forces poured through Belgium in a race towards the French frontier. Their troop trains even carried portable wooden platforms stacked on their roofs so that when the men alighted from their carriages between stations they would not get their boots dirty and would look smart as they marched through captured villages. Arms, supplies and materials were organized with meticulous precision to keep up with the army's advance. Belgian forces resisted the Geman onslaught to the best of their ability, helped by as many French as could be sent to their aid and by the 160,000 men of the BEF on the Continent – the men referred to by the Kaiser as 'this contemptible little army'. At Mons the British and the Gemans clashed for the first time. The rifle fire of the highly-trained British troops was so rapid and accurate that the Germans thought they had run into nests of machine guns and fell back. There were massed cavalry charges for about the last time in modern warfare. But the efficient organization and sheer weight of numbers of the Germans meant that the struggle could have only one outcome. Liège resisted for a week before it fell; Namur, Brussels, Malines and Louvain followed swiftly afterwards, although Antwerp held out until the autumn. Belgium was overrun, but its gallant resistance had been of great value in providing a breathing space for the allies to get their troops into position; without this, Paris might easily have fallen in the first few weeks of the war.

The French and British fell back slowly to the Marne, fighting stubbornly and suffering heavy casualties. By September the Germans had pressed on even further, crossing the Petit Morin and the Grand Morin. The pounding of artillery could be heard in Paris, only twenty miles to the west. The German commander, von Kluck, swung his right inwards to overwhelm the allies' left wing, but in doing so exposed his flank to counter-attack. The governor of Paris, Galliéni, sent troops up to the front in taxicabs, causing more German soldiers to be diverted to meet them and thus creating a hole in the advancing German front through which the British and the French counter-attacked. German lines of communication were already dangerously overstretched, their high command nervous and their timetable breaking down; so German commanders thought it prudent to withdraw and regroup themselves safely behind the Aisne front. There both sides proceeded to dig themselves in, and from these positions the fighting front shifted very little for the duration of the war.

As the two sides ground to a halt in Champagne, a front line was created which consisted of an elaborate pattern of zig-zag trenches and dug-outs. In efforts to outflank each other the two armies extended their lines in a northerly direction, abandoning these tactics only when they reached the sea near Nieuport. German attempts to capture the Channel ports failed, and though fierce battles were fought along the Yser and on the higher ground at Ypres the lines of communication between the French and their British allies remained secure for the duration of the war.

3 ▷ THE WAR FRONTS

THE WESTERN FRONT

The lines of trenches from the Swiss border to the Channel coast were the main theatre of the conflict for four years, in which boredom, frostbite and typhus--carrying lice competed to destroy human life and morale, and where enormously costly set battles such as the Somme (1916) and Passchendaele (1917) occasionally erupted. The trenches were subjected to unendurable artillery bombardments. In the two days before the battle of Messines Ridge, for example, in 1917, no fewer than 4.25 million shells were directed against a short stretch of front, and the continuous roar of more than twenty shells per second not only unhinged the minds of the soldiers experiencing the bombardment but also utterly wiped out the landscape and turned it into a desolation. Though the latest in military technology was employed, neither side really secured permanent penetration of the other's lines, and any temporary advance was purchased only at the cost of thousands of lives. So inhuman was the suffering that by 1917 the French army was on the verge of mutiny, and for much of the last year of the war the main burden of western defence fell on the British, and later the Americans.

THE EASTERN FRONT

German plans here were based on two assumptions: the first that the western allies could be swiftly defeated in a *blitzkrieg* that would be over in about six weeks, and the second that Russian mobilization would be so slow that a token force in the east could hold them at bay for long enough to end the war in the west and so avoid a war on the two fronts. Both ideas failed to work out in practice. In the west, Belgian resistance prevented a crushing blow being dealt to the French; whilst in the east, Russian troops took the field much more quickly than was ever thought possible. By the end of August they had completely overrun East Prussia. They were, however, badly trained and under-equipped, and the Germans dealt them crushing blows, first at Tannenberg in 1914 and then at the Masurian Lakes in 1915. The Austrians, however, fared less well. Their troops were crushed at the battle of Lemberg, and shortly afterwards they were forced to evacuate almost the whole of Galicia. All the same, during 1915, Russian forces failed to achieve success. German troops from the north and Austrian troops from the south threatened to bite off what was sometimes called the 'Polish tongue', a vast salient of territory which stretched westwards from Russian-occupied Warsaw and came within 180 miles of Berlin. Losing nearly a half million men in their efforts to stave off this pincer movement, Russian commanders eventually withdrew from Poland altogether, shortening their lines almost due north–south from Riga to the Romanian frontier. After this, the Russians never seriously threatened the central powers again, though in 1916 and 1917 they sacrificed many men in their efforts to do so.

THE BALKAN FRONT

In 1915, in a desperate effort to end the stalemate on the western front, the allied high command launched an attack against the Turks, who had recently joined the central powers. This attack was on the Straits connecting the Mediterranean with the Black Sea, on which the Turkish capital, Constantinople, stood. The immediate cause of the Gallipoli campaign was a Russian request for a diversionary attack to relieve the pressure on them on the eastern front. But the attack had much wider possibilities: it would knock out Turkey, secure the Middle East, aid Serbia, persuade Romania to join the war on the allied side, relieve the pressure on France and break the virtual blockade of Russia, thus making it possible to supply them with much needed armaments. Unfortunately the Turks were given plenty of advance notice by preliminary naval bombardments, and the invasion, when it came, was a costly failure. Turkish snipers and machine-gunners inflicted dreadful casualties on troops who had little cover, and in hand-to-hand fighting they inflicted gruesome injuries on British and Commonwealth troops by means of their serrated bayonets. Even where they fell back they sometimes poisoned the wells so as to deprive the invaders of safe water supplies. In the end British, Australian and New Zealand troops were compelled to withdraw, the last men leaving a hastily-chalked notice on equipment they had abandoned on the beach: 'You can keep your bloody peninsula.' Meanwhile Serbia was invaded by Austria and taken in the rear by the Bulgarians, and the Serbs were cut off from Salonika where British and French forces had been sent to their assistance. Some of the forces returning from Gallipoli also went to Salonika in December, but during the rest of the war they achieved very little and were not able to prevent both Serbia and Romania being overwhelmed by the central powers. There were over a quarter of a million men in the Salonika bridgehead by 1918, and the German commander of the besieging forces was able to boast that it was 'the biggest prisoner-of-war camp in Europe'.

THE ITALIAN FRONT

In 1915 Italy joined the war – but on the side of the Triple Entente. It was encouraged to take this decision by agreement with the allies in the Pact of London to the effect that at the end of the war they should be given those Italian-speaking areas which most nationalists felt were rightly theirs. The Italians had some successes in Venetia in the foothills of the Alps during 1916, launching almost a dozen offensives in this area in about eighteen months. However, in October 1917 the Austrians, reinforced by six German divisions, overwhelmed the Italians at Caporetto and the Italian position collapsed. Italy lost about 250,000 men in the battle and there were about a further 400,000 desertions. The Italian rout ended only with the arrival of British and French reinforcements along the line of the River Piave, a few miles north of Venice. It was not until the battle of Vittorio Veneto in 1918 that the Italians were able to recapture the initiative and start to drive out the invading Austrians.

THE WAR IN THE MIDDLE EAST

> **The World War also took place outside Europe.**

At the end of 1914, British and Indian troops landed at Basra on the Persian Gulf and began to advance up the Tigris against Turkish forces defending Mesopotamia. They inflicted several defeats on the Turks at Kurna, Shaiba and Amara, and came almost within sight of Baghdad. Lack of supplies and ammunition forced them back to Kut where in 1916 they found themselves besieged for five months and were eventually forced to surrender. Another expedition, however, retook Kut in 1917 and by 1918 pressed on to take Baghdad and Mosul.

Other Turkish forces in 1915 invaded Egypt, nominally a Turkish territory, and soon were threatening the Suez Canal, a vital lifeline in imperial communications. Repelling these attacks, British and Commonwealth forces were able by 1916 to cross the desert and invade Palestine. Though initially defeated at Gaza, the British won an impressive series of victories over their enemies, defeating the Turks at Beersheba, Askelon and Jaffa, occupying Jerusalem and smashing the Turkish forces completely at Megiddo in September 1918. By the end of the war Britain had occupied virtually the whole of Palestine, Syria and Mesopotamia.

THE WAR IN THE COLONIES

In the course of the war, cut off from communication with Germany because of their loss of control of the seas, German colonies fell into the hands of Britain, France and their various allies.

In Africa, Togoland fell to the allies by the end of 1914, and Cameroon was divided up between the British and the French in February 1916. In German South-West Africa, Generals Botha and Smuts, though hampered by a rebellion of Boer nationalists, overcame German resistance and occupied Windhoek in 1915. German South-East Africa offered tougher resistance. The German commander, Lettow-Vorbeck, at the head of a force including fewer than 300 Europeans, fought gallantly, and when the cruiser *Königsberg* was forced to take refuge in the Rufiji River and was sunk there, he even employed its heavy guns in the defence of the colony. At the end of 1918 he was driven into Portuguese territory, but he returned to invade Northern Rhodesia, where he captured Kasama. At the end of the war he was still fighting, boasting with some exaggeration that he had engaged the attention of no fewer than 137 generals and over 300,000 troops and had still survived.

In the Pacific, New Zealand occupied Samoa; Australia New Guinea and the Bismarck Archipelago; the Japanese the Marshall Islands; and a joint Anglo-Japanese force Kaiochow, all before the end of 1914. By 1915 nothing remained of the German empire in the Far East and Pacific area.

THE WAR AT SEA

Supported by naval forces of the French and later the Italians, the British navy in the early days of the war faced formidable tasks. Not only did it have to protect the British Isles from invasion; it had also to secure the flow of foodstuffs and supplies into Britain for the war effort, and to keep open the lines of communication between Britain and the many theatres of war in which allied troops were engaged. It also had to maintain a blockade of Germany and the central powers, so that they could not obtain military supplies from neutrals, and it had to sweep German naval raiders from the seas. In the first few weeks of the war, three German cruisers were sunk off Willhelmshaven in the Heligoland Bight, then the *Karlsruhe* after a brief career in the West Indies, the *Kaiser Wilhelm der Grosse* off West Africa, and the *Königsberg*, operating near Zanzibar. A more important victory came with the sinking of the *Gneisenau*, *Scharnhorst*, *Leipzig* and *Nuremberg* in the battle of the Falkland Islands in December 1914 – only the *Dresden* escaped, and she was later tracked down and sunk in 1915. Meanwhile much damage was being done by the cruiser *Emden*, but she was pursued across the Indian Ocean and back and eventually sunk off the Cocos Islands by the Australian cruiser *Sydney*.

In 1914 and 1915 a number of English east coast towns, such as Scarborough, were bombarded by German ships, but after the battle of the Dogger Bank these attacks ceased. The greatest naval battle of the war did not occur until May 1916, when the German high seas fleet encountered the British grand fleet under Admiral Jellicoe at Jutland and 145 British ships and 110 German ships were engaged. Both sides suffered grievous losses, British losses in men and ships being marginally greater than German; but it was the German fleet which broke off the action and retired to port, not to re-emerge until it sailed into captivity at the end of the war. Nevertheless, even in harbour German battleships tied down British vessels which could have been more profitably employed elsewhere, especially in keeping open the western approaches.

In the meantime, Germany began to rely increasingly on submarines to attack allied shipping. Already they had torpedoed the transatlantic liner *Lusitania* off the south coast of Ireland in May 1915, and soon they were inflicting heavy losses on the merchant marine. By 1917 the submarine menace entered its gravest phase when Germany declared 'unrestricted' submarine warfare, sinking unarmed merchantmen, hospital ships and anything afloat whether belligerent or neutral, without surfacing to give warning. British losses rose from 181 ships (300,000 tons) in January 1917 to 423 ships (850,000 tons) in April. Britain hovered on the brink of total defeat. But in the nick of time the adoption of the convoy system and other preventive measures such as hydrophones and depth-charges enabled the supply ships to survive. By the end of the year, 99 per cent of the merchant ships and their destroyer escorts were getting through. By 1918, the Dover patrol was culling U-boats fairly successfully, and successful attacks also took place on the German U-boat pens at Zeebrugge and Ostend. Perhaps more decisively, the submarine campaign led to the intervention of the USA in the war and the timely strengthening of the allied side.

THE HOME FRONT

❝Effects of the war in Britain❞

This war was perhaps the first 'total' war ever experienced in Britain, with large civilian populations being caught up in it either directly or indirectly. After coastal bombardments came aerial attacks, first by Zeppelins and later by airplanes. For the British people this was a new experience, and though fewer than 4,000 casualties were inflicted, the effects at first were frightening. Generally, however, the British submitted good-humouredly enough to encroachments on their liberties that would not have been acceptable at other times. The Defence of the Realm Act, abbreviated to its affectionate acronym DORA, enacted a mass of restrictions and regulations, such as the internment of suspected spies without trial and the imposition of stiff prison sentences for food hoarding and profiteering. Trade union activities were also curbed. Industrial output was largely converted to warlike purposes, and the output of steel, armaments and ships was stepped up. The burden of taxation was greatly increased, and government borrowing rose sharply. Prices also went up, especially of foodstuffs, and housewives stood for hours in queues to buy even such basic commodities as bread and potatoes. The manufacture of luxuries almost ceased, and even such things as coal were rationed for domestic use. By the end of 1916 a massive scheme was brought into being for food rationing, and in this year also, breaking with long tradition, military conscription was introduced for those between the ages of 18 and 41. In the last year of the war this latter age was raised to 51.

A great many social changes were also taking place in the country. Handicapped by an acute shortage of skilled labour, unions acquiesced in the 'dilution' of labour, i.e. they permitted skilled jobs to be performed by less skilled operatives; and in the interests of national survival they even agreed to abandon the strike weapon. Women increasingly came to play a part in the nation's life, driving trams, delivering letters, working on the land and even working in armaments factories as well as serving as nurses at the front. Their style of clothing changed, and they began to wear trousers. It was not now unusual to see them smoking or visiting pubs. Even so, the consumption of alcohol as a whole diminished, and the statistics of drunkenness sharply declined.

Politically Britain was governed by a coalition government composed of both Liberal and Conservative ministers, united first under H.H. Asquith and from the end of 1916 under Lloyd George. As the war progressed a deep sense of moral purpose and determination emerged, and the country began to look forward to better times in future. An Education Act was passed in 1918, and women for the first time were given the vote. It was hoped that the end of the war would usher in the dawning of a new world.

4 THE NEW TECHNOLOGY

War is sometimes said to be the catalyst of economic change, speeding up processes which have already begun. Certainly the First World War was a scientific war in a quite unprecedented way. Traditional forms of combat – the manoeuvring of cavalry on open ground and the use of highly-trained riflemen responding to their orders with almost parade-ground precision – seemed now to be things of the past, and a new style of fighting and movement took over. Motor vehicles were used for transporting men and materials; armoured cars and even armoured trains were introduced. At Cambrai in 1916 the tank – perhaps the only certain way to breach the enemy's lines – made its appearance for the first time. Other new weapons also made their appearance: flame-throwers, more accurate machine guns and poison gases such as chlorine and phosgene. Barbed wire, used rather more than ten years earlier during the Boer War, was also used in deadly entanglements to protect the line of the trenches and to discourage attacks across No Man's Land between the trenches.

At sea there were many new developments. Great engineering skill and precision went into providing ever more accurate naval artillery, to culminate in great guns which could fling shells of 16-in diameter upwards of 16 miles with deadly precision, and also a variety of smaller weapons which were nevertheless equally effective in their own way. Armoured plate up to 6 or 9 inches thick was used to protect these 'ironclads', increasing their weight enormously and causing them to wallow in the water. Because of torpedoes aimed below the water line, it was necessary to armour the ships even lower down their hulls, and in the end battleships became floating steel coffins for their crews. Smaller vessels were perfected to deal with other dangers: corvettes, mine layers and sweepers, frigates and Q-boats (disguised merchantmen with a deck-gun to use against attacking U-boats). Explosive mines were laid over wide areas of sea to bar the access of shipping through forbidden waters. Depth-charges and hydrophones were perfected to use against U-boats, and with the introduction of the convoy system lightly armed destroyers capable of moving at very high speeds were developed to deal with the U-boat menace.

In the air, too, technology made great strides. At first the lighter-than-air dirigible, the Zeppelin, moving almost noiselessly by night, was used for reconnaissance and aerial attack, but it proved to be too vulnerable to searchlights and anti-aircraft guns; later, piston driven propeller planes were developed both as fighter and bomber aircraft. Fighters were equipped with machine guns on the engine cowling synchronized to fire between the blades as the propeller turned. Bomber crew at first simply heaved the bombs over the side of the cockpit when they were over the target, but later they were provided with quite intricate launching equipment.

Similar improvements were made during the war in medicine and surgery in order to deal with the massive casualties involved in the new forms of warfare. The effects of these, happily, were to save lives rather than to take them, but even so the deaths and injuries far outstripped anything seen before in history. Medical and surgical services were heavily overloaded and the suffering was enormous. One of the reasons why men were so determined that no war should ever recur in the future was the memory of this hideous pain.

IDEAS AND PRINCIPLES

CAPITALISM

An economic system based on the private ownership of property, including land and industry, and operating on the profit motive. Individuals control their own money and possessions (capital), and employ them in such a way as to increase them and make them richer than other people. Theoretically the whole system is based on equal opportunity and on free enterprise and competition.

CENTRAL POWERS

At the time of the First World War these were the allies in central Europe: Germany, Austria-Hungary and Italy. They were supported at first by a number of smaller powers, such as Romania. In practice, when the war started, Italy and later Romania joined the allied side.

COALITION GOVERNMENT

A parliamentary government in which more than one party is joined to form a government. This may occur where no single party has an overall majority in parliament (a 'hung' parliament) or in the event of a national emergency such as a war, when unusual unanimity is required.

ENTENTE

A diplomatic arrangement rather less formal than an outright alliance, in which powers are pledged to mutual agreement and support. The word derives from a French word which means 'understanding'.

GUTTER PRESS

This is composed of cheap sensationalist newspapers for the lower end of the popular market. The expression is a term of abuse applied by those advocating a more responsible approach by the press.

TOTAL WAR

A war fought in many theatres and employing a wide variety of weapons, often of a very lethal character and indiscriminate in their effects; a war, furthermore, involving all the efforts of the populations of the states involved, and going some way towards obliterating the distinction between combatant and non-combatant.

'TWO-POWER' STANDARD

A phrase used at the time of the First World War to describe British naval policy, i.e. the British government's insistence that the strength of the British navy should be as great as that of its two most powerful neighbours combined. Since British resources were incapable of keeping pace with German or US resources, let alone a combination of the two, the importance of this concept was to a large extent propagandist.

ULTIMATUM

A list of final terms, a last offer or demand. Usually applied to the final requirement made by one government of another before a declaration of war.

APPLIED MATERIALS

Texts

S.R. Gibbons and P. Morican, *World War One*, Longman, 1965.

R. Musman, *The First World War*, Chatto & Windus, 1968

Roger Parkinson, *Origins of World War One*, Wayland Documentary, 1970

Fiona Reynoldson, *First World War (Books 1 & 2)*, Heinemann, 1987

R.R. Sellman, *The First World War*, Methuen, 1961

A.J.P. Taylor, *The First World War*, Penguin, 1967.

Jack Watson, *European History, 1815–1941 (Units 17 & 18)*, Murray (Success Series), 1981

Empathy

J. Simkin, *Life in the Trenches*, Spartacus (Voices from the Past Series), 1986.

Audio-visual

Audio Learning (slide packs),
Origins of the First World War, EM/1250/12.
First World War – Combatants and their Arms, EM/1251/12.
First World War – Civilians and Morale, HA/1252/12.
France During the First World War, 39/A3/10.
Audio Learning,
The First World War, HM0005
AVP History,
The First World War, 1914–18, Audio Cassette 940/1–9
The First World War, Slide/Filmstrip 781–6

EXAMINATION QUESTIONS

The Origins Of The First World War
Source A

Note to the cabinet from the Prime Minister, Lord Salisbury, in May 1901.

'The British Government cannot undertake to declare war, for any purpose, unless it is a purpose of which the people of this country would approve. . . I do not see how we could invite nations to rely upon our help in a struggle which must be formidable, where we have no means whatever of knowing what may be the attitude of our people in circumstances which cannot be foreseen.'

Source B

Extract from an interview with Kaiser Wilhelm II published in the *Daily Telegraph*, 28 October 1908.

'You English are like mad bulls; you see red everywhere! What on earth has come over you, that you should heap on us such suspicion? What can I do more? I have always stood forth as the friend of England...'

Source C

From a speech made in the German Reichstag, November 1911.
'Now we know where our enemy stands. Like a flash of lightning in the night, these events have shown the German people where its enemy is...when the hour of decision comes we are prepared for sacrifices, both of blood and of treasure.'

Source D

Lenin in 1911.
'A war with Austria would be a splendid thing for the revolution. But the chances are small that Franz Josef and Nicholas will give us such a treat.'
British diplomat in July 1914.
'I have my doubts as to whether Austria will take any action of a serious character and I expect the storm will blow over.'
Franz Josef in July 1914.
'How can we wage war if they all jump on us, especially Russia?'

Source E

The cartoon 'A chain of friendship', published in the *Brooklyn Eagle*, July 1914.

Source F

Telegram from Nicholas II of Russia to George V of England, sent on 2 August 1914.
'Ever since the presentation of the Austrian ultimatum at Belgrade, Russia has devoted all her efforts to some peaceful solution of the questions raised by Austria's action. The effect of this action would have been to upset the balance of power in the Balkans which is of such vital interest to my Empire. Every proposal put forward was rejected by Germany and Austria...'

1. (a) Which event had brought about the 'Austrian ultimatum at Belgrade' referred to in Source F? (1 mark)
   (b) Explain briefly how the situation shown in Source E had come about in the twenty years before 1914. (4 marks)
2. (a) Explain why Russia was so concerned about 'Austria's action' (Source F). (4 marks)
   (b) What caused the German outbursts in Sources B and C? (4 marks)
3. Sources A and E show that a considerable change took place in British foreign policy between 1901 and 1914.
   (a) Using Sources A and E explain what this change in policy was. (2 marks)
   (b) Using any of these sources, and your own knowledge, explain why this change in policy took place. (4 marks)
4. How do Sources D, E and F help to explain Austria's part in the coming of European war in 1914? (5 marks)

5.   'Nobody really wanted war in 1914'. How useful are these sources in helping you to decide whether this statement is true or not? (6 marks)

(TOTAL 30 marks) (MEG)

OUTLINE ANSWERS

It is not unusual in this examination to have a number of short extracts and other sources used as the basis for a question; in this example, the question takes up about 45 minutes and comprises half an examination paper. It is essential, therefore, to study the sources closely before embarking on your answers.

QUESTION 1

You will observe that only 1 mark is awarded for the answer to 1 (a), and that a very brief answer will suffice – though you are obviously expected to know that Belgrade is the capital of Serbia, if you are to make any sense out of the question. Part 1 (b) is given rather greater weighting. When you examine the cartoon, you will see that it refers to the various links in the alliance system, and asks for an explanation of how these links came about in the twenty years before 1914. Some knowledge of the Franco–Russian alliance and the two ententes will be expected, but detailed information about developments before 1894 will not be required.

QUESTION 2

Question 2 (a) enquires into Russia's reasons for supporting Serbia in the Balkans and for being concerned about Austria's ambitions in this area. You will note that the document refers to a 'peaceful solution', but since it originates from the Tsar such a stance is only to be expected. 2 (b) refers to two documents, B and C, and asks for explanations of German indignation. It should be noted that both relate to earlier crises – the first the Austrian annexation of Bosnia in 1908, and the second the Agadir crisis of 1911 – furthermore, both of them are very public pronouncements, the first in a newspaper, the second in the German Parliament, and have more than half an eye on their propaganda impact; hence they may be expected to lack some of the cool logic of more official diplomatic documents.

QUESTION 3

Question 3 seeks to contrast the situation of Britain in 1901, the last year of its 'splendid isolation', with 1914, when it was a member of the Triple Entente. Part (a) asks for an indication of the nature of this change from isolation to involvement, and scores 2 marks; (b) invites an explanation of the change, for 4 marks. It is worth noting that any of the sources may be employed to give this explanation, and that answers are not limited to the sources but may contain information recalled from your own knowledge.

QUESTION 4

Question 4, for 5 marks, requires reference to each of Sources D, E and F. The extracts from Lenin, the Emperor Franz Josef and the British diplomat in D show that Austria and Russia are on opposite sides, that the Austrians have a sense of being the victims of an international conspiracy, and that at least one responsible British figure at the time of the final crisis did not take the likely effects of the Archduke's assassination too seriously. The cartoon 'A chain of friendship' in E illustrates Austria's position in the alliance system, threatening Serbia and in turn being threatened by Russia. Source F presupposes a more detailed knowledge of the Austrian ultimatum, and some knowledge of Austria's (and Germany's) rejection of the Serbian response. If your answer does not refer to all these sources, you cannot expect to get the full quota of marks.

QUESTION 5

All six sources should be used in Question 5 in your attempt to show whether the quotation – 'Nobody really wanted war in 1914' – is true or not. There seems to be little evidence that anyone, except possibly Lenin, actually wanted war, though no one except the British diplomat seems to have been taken by surprise by its outbreak. Far from wanting a war, both the Austrian Emperor and the Russian Tsar adopt an attitude of 'more in sorrow than in anger'. It must be remembered, however, that this evidence is very limited, and there may be masses of other evidence that is much more conclusive than this seems to be.

SUGGESTIONS FOR FURTHER WORK

1. Write two news reports of the assassination at Sarajevo in June 1914, as they might have appeared a) in an Austrian newspaper and b) in a Serbian newspaper.
2. Use an atlas to reconstruct the last voyage of the cruiser *Emden*, sailing to the Mariana Islands from Kaiochow, then to Madras and Pondicherry, to Diego Garcia and finally to the Cocos Islands. Calculate the mileage of such a voyage, and suggest reasons why this mileage is probably an underestimate.
3. Collect photographs and other illustrations of aircraft and warships taking part in the First World War, and list some of the differences between these and their modern equivalents.
4. Construct and label maps of the campaigns of the First World War on (a) the Russian front and (b) the Italian front. Which of these fronts involved the greater degree of movement, and why?
5. Find out what you can about the career and importance of Colonel T.E. Lawrence at the time of the First World War.
6. As a soldier involved in the fighting at the third battle of Ypres (1917), write a letter home to the mother of one of your friends killed in the course of the battle, explaining how he died and offering your sympathy on his death.
7. Find out what you can about the War Poets, and read some of the poems of Edmund Blunden, Siegfried Sassoon and Wilfred Owen. How do you explain the fact that they sometimes seem to hate their own leaders worse than their German foes?

STUDENT'S ANSWER – EXAMINER'S COMMENTS

Question

How reliable would you regard the following sources of evidence if you were preparing a report on life in the trenches on the Western Front?
(a) poems written by soldiers who were there;
(b) photographs;
(c) accounts given by soldiers on the front line.

(MEG) (4 + 4 + 4)

> **Much of the information on Brooke is about his life (i.e. biography) rather than about his writings on the war. Even then much of it is wrong, e.g. he died of blood poisoning on the Greek islands, not in action on the Western Front.**

(a) Rupert Brook was educated at Cambridge and lived in the Old Vicarage Grantchester. When war came he was among the first to volenteer and went to the western front to prove his manhood but he was killed by a German sniper bullet in the first battel of Ypres in 1915. He wrote many famous patriotic poetry and there were others who were also there like Siegfried Sassoon and Wilfred Blunt and T.S. Elliott who later wrote 'Murder in the Cathedral'. All these were very much effected by the war, especially if they had received white feathers from their admirers.

> **The impression that Brooke was one of a company of soldier-poets is quite inaccurate, especially in the case of T.S. Eliot. Wilfred Blunt was not even a poet!**

> **The whole of this response is broadly irrelevant and would not score much at all. NOTE that the question is about the reliability of the evidence found in the war poets' writings.**

> **This answer should be more critical of the staging, editing and doctoring of photographic evidence. It would score less than half the marks available.**

(b) The camera was a British invention and primative early cameras was often used for taking photographs on the western front. These give a lot of evidence about life in the trenches and what the soldiers eat and wear and the dangers to which they were exposed, cameras canott lie and so the evidence they gave is good evidence and tells us how brutal the Hun were.

> **This is a good point and will score well: soldiers were often reluctant to tell their families the whole truth, and in any case military censorship discouraged this.**

(c) Soldiers at the front spent a lot of time writing letters to keep in touch with their families and sweethearts at home, so they produce a lot of evidence about conditions in the trenches. They wish to spare the feelings of their loved ones and so do not always tell the truth about what they saw and keep a stiff upper lip especially if there is carnage and bloodeshed in their lives. Conditions was often so bad they wished to 'get a Blity one' so that they can return home e.g. a bad wound that would get them invalidded out. Also what the soldiers write is often bias. This is because they know that if they write the truth it will be cencored.

> **'Is bias' is a very common mistake . Learn to say 'shows bias' or 'is biased'. You should also try to avoid many of the mistakes in spelling and grammar present in this answer.**

> **NOTE that 4 marks are available for parts (a), (b) and (c) of this answer. The answers offered here are rather weak and often miss the point of the question.**

GETTING STARTED

In November 1918 Germany had agreed to an armistice. There were some German generals and politicians who thought that the war could be renewed if peace talks went badly, but Germany was in no position to fight again. Germany's fate therefore depended on the Paris discussions, from which she was excluded. She could expect little mercy from France, whose leader, 'Tiger' Clemenceau, was determined to make Germany pay for the enormous suffering France had endured since 1914. Lloyd George, the British Prime Minister, talked tough to the British people in order to retain public support at home, but at Versailles he was more inclined to take a moderate course. Orlando of Italy had little interest in punishing Germany, but much interest in getting all he could for his country. Perhaps only Wilson, the United States' President, wanted a fair treaty, based on his own notions of justice as set out in his fourteen points. It was not surprising that what emerged was a series of compromises in which Wilson's points were the ideal, but in which practical solutions were often preferred.

**HOW GERMANY AND
AUSTRIA WERE
DEALT WITH
HOW BULGARIA AND
TURKEY WERE
DEALT WITH
THE LEAGUE OF
NATIONS
INTERNATIONAL
PEACE IN THE
1920S**

HISTORICAL DEVELOPMENTS

The Germans learnt their fate at Versailles, where the German delegates signed under protest in June 1919; the Austrian delegates accepted the Allied terms at St Germain three months later. Political uncertainty in Hungary delayed the Treaty of Trianon until 1920. All three treaties took on board President Wilson's concern to draw frontiers along national lines, taking the wishes of local populations into account. This was the so-called principle of self-determination, and the treaty--makers adopted the idea of local plebiscites to help determine the fate of disputed territories. Unfortunately the treaties were not very consistent: the plebiscites held in 1920–21 led to German losses of territory in Northern Schleswig, Upper Silesia, part of East Prussia and Eupen and Malmédy, but no plebiscite was risked in Alsace and Lorraine which were returned to France, nor were plebiscites held in much of the territory taken from Germany to form part of Poland's western provinces. Again, in the St Germain treaty no plebiscite was held in those parts of the Tyrol given to Italy, the Sudeten Germans were refused one, and the ban on any proposed union between Germany and Austria seemed to conflict with the principle of nationality. Moreover, the Treaty of Versailles did not apply the principle of self-determination in respect of Germany's colonies, for it was still believed that overseas territories required European or white government and administration. Germany lost all her colonies, and these were entrusted as mandates to the various victorious powers. Britain and France shared out the German colonies in central Africa, while South Africa acquired the mandate of German South-West Africa. In the Pacific, Germany's scattered small islands were granted to Australia and New Zealand, and even to Japan. The mandatory powers were to hold the territories in trust for the League of Nations and were to report to the League on how they carried out their responsibilities. Self-determination was eventually intended for these former colonies, the timing depending on their stage of development, but for the former German colonies, at any rate, independence seemed a long way off.

DISARMAMENT

Now that Germany had lost all her colonies there was no real need for her to possess a great fleet, and the continued existence of her army posed a potential threat to the victorious allies. So, although Germany was to be disarmed partly as a punishment and partly because her armaments were no longer necessary, it was the aim of the allies to make German disarmament the prelude to world disarmament. The Versailles treaty compelled Germany to remove all troops and fortifications from her territories to the west of the Rhine, and from land 32 miles in depth to the east of the Rhine. This local disarmament was called demilitarization. In addition an allied army of occupation was to control the Rhineland and several bridgeheads over the Rhine for fifteen years. The French had hoped to detach the Rhineland from Germany altogether, but were obliged to make concessions. They did, however, secure the important coal-producing area of the Saar; even though the area had a predominantly German population it was to be placed under international administration for fifteen years, which meant that it was effectively under French control. French security was further strengthened by the reduction of the German army to 100,000 men, with conscription banned. Germany lost her airforce entirely, and her fleet was restricted to six second-class battleships and a few smaller vessels necessary to protect her sea-lanes and coast. Germany was not allowed to retain or build any submarines. The Treaties of St Germain and Trianon imposed similar disarmament restrictions, leaving Austria and Hungary with small armies but without air forces and with virtually no navies.

1 ▷ HOW GERMANY AND AUSTRIA WERE DEALT WITH

'WAR-GUILT'

The 'war-guilt' clause, imposed on Germany at Versailles, was generally taken to imply that Germany alone was responsible for starting the war. The clause seems to have been thought necessary as the basis for the compensation the allies were seeking for their enormous war losses. The allies insisted in principle that Germany should pay, partly by the trial of German war criminals (e.g. the Kaiser), though most of them in fact were never brought to trial, and partly by imposing on Germany the total allied war costs. This demand for reparations was not settled at Versailles but detailed demands were entrusted to a reparations commission. In the meantime Germany was to pay one thousand million pounds on account. Not until 1921 was the sum Germany had to pay fixed at £6,600,000,000.

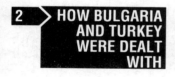

Germany didn't like being given the blame...or having to accept a dictated peace.

Germany was not allowed to haggle with the allies over the details of the Versailles treaty. German delegates may well have felt aggrieved about losses of territory, particularly those containing German populations. And they criticized the disarmament and Rhineland arrangements as leaving Germany defenceless. But above all they strongly objected to the unhistorical implication (in the war-guilt clause) that Germany alone was responsible for the war, and they could assert with some justice that signing the treaty was giving a blank cheque to the reparations commission because Germany was signing an agreement to pay a sum as yet unspecified. Threatened with the renewal of hostilities, the German delegates had no choice but to sign the treaty in the Great Hall of Mirrors at Versailles where France had been humiliated in 1871. There was, however, no major protest from the Austrian empire: it had fallen apart. The Treaties of St Germain and Trianon were respectively treaties with a separate Austria and separate Hungary, from which Czechoslovakia had already been created and from which Yugoslavia had in part already broken away. The Italians gained the South Tyrol, Trentino and Istria from Austria, Romania gained Transylvania from Hungary and Galicia was restored to Poland. Both countries accepted responsibility for reparations, but none was ever paid.

2 ▷ HOW BULGARIA AND TURKEY WERE DEALT WITH

Bulgaria's main loss, by the Treaty of Neuilly, was western Thrace, which was given to Greece. Bulgaria had thus lost its outlet to the Aegean Sea and to the Mediterranean. The Treaty of Sèvres emphasized the fact that the Ottoman empire had lost the loyalty of many of its subject peoples. Arabia became independent, Turkey lost Syria as a mandate to France, and Palestine, Transjordan and Iraq as mandates to Britain. Turkey gave up all claim to Cyprus, which the British had held since 1878. Italy gained the Dodecanese Islands in the Aegean, including Rhodes, and Greece gained eastern Thrace. But by placing the Straits under international control and allowing the Greeks a foothold in Asia Minor, the allies appeared to threaten Turkish independence. Mustapha Kemal overthrew the Sultan and expelled the Greeks from Asia Minor in 1922. By the Treaty of Lausanne in 1923 the Treaty of Sèvres was modified: the Greeks accepted their loss both of eastern Thrace and their territory in Asia Minor, control of the Straits was restored to Turkey, and the Turks accepted the loss of their Asian and African territories outside Asia Minor. The first major modification to the Paris Peace Settlement had taken place. Already some Germans, of whom the still comparatively obscure Hitler was one, looked to the Turkish example as a precedent and hoped that Germany would not be long in following it.

3 ▷ THE LEAGUE OF NATIONS

The Covenant (or constitution) of the League of Nations was the first clause in all the peace treaties. It represented the aim of the allies to ensure the maintenance of peace in the future. It was the creation of the victorious allied powers, and in every case it was part of the dictated peace imposed upon the losers of the war. It might, perhaps, have been better not to have associated the League of Nations with the Paris settlement. As it was, the League was often seen and criticized as the instrument of the victorious powers with whose interests it was closely identified.

Nations free from war.....and peace organised .

The League of Nations was originally to be confined to the allied powers and thirteen neutrals, but it actually started life with forty two members. Each of these states had one vote in the Assembly of the League, and a two-thirds majority was necessary for the admission of new members. Thus the defeated powers were excluded at first from membership, but by 1923 Austria, Bulgaria and Hungary had joined, and there seemed no reason why a sincerely repentant Germany should not eventually gain sufficient votes to secure entry. The Assembly controlled the League's budget and supervised the various activities of the league. Decisions in the assembly had to be unanimous, however, and this weakened the capacity of the assembly for decisive action.

The Assembly met annually, but the Council of the League met at least four times a year and at extra times if there was a crisis. The four victorious powers had automatic seats on the Council, but the USA had refused to join. The Council was also to have four members elected by the Assembly and by 1926 this number had grown to nine. The Council was expected to deal quickly with disputes as they arose, but again council decisions had to be unanimous, while the Council's power to enforce its decisions was limited. Although the League could raise an army by asking its members to contribute troops, this might have proved difficult to work in practice. In fact this provision of the Covenant was never used. The League tended to hope that its orders would be obeyed, even by non-members, and that economic sanctions (trade restrictions) on offending countries would be a sufficient deterrent against aggression. It was assumed that threats to peace would come from the smaller powers; the great powers could effectively block any moves to deal with their own threats to peace.

The League was serviced by a large staff of civil servants, who formed the secretariat. Despite chronic shortage of funds, the secretariat supervised the work of the agencies of the League of Nations throughout the world. Much of this work did not seem newsworthy and went largely unrecognized at the time. The International Labour Organization did much good work in improving working conditions and trade union rights, particularly in countries which had not yet achieved democratic government. The Health Agency tackled epidemics and provided help in both prevention and cure. Special committees dealt with drugs and refugees. There was a special commission for disarmament which worked hard but without much success, and a special commission for minorities which had partial success in dealing with problems of national minorities arising out of the peace treaties. The mandates commission kept a close eye on the way in which the new owners treated the former German colonies. A permanent Court of Justice at The Hague dealt with legal disputes (not political ones) between two or more states, provided that all parties agreed in advance to accept the court's ruling.

4 ▷ INTERNATIONAL PEACE IN THE 1920S

The achievements of the League of Nations in the medical and social field were considerable but received little publicity, although the Norwegian explorer Fridtjof Nansen managed to hit the headlines with his valuable work for refugees. But the success of the league would be measured not by its social achievements but by how far it succeeded in its principal aim, the maintenance of international peace. The absence of the USA was a grave handicap, and so was that of Russia, which had been left to fend for itself by a peace conference which ignored it. Although the 1920s was a decade of relative optimism, the League's early efforts had rather mixed results. Although Poland was a founder member of the League, Poland not only went to war with Russia in 1920 – a defiance of League principles – but also seized Vilna from Lithuania and refused to give it up. In 1923 Mussolini sought revenge against Greece by bombarding and occupying the island of Corfu. It was the Conference of Ambassadors rather than the League which settled both the Vilna and Corfu disputes. It was even less likely that the League could deal with the French and Belgians who occupied the Ruhr in January 1923: League pressure and world opinion failed to prevent the French from remaining in occupation for two years.

❝The limited successes of the 1920s.❞

The League's great success in these early years was in settling the dispute between Sweden and Finland. The Aaland Islands in the Baltic were claimed by both countries, and it is to Sweden's credit that in 1921 it accepted the League's award of the islands to Finland. The League also settled a number of minor disputes between neighbouring states in Central and South America. An attack by Greece upon Bulgaria led to League intervention and the Greeks were compelled to withdraw. Turkey, although not yet a member of the League, accepted League arbitration in a dispute with Britain over Mosul in 1926.

These successes, although limited, gave cause for hope that the League's growing stature and experience would give it the muscle to handle major issues, especially as there was in the 1920s a considerable international effort to make peace permanent. The Washington Naval Agreement of 1921 effected a cut-back in the naval programmes of Britain, the USA and Japan. The Geneva Protocol of 1924 wanted to enforce arbitration in international disputes, but Britain refused to accept it. But Britain did sign the Locarno treaties of 1925 in which Germany's western frontiers were guaranteed, and Germany accepted the demilitarization of the Rhineland. Germany was admitted to the League in 1926. In 1928 the spirit of the Geneva Protocol was revived in the Kellogg-Briand Pact. It secured almost universal signatures as the world's states, including the USA and the USSR, hastened to renounce war. And although the pact contained no sanctions against aggressors and permitted defensive wars, it seemed a step in the right direction. Even France seemed to have caught the right mood when French troops evacuated the Rhineland in 1930, five years earlier than necessary.

But with the 1930s the international atmosphere darkened. Japan showed the League's impotence by successfully seizing Manchuria in 1931, brushing aside the advice of the Lytton Commission. A disarmament conference which met at Geneva in 1932 spent more time talking about German rearmament than world disarmament. When Hitler's delegates arrived there in 1933 and France showed even less willingness to make concessions to Germany, Hitler took his country out of both the conference and the League. The Saar plebiscite in 1935 encouraged growing German nationalism, but did not flout the Versailles treaty. But Hitler's reoccupation of the Rhineland, itself partly inspired by the Saar vote, certainly did so. It was a bold stroke that succeeded; the League could only utter feeble protests. When German rearmament, including conscription, was condoned by an Anglo–German naval agreement providing for the construction of a German fleet, it hardly seemed worthwhile for the League to object. The League's authority was further weakened by its inability to make a stand over Abyssinia in 1935–6. The common expansionist interests of Germany and Italy pushed the League into the background and Britain and France into the foreground. The new partners, Hitler and Mussolini, intervened in the Spanish Civil War directly to assist Franco; the League's efforts to secure non-intervention merely gave the dictators a free hand there.

Appeasement (see Chapter 8) was now the key to international relations. Britain and France tried to avoid war by making concessions. When Hitler joined Germany to Austria in direct contravention of the Treaty of Versailles, the League could only protest. The League was not involved in the Munich deliberations of 1938, nor could it do more than discuss and protest at the extinction of Czechoslovakia and Albania in 1939. It could do nothing to prevent the outbreak of the Second World War in September 1939. The expulsion of Russia from the League in December 1939 as a punishment for the Russian attack on Finland was a last defiant League gesture before the League itself was swept away by the tide of events.

IDEAS AND PRINCIPLES

ARBITRATION

A means of settling disputes by which the parties to the dispute submit their case to a third and independent party. The third party acting as arbitrator gives a ruling which may be a compromise or may favour one side more than the other. It is usual for those who agree to arbitration to agree in advance to accept the verdict of the arbitrator, otherwise the arbitration will have been nothing more than time wasting.

CONFERENCE OF AMBASSADORS

A permanent conference of representatives of the four victorious powers of the First World War, i.e. Britain, France, Italy and Japan (but not the USA), established in Paris under French chairmanship. Its task was to deal with matters arising from the Paris peace treaties. In dealing with problems such as Vilna and Corfu it sometimes seemed to be exceeding its powers and trespassing on the work of the League of Nations, but the conference was not finally disbanded until 1931.

DEMILITARIZATION

The withdrawal of an area from military control, and the removal from it of certain specified armaments, or of all armaments.

MANDATE

The covenant regarded the development of the colonial peoples as one of the duties of the more advanced nations. The former colonial territories of Turkey and Germany were thus handed over to the League of Nations after 1918. The land was held 'in mandate' by powers known as 'mandatories', the word 'mandate' implying a legal right granted by a superior authority. Such territories under the United Nations were known as trust territories and were held by a trustee.

PLEBISCITE

A popular vote taken on some specific issue, usually relating to the state to which in future the area voting is to be attached. In the 1920s and 1930s plebiscites were often held for this purpose in respect of certain areas e.g. Upper Silesia, or even for whole countries e.g. Austria in 1938. The outcome of a plebiscite is often a foregone conclusion, and confirms the wishes of the authority which arranges it.

REPARATIONS

A form of international compensation, generally applied to the defeated powers after the First World War. They were intended to compensate for death and injury to armed forces and civilians, and for material destruction and damage. Attempts to add indirect losses to reparations (e.g. loss of business – as distinct from loss of goods – arising out of submarine warfare) were abandoned as impracticable. German reparations were assessed at £6,600,000,000 in 1921, but were reduced in 1924 and again in 1929. The payments ceased altogether in 1931 and Hitler made it clear in 1933 that he had no intention of resuming them. Total payments made by Germany in reparations amounted to less than two thousand million pounds most of it in goods (e.g. coal) rather than money. The USA lent Germany money to help with reparations payments, money which for the most part was never repaid.

APPLIED MATERIALS

Texts

John Chadwick, *International Organizations*, Methuen (Twentieth-Century World), 1969

S.R. Gibbons and P. Morrican, *The League of Nations and UNO*, Longman, 1970

M.L.R. Isaac, *A History of Europe, 1870–1950*, Arnold, 1963; Chapter 10

I. Richards, J.B. Goodson and J.A. Morris, *Sketchmap History of the Great War and After*, Harrap, 1965

R.N. Rundle, *International Affairs, 1890–1939*, Hodder & Stoughton, 1979; Chapter 10

John and Gwenneth Stokes, *Europe & the Modern World* (Longman) Chap. 19, 1970

Documentary

J.H. Bettey, *English Historical Documents, 1906-1939*, Routlege & Kegan Paul, 1967

R.W. Breach, *Documents and Descriptions, The World Since 1914,* Oxford, 1966

R. Brown and C. Daniels, *Twentieth-Century Europe*, Macmillan (Documents & Debates), 1983

EXAMINATION QUESTIONS

QUESTION 1

(a) In what ways can the Treaty of Versailles be said to have punished Germany?

(b) How far had the terms of the Treaty of Versailles been broken by the end of 1938?

(30 marks) (SEG)

QUESTION 2

The European powers and their membership of the League of Nations in the 1920s and 1930s.

Britain	1919 ——————————————→still a member in 1939	
France	1919 ——————————————→still a member in 1939	
Japan	1919 ————————→1933	
Italy	1919 ————————————→1935	
Germany	1926 ———→1933	
USSR	1934 ————————→still a member in 1939	

(a) What were the special circumstances of the year 1919 that led to the forming of the League of Nations?

(b) (i) Why did Germany not become a member of the league until 1926?
(ii) Why did Germany leave the league in 1933?

(c) Why did the Soviet Union not become a member until 1934?

(d) The diagram shows that Japan left the league in 1933 and Italy left in 1935. How far were the circumstances of the two events similar?

(e) Why were Britain and France so important for the success of the league?

(30 marks) (SEG)

OUTLINE ANSWERS

ANSWER 1

In 1 (a) an indiscriminate list of the terms of the Treaty of Versailles will not get you beyond Level 1. It is important to recognize that while taken as a whole the terms may be regarded as a just punishment, some terms were more concerned with justice and the righting of previous wrongs than with punishment. Thus Germany's loss of Alsace-Lorraine could be regarded as justice for France rather than punishment for Germany. And Germany's territorial losses elsewhere in Europe were less of a punishment if they resulted from plebiscites than, say, the loss of the Polish Corridor, where a plebiscite might well have given a German majority. It is worth considering also whether the enforced German disarmament was intended as punishment or whether it was intended as the first step towards achieving permanent peace in accordance with the principles of Wilson's fourteen points. It may be difficult to see Germany's loss of her colonies as anything less than punishment, but reparations from the allied viewpoint were regarded as compensation: had they wished to punish Germany financially they would have imposed an indemnity.

Again, in 1 (b) a narrative approach would not score highly. The question asks 'How far' and it would be useful to suggest that the changes in the 1920s were modifications of the treaty rather than breaches, particularly with regard to reparations. The territorial provisions and disarmament provisions remained virtually intact throughout the 1920s. The coming to power of Hitler resulted in a series of breaches, all of which should be referred back to the treaty; i.e. Rhineland, rearmament, *Anschluss*. Remember that the Sudetenland issue is not relevant to Versailles. As the question asks 'How far', it should be pointed out that many of the territorial provisions of the treaty – territories lost to Poland, France, Belgium and Denmark – remained intact in 1938, and that the former German colonies remained as mandates, although reparations had been abandoned.

ANSWER 2

In 2 (a) the creation of the league should be linked with the First World War and the Paris settlement, as well as the determination to create the framework in which peace could be constructed on a permanent basis. In 2 (b) (i) Germany's original exclusion as a defeated power was followed by the repeated efforts of a co-operative Germany to secure admission, despite obstruction by countries such as Brazil and Spain which delayed Germany's entry longer than that of most defeated powers. In 2 (b) (ii) the withdrawal of Germany will relate to Hitler's rise to power and the failure of disarmament. The Soviet exclusion in 2 (c) is partly the result of world hostility to Bolshevism but also to the partially self-inflicted isolationism of Soviet Russia. In 2 (d) elementary answers will see the common element in the aggression of the two powers, and may develop it further by pointing out that the League reaction to the aggressions differed, and that the Italians, while following the Japanese lead, had an even weaker case in Abyssinia than did the Japanese in Manchuria. To say in 2 (e) that Britain and France were major powers and were permanent members of the Council takes the answer part way, but the absence of the USA and the nature of the League membership gave the League a strong European flavour, and in the 1930s the duty of holding the line against the dictators inevitably fell to Britain and France.

SUGGESTIONS FOR FURTHER WORK

1. List the territorial changes made in Europe by the peace treaties of 1919–20, and check them against a map of Europe.
2. As German delegate at Versailles, list your objections to the Versailles terms offered by the Allies. Give the Allied reply to these objections.
3. Make a detailed study of the work of one or more of the following: the Commission for Minorities; the Mandates Commission; the Health Agency; the International Labour Organization; the Special Committee for Refugees.
4. Write a report for a newspaper of a public debate which took place in 1920, in which a heated argument arose over the aims and likely effectiveness of the League of Nations. A public debate on the same subject took place fifteen years later. Write a report for your newspaper on this debate, highlighting the differences between this debate and the one held fifteen years earlier.

STUDENT'S ANSWER – EXAMINER'S COMMENT

Question

Write an editorial for a German newspaper in June 1919 on the subject of the Versailles peace terms.

A good first paragraph.

The Diktat reference is a bit early, this was invented in the 1920's and was made into an everyday word by Hitler.

Reparations were not fixed in 1919. The actual sum was only decided in 1921.

The second paragraph is merely a list of terms and contains no commentary on the terms listed.

Good spelling in much of the work. But technical terms such as armistice, plebiscite, Alsace and Lorraine could have been practised <u>before</u> the exam..

The final two paragraphs show 'empathy', i.e. seeing events as they appeared to people at the time..

So now we know the worst. All the Allied terms have been presented, not to be negotiated, but to be accepted without being changed. Allied armies are ready to enter Germany if the terms are rejected, and the British navy is only too ready to renew the blockade and starve the German people into giving in. No wonder many people are calling it a Diktat.

Germany is to lose Alsase and Loraine. The Rhineland is to have no military at all, the army is to be reduced to 100,000 men, there is to be no German airforce, and the navy is to lost most of its fighting ships. £6,600,000,000 has to be repaid and plebisites are to be held in some areas to decide whether they are to cease to be part of Germany.

When germany asked for an armistise it was assumed that the basis of the armistise would be President Wilson's Fourteen points, but it is clear that Germany has been mistaken. There is to be no plebisite in Alsase and Loraine. Nor, even if they wanted to, are the peoples of Austria and Germany allowed to unite. In his search for justice for Poland, Wilson seems prepared to allow large number of Germans to come under Polish rule. The Allied concern for Germany's colonies, the mandates and the eventual independence, would be more impressive if the Allies themselves were prepared to lead their own colonies to indpendence. But in fact the mandate system will be merely a cloak to hide the fact that Britain and France have expanded their empires at Germany's expense.

The basis of the whole Treaty is the assumption that Germany is solely responsible for causing the war. A crippled country has to pay a savage war penalty on the assumption that French ambitions, Russian policy in the Balkans, and Britain's insistence on dominating the seas had no part in bringing about the war. Wilson wants to see a world committed to disarmament. We doubt if France does. While France remains armed to the teeth, her forces ever ready to take advantage of Germany's weakness, Germany is the only country to disarm. It is not Germany who threatens future peace, but the Allies.

The German people have no alternative but to accept this Treaty. It will be for Germany's future generations to avenge her present sufferings.

Overall, some good material, reflecting the feelings of many Germans at the time. There could perhaps have been a little more individuality in the views of the Editor – instead of taking such a typical German approach to the peace terms.

THE RUSSIAN REVOLUTION AND THE RULE OF LENIN

THE CONDITION OF RUSSIA

THE FEBRUARY REVOLUTION OF 1917

THE OCTOBER REVOLUTION

POLICIES OF LENIN

THE CHARACTER OF RUSSIAN GOVERNMENT

COMMUNISM

CONTRIBUTION OF LENIN

GETTING STARTED

In the early years of the twentieth century the condition of Russia was not an enviable one. It was a peasant country with a low standard of living. Its peasantry were poor, ignorant and superstitious, working hard with their simple tools just to keep themselves alive. Serfdom had by this time been abolished but rural conditions were still backward. As far as industrial development went, Russia was in some ways behind its more powerful neighbours and dependent on them for much of its investment funds. Unlike Britain, it lacked an active middle class. When social and economic change came, it burst on Russia like a storm. As a result, working-class economic and social agitation emerged late upon the scene, prompted by bad conditions arising from rapid industrialization and poor urban living conditions. Trade unions were banned, and political opposition was likely to attract the attention of the political police. To complicate matters further, only about half the country's 150 million population were Russians; there were over fifty other national groups subjected to them, some of whom, like the Ukrainians and the Poles, resisted 'russification'.

HISTORICAL DEVELOPMENTS

THE CONDITION OF RUSSIA

At the time, Russia was a country under the personal rule of the Tsar, Nicholas II. In comparison with many western governments, and in the light of the aspirations of the Russian people, this system of government was already hopelessly out of date. The Tsar's leadership was by 1917 thoroughly discredited. Waste, corruption and incompetence were in evidence throughout the system; the bureaucracy of paid officials was selfish and unimaginative, and the police and the courts were used repressively. Efforts had been made after 1906 to govern Russia through a representative parliament, the Duma, but these had largely failed. Opposition politicians found it just as difficult to get on with the Tsar as he did with them, and foreign loans had in practice given Nicholas the means of being independent of their advice. Throughout Russia the influence of the aristocracy, the upper classes and the church discouraged change, whilst Nicholas had inherited from generations of ancestors the high sense of moral duty which prevented him from adapting himself to the role of a limited monarch.

66 **This is how the old world came to an end.** 99

But it was the First World War which finally hastened the revolution. The serious defeats and heavy casualties of the war aggravated the shortcomings of the system, whilst industrial backwardness led to desperate shortages of materials and munitions. The government and the army placed considerable reliance on the railways for transportation, and these broke down as the war progressed. Even the horses were subject to conscription for fighting at the front. The drain on Russian resources, together with enemy occupation of some of Russia's eastern provinces, produced bad effects on the country's farming, and acute shortages, queueing at the shops and high inflation became commonplace. Citizens of large towns often faced situations little short of famine. At the same time taxation was cripplingly heavy; before the end of the war about half the national income went on paying interest on earlier borrowings, many of them from foreigners. The months before the revolution saw a complete breakdown in the Tsar's public relations. Many Russians believed the war to be no more than a personal whim of Nicholas II, whilst his wife, the Tsaritsa Alexandra, was feared and disliked because she was popularly supposed to have pro-German sympathies and German agents were suspected of having gained access to Russia's innermost secrets. A series of disastrous advisers were appointed by Tsar Nicholas, and he and his wife were much influenced by the ruffian Rasputin. He was a coarse Siberian peasant who, though he had never taken holy vows, had achieved for himself the reputation of being a holy man; but he soon got Russia into a most unholy mess. His assassination in December 1916 opened the way to the events which finally led to the revolution.

THE FEBRUARY REVOLUTION OF 1917

This was not so much directed against the Tsar as against the government's mishandling of the war. Demonstrations, protests and raids by hungry people on food shops in Petrograd in early March led to the calling of a general strike in factories and offices on 11 March, and prompted immediate counter-measures by the authorities, resulting in mass arrests and some loss of life. Two days later a committee of the Russian Duma took over power. On 15 March the Tsar abdicated from the throne; though the throne was offered to his brother the Grand Duke Michael, it was refused and Russia became to all intents and purposes a republic. In the chaos which followed, a provisional government was set up to rule the country until a constituent assembly could be called to establish a constitution on a more permanent footing. Its first prime minister was an aristocrat, Prince George Lvov. Alexander Kerensky, a socialist, was his minister of justice, then war minister and finally in July, on the fall of Lvov's second cabinet, prime minister in his turn. This government, however, was never very firm, and collapsed in the autumn.

66 **A revolution and a new government** 99

The provisional government failed to fulfil popular expectations, and lacked the wide support which might have made it a success. Its ministers, including Kerensky himself whilst he was at the War Office, wished to continue the fight against the Kaiser and feared that if they sought a peace treaty they would be heavily punished by its terms as well as being regarded as traitors by their war-time allies. The catastrophic failure of the summer offensive of 1917 put paid to all chances of the country's continued participation in the war, though it took a long time for the government to face the reality of this defeat. At the same time, the provisional government was handicapped by its own failings, and even by the political beliefs to which its supporters subscribed. Because many of them were liberals and in revolt against the tyranny of the Tsar, they felt obliged to release political prisoners and free the press from government control. Unfortunately this provided their less scrupulous opponents with opportunities to campaign against them and even to challenge the whole basis of political freedom. Likewise they hesitated to act improperly or illegally, and insisted on deferring reform schemes until elections had taken place and the wishes of the people had been made known. In particular, they refused to nationalize land or other property until they were sure they could give adequate compensation to former owners.

Their opponents seized on this inaction, suggesting that the provisional government lacked the will to reform. During the summer of 1917, too, inflation continued to race ahead, chiefly because of chronic shortages, the government's continuing financial demands and the uncertainties of the future. Opponents believed that the provisional government had no wish to curb inflation; indeed it was thought that many of them were doing very well out of it. The real truth was that no one, not even the opponents themselves, had the least idea how to deal with inflation.

Steadily, during the spring and summer of 1917, support for the soviets (councils of workers, peasants' and soldiers' deputies) grew. Many of their members were communists, and through this group was split into Mensheviks and the more extreme Bolsheviks, they began a steady rise to power. They held a few seats in Lvov's second cabinet, and it was through their co-operation that the supporters of the Petrograd Soviet did much of the work of the provisional government. There was an all-Russia Congress of Soviets in June, and the Bolsheviks even felt strong enough to try to stage a coup in July, though the effort was unsuccessful. Lenin, the leader of the Bolsheviks, had returned to Russia from Switzerland, where he had been in exile, soon after the February revolution, and no sooner had he arrived in Petrograd than he issued the April Theses, in which he set out a bold plan for a Bolshevik take-over. Those who knew him were much impressed by his single-mindedness and intelligence, and though (as the Menshevik opponents thought) he lacked practical experience in government and put forward a number of rather impractical policies, he soon built up a dedicated band of followers determined to put his brand of communism into practice. Meanwhile the provisional government found its foundations being slowly eroded by its failures. Its bourgeois foundations had always been perilously narrow, and they were now narrowed even further by desertions to the right of those who thought that only a sharp dose of repression would ease Russia's problems, and desertions to the left of those who were disappointed in Kerensky's performance and thought that Lenin promised to do better. In September a former Tsarist general, Kornilov, moved to crush the extremer elements of the revolutionary rabble and sought Kerensky's approval to restore a little of the country's former discipline. Kerensky hesitated. If he went with Kornilov he branded himself as anti-revolutionary and an enemy of the people; if he went against him he weakened discipline further and left the radicals in possession. In the end he invited the Bolsheviks to help him suppress Kornilov, and even armed them for that purpose. Thereafter he was at their mercy.

3 THE OCTOBER REVOLUTION

There was a carefully-timed Bolshevik coup on 7 November. Immediately before, Kerensky had tried to replace the Petrograd garrison with soldiers who were more reliable and to transfer the Russian capital to Moscow, but the Bolsheviks, who were strongest in Petrograd, resisted this move. Trotsky's Red Guards occupied key points in the city and seized the Winter Palace, forcing the provisional government to surrender. Kerensky fled in a car bearing the insignia of the American ambassador and escaped detection later only by disguising himself as a sailor. Power now passed almost without bloodshed into the hands of the Bolshevik-dominated Council of People's Commissars, with Lenin as its chairman. At once it embarked on a flood of reforming decrees: 193 were passed between 8 November and 31 December 1917. Lenin offered freedom to all the subject peoples of Russia; he gave the land to the peasants and the factories to the workers; he abolished money; he took over the church and attempted to destroy religion; he even began to plan revolutions of a similar communist character all over the world. From being the leader of a lunatic left wing, Lenin had suddenly become a force to be reckoned with.

And then another government.

Undoubtedly Lenin's cleverness was the key reason for his sweeping success. At the same time, the party he had built up contained a body of men who were disciplined and ruthless, determined to profit from every division of their opponents. Lacking in the democratic niceties, they were not constricted by the scruples of their more liberal opponents, and eliminated them in large numbers. Lenin himself was a skilled propagandist, offering the people promises that he could not afterwards fulfil or apologizing for the changed circumstances which compelled him to break promises. Thus, ending the war with a 'peace without indemnities and without annexations' turned out to be as impossible as Kerensky had predicted; and 'handing over the land to those who worked it' meant that peasants had a free use of their holdings, but that legally they belonged to the state. Even the factory worker, promised industrial democracy, found himself subject to the control of a newly appointed 'bourgeois specialist', who gave him much the same sort of orders as his old boss. None the less, at a time when the opponents of the Bolsheviks were deeply divided amongst themselves, and when they could count on the political inexperience of the Russian public, Lenin was able to make the best of his chances. With the country so deeply in danger from internal and external enemies, he could also appeal to the fundamental patriotism of the people.

4 ▷ POLICIES OF LENIN

PEACE

The Bolsheviks agreed an armistice with Germany in December 1917, and negotiations began with the Germans in the new year with a view to arranging suitable peace terms. The new foreign minister, Trotsky, however, found to his horror that the German terms were far too harsh to accept, and was forced into making endless speeches at the conference so as to slow matters down. Lenin knew that he could not continue the war, and he ordered demobilization, demanding 'peace at any price' as a 'breathing-space' for the revolution. In the end, Trotsky refused to sign, and it was a former Tsarist official, Chicherin, in formal morning suit, who signed the Treaty of Brest-Litovsk in March 1918. By this treaty, Russia paid a war indemnity of 300 million gold roubles, and agreed to sign away a third of its population and the greater part of its iron and coal resources. Russia yielded up Kars, Ardahan and Båtum to Turkey (though much of this land was later returned) and agreed to the setting up of an independent Ukraine, a million tons of whose wheat was ear-marked for use by the victorious central powers; an independent Poland, much of which was subject to a German-controlled government; and independent Baltic states – Latvia, Esthonia and Lithuania – all largely dominated by German governments. Finland was to be independent, too, but was placed under a German prince. Though the Russian people as a whole were grateful for the ending of the war, there were not many of them who were enthusiastic about the peace terms.

LAND

Lenin's decree on land abolished the private ownership of land at a stroke and guaranteed that the peasants would be free to work the land they occupied, without compensation to the previous owner. Thus the Bolsheviks solved the problem that had for so long delayed their liberal opponents: state, church and landlords' estates were to be confiscated and distributed by village councils to the poorer class of peasants. Richer peasants, too, often the object of popular hatred, might find some or all of their land taken from them on the ground that they already possessed more than they needed. Such a step encouraged the poorer peasants to plunder the holdings of the better-off, and even to plunder each other. The main effect was to weaken title to land, the ownership of which in any case was not vested with the individual peasant but with the state, and this all helped to add to the ferment in the countryside.

GOVERNMENT

Though the Bolsheviks had secured control of Russia by their coup of October, they still existed only in small numbers. Lenin, who actually took pride in the limited number of his followers – describing his party as 'little but good' – none the less asserted that with his 200,000 supporters he had as many men working for him as the Tsar had ever had. All the same, he found the business of winning a majority in an election a very difficult thing. Hence, when the long-awaited constituent assembly finally met in January 1918, the Bolsheviks held only a quarter of the seats. Lenin immediately dissolved the assembly, employing his newly established political police, the Cheka, to arrest the more prominent of his opponents and to seek out any other political groups that were likely to prove troublesome to him. In July 1918 the Bolsheviks produced a new constitution which announced Russia as a socialist republic, a constitution which, though it made no specific mention of the Bolsheviks, left the country entirely under their control. In the same month Nicholas II and his family, who had been held as political prisoners away from the centre of events for some time, were shot by their captors and their remains dropped down a mine in Ekaterinburg in Siberia. They were less dangerous to Lenin as dead martyrs than as a living focus for further opposition.

BREAD

Continuing food shortages and the breakdown of the industrial economy all accelerated the decline of the country into chaos. Normally the countryside depended on the urban areas for its manufactured products and in exchange for them provided the foodstuffs with which the towns were fed; but by 1919 the towns had little or nothing to give in exchange. At the same time, inflation had destroyed the value of money and the Bolsheviks had tried to do away with it altogether. The commodity cards which they issued instead were of little value to the peasants, who, with the usual peasant realism, refused to work for nothing and planted only as many crops as they needed for their own purposes. The Bolshevik authorities, based chiefly in the towns and cities, were therefore compelled to resort to requisitioning at the point of the bayonet in order to ensure that their own supporters had enough to eat. Their attempts to introduce co-operative or collective farming methods came up against age-old peasant conservatism, and the whole rural economy broke down. Widespread famine was the result, and thousands starved.

CIVIL WAR

Use a map to sort out civil war and foreign intervention.

With or without the Tsarist resistance, Bolshevik power grew rapidly in many areas of Russia, and soon Trotsky's Red Army found itself faced by a variety of anti--Bolshevik forces. Some were ex-Tsarists, some were liberals and Mensheviks and yet others fought for the liberation from Bolshevik control of subject peoples within the old Russian empire. Many of them were known as 'Whites', on account of their supposed royalist leanings, though in fact nearly all of them were a loose alliance of different groupings, without much internal cohesion when things were going badly. In the Baltic provinces, Marshal Yudenich pushed his tank columns in the direction of Petrograd until he ran out of petrol; General Denikin, in the area of the River Don, and General Wrangel, in the Crimea and the Ukraine, aimed to advance on Moscow from the south; whilst former Tsarist Admiral Kolchak pressed along the Trans-Siberian Railway as far as Kazan in a bid to take Moscow from the east. White governments were proclaimed in Samara, Omsk and Archangel. The counter-revolutionary forces were assisted by Americans and Japanese in the Far East, though neither of these came any further west than Lake Baikal; and by British and French in the west, in the Arctic Circle near Archangel and Murmansk and in the Baltic, especially in Poland. For a time, Bolshevik control was narrowed to an area around Petrograd and Moscow, and it looked as though Lenin's revolution might be snuffed out almost before it had time to get under way.

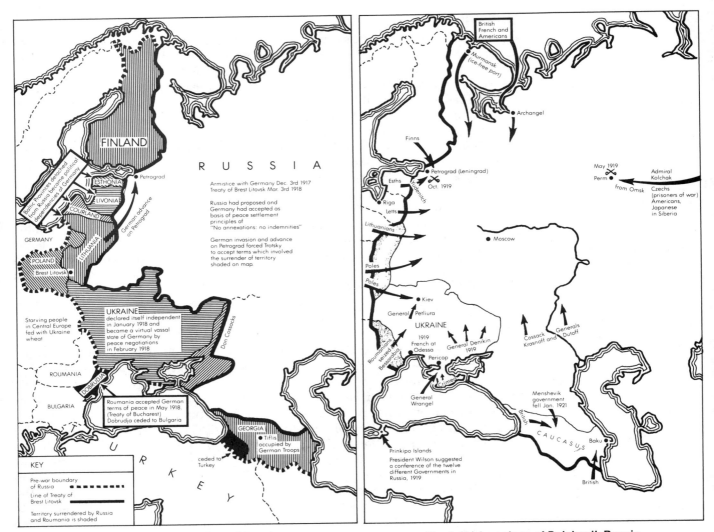

Fig.4.1a) Treaty of Brest Litovsk   **Fig.4.1b) Invasions of Bolshevik Russia**

RUSSO–POLISH WAR

The Poles seized the chance to extend their territories to the east of the Curzon line, which was set up to divide Poland from Russia at the time of the Versailles treaty. In this, they were encouraged by foreign anti-Bolshevist forces. Britain sent a financial mission to Poland to help the Poles in their struggle; the French sent a military mission under General Weygand with the same idea. Poland soon became a focus for anti-Russian and anti-Bolshevik sentiment. In the early stages of the war the Poles were successful; they advanced towards Kiev and penetrated up to 200 miles into Russian territory. They were then, however, defeated, and forced to fall back to Warsaw, where they rallied successfully and once again drove the Russians out and advanced beyond their frontiers. Finally, by the Treaty of Riga in 1921 the Poles gained large areas east of the Curzon line, an action of which the western powers, frightened as they were of communism, thoroughly approved. Generally, however, in these civil wars, Trotsky's troops were enormously successful. This was partly because of his own inspired leadership, and partly because of the ruthlessness of the Cheka in eliminating opponents. It should also be noted that most of the strategic advantages lay with the Reds, e.g. interior lines of communication and the control of the central railway network. Furthermore, foreign help for the Whites was scattered and ineffective, whilst the Reds were able to call on the simple patriotism and loyalty of the mass of the peasant partisans. For the most part, of course, the peasants had no love of the Reds, who threatened to nationalize their lands and seize their crops; but White brutality and the conspicuous corruption of their regime alienated peasant sympathies and led to the alignment of neutral groups with the Bolshevik forces. Finally, it should be said that there was not simply one war, but a number of ill co-ordinated campaigns in which the single-mindedness of the Bolsheviks was able to triumph.

WAR COMMUNISM

This was not only introduced as part of the later stages of the war against Germany, but also as part of the campaign designed to establish a communist regime in Russia in place of the capitalist regime which already existed. It was swept along by the force of its own convictions and was inclined to make no compromises. Land, industries and businesses were all nationalized, and banking, insurance and foreign trade were all taken over by the state. A supreme economic council was set up to plan the economy, the old market economy being replaced by a thorough-going system of planning. Social insurance, an eight-hour day and better wages and conditions were decreed. The system operated through the co-operation of workers' organizations, enlisting the support of the trade unions in the running of the factories. Unfortunately the removal of the management and the in-effectiveness of the new workers' committees led to a sharp deterioration in the relations between the Bolshevik leadership and the workers' leaders, and the result of this was that the discipline was tightened and the Bolsheviks paid increasingly little regard to worker democracy. War casualties, starvation and the dislocation of the economy weakened the country and made the Bolsheviks more determined to override the minor objections of the work-force in an all-out effort to make the system work. The result of this high-handed treatment was sour dissatisfaction on the part of the working rank and file, and disillusionment that the people's revolution had not brought about the freedom that popular control seemed to promise. Thus in March 1921 the sailors of Kronstadt – 'the pride and glory of the revolution', as Lenin had called them – rose in revolt alongside the mass of Russian workers, demanding an end to the dictatorship of the Bolshevik leaders and also true industrial democracy. They wanted free elections, freedom of speech and the right of all left-wing parties to participate in the new government. Lenin was thoroughly frightened, representing the affair as a White conspiracy. Trotsky ordered the Red Army across the ice to Kronstadt ruthlessly to crush popular resistance to Bolshevik control; for the Bolsheviks, as Lenin put it, it was the 'lightning flash which lit up reality'.

NEP

66 Making communism work by modifying it. 99

This replaced war communism after April 1921. Pure communism had to be set aside in order to make the system work and to enable the economy in Russia to re-cover from the hammer blows dealt to it by the war and the dislocation following it. The Russian people were no longer asked to work selflessly for the benefit of the state; in future they were to be allowed to work for their own profit. As far as agri-culture went, forced requisitioning was to be replaced by a state tax to be paid in foodstuffs; the surplus could be sold for private profit. In industry, businesses em-ploying fewer than twenty were to be returned to private ownership or to local co-operative concerns. Private enterprise was to be restored in the small retail trade. Incentives and bonuses were permitted to encourage production. An economic sys-tem very like a 'mixed economy' was brought into being, but the commanding heights of the economy – the coal mines, the steel mills, the railway system and the central planning mechanism – were to remain in the hands of the state. This was a 'Brest-Litovsk on the economic front' – an attempt to secure a breathing-space until Russia was ready for its next moves towards socialism.

5 ▶ THE CHARACTER OF THE RUSSIAN GOVRNMENT: A BRIEF NOTE

(1) It was a one-party dictatorship, imposing a system of government known as 'democratic centralism'. The Bolshevik Party claimed to represent the true wishes of the Russian people, regarding other parties as against the public in-terest; other nationality groupings even, (though they had been promised their right to freedom), were said to be deluded if they wished to break away. Bolshevik supporters were required to follow the 'party line' and were 'purged' if they did not; political opponents were suppressed altogether.

(2) It imposed strict controls on the country and did not hesitate if necessary to use methods of terror. It was highly bureaucratic, even repressive. There were many restrictions on people's lives: on their movements, on their rights of meeting and on their membership of other bodies. There were even efforts to control their thoughts and beliefs, through strict censorship of the press and the supervision of the other media. Detention and labour camps were used for dealing with opponents, and the political police (first the Cheka, and then afterwards similar organizations like the OGPU, the NKVD and the KGB) exercised wide powers.

66 New tyrannies for old. 99

(3) It opposed the Christian churches, especially the Orthodox Church of Russia. Priests were driven from office, many of them being shot or imprisoned; their churches were ransacked, valuables stolen and the buildings themselves made over to other purposes; church estates were broken up and church lands taken over by the state. There was to be no religious teaching in schools, and the public celebration of the Christian faith was prohibited.

(4) It imposed strict controls on the economy, substituting the planning mechanism (which was called the 'command economy') for the machinery of individual enterprise, governed by supply and demand in the interests of profit making (the 'market economy'). Planning was often cumbersome and slow moving, and the consequences of its errors could be disastrous.

(5) At the same time, however, Bolshevik government produced for the average Russian a number of worthwhile improvements. Unemployment was abolished, factory conditions improved, free medical and dental treatment was introduced, working-class flats were constructed to replace appalling slums and a school building programme for all children was undertaken. Homes for the elderly, holiday facilities for workers and many other things all tended to improve the quality of life, though improvement came only slowly, and there were times of desperate shortage and hardship.

IDEAS AND PRINCIPLES

COMMUNISM

This was the product of the thoughts and writings of the German scholar Karl Marx (1818–83), and is sometimes known as Marxism. Marx believed that in the past property had been controlled and ideas imposed on society by the ruling group – in capitalist society, the bourgeoisie. Society was always evolving as new forces from below emerged to challenge the domination of this ruling group. History was thus composed of a series of class struggles, and political power gravitated downwards as the ruling group was ousted by these submerged forces. In capitalist society there existed a deepening tension between the bourgeois property owners and the proletarian working class which they exploited; the interests of these two classes were diametrically opposed and out of their conflict new political forms emerged. Marx believed that the capitalist class 'digs its own grave' by its increasing exploitation of the proletariat; eventually the injustices will become so blatant that the workers will rise against their masters and the old order of society will be revolutionized. In this sense the revolution is inevitable. That is not to say that it will happen automatically without anyone having to worry about how to organize it, but that eventually workers' organizations will be stung into taking action on behalf of the unfortunate multitude. When this happens, the old order will be overturned, those formerly exploited will exploit the exploiters, and a new form of society will emerge, radically different from the old one in that power will now be in the hands of the representatives of the underdog. Gradually, however arbitrarily, the worst abuses of the old system will be destroyed, and society will edge a little closer to true justice. Eventually, Marx predicted, the need for coercion will cease, a 'classless society' will follow and so the state will 'wither away'. Marx drew up no actual blueprint of this ideal form of social organization, since he saw himself as being in the business not so much of prophecy as of social analysis. Thus when the revolution did actually take place, years after Marx's death, it is hardly surprising that Lenin found himself in entirely uncharted waters.

CONTRIBUTION OF LENIN

Lenin's contribution to the development of Marxist communism was a significant one. He found himself not only called upon to put the tenets of Marxism into operation, but to flesh out Marx's balder statements with greater detail. From the early 1920s, therefore, the theory comes to be referred to as that of Marxism-Leninism. In those stages of the old capitalist order, for example, that had largely developed after Marx's death, Lenin saw imperialism as the last, and highest, stage of monopoly capitalism, when the capitalist classes turned to colonial exploitation in their desperate attempt to disguise the increasing injustices of the system; and with colonial exploitation came arms and naval races, both of which acted as shots in the arm for the flagging vitality of capitalist production. In the end, however, Lenin believed that capitalism was bound to fail and the revolution would be all the more bloody when it came. He had views, too, on the work of the party – a detail with which Marx had never concerned himself – in bringing about the revolution and master-minding it whilst it was in progress. He believed the party should be kept small and highly disciplined, working loyally towards the objectives which the leadership had set down. Lenin despised the bourgeois parties, where policies were trimmed and the current issues fudged with a view to capturing the fleeting approval of a mass electorate; he favoured a selfless and dedicated band of leaders who would pursue the true path to progress with a single-mindedness that was almost religious in its conviction. Lenin was also called upon to explain why the coming of the classless society which was the final goal of communists was so long delayed in coming, and why the 'dictatorship of the proletariat' seemed to show no sign of coming to an end. His explanation was that the bourgeoisie were cunning and persistent, lurking always ready to make their comeback, and that the leadership had to continue to be vigilant if it wished to prevent a counter-revolution. Lenin believed that the post-revolution period fell into two phases: the intermediate, and socialist, phase where the tyranny of the proletariat had to be continued and the apparatus of the state maintained, and the final, or communist, phase in which – eventually – as Marx had predicted, the communist utopia would arrive. To this view, at least officially, the Russian leadership continued to subscribe throughout the period of communist rule.

APPLIED MATERIALS

Texts

P.D. Allan, *Russia and Eastern Europe*, Arnold, 1983
J. Aylett, *Russia in Revolution, 1900–24*, Arnold, 1987
J.Brooman, *Russia in War and Revolution*, Longman (Modern World History), 1987
L. Hartley, *The Russian Revolution*, Evans, 1980
T. Howarth, *Russia, 1900–53*, Longman (History Series), 1978
N.C. Jackson, *Russia in the Twentieth Century*, Wheaton, 1978
D. Mack, *Lenin and the Russian Revolution*, Longman, 1970
J. Quinn, *The Russian Revolution*, UTP, 1978
J. Robottom, *Lenin and the Revolution*, Longman, 1972

Documentary books

A. Cash, *The Russian Revolution*, Jackdaw,
J.L. Taylor, *Russia in Revolution*, Holmes McDougall, 1986

Computer programme

Scott and Wilkes, *The Russian Revolution*, Sussex Tapes

EXAMINATION QUESTIONS

QUESTION 1
Why were there two revolutions in Russia in 1917?

(NICCEA)

QUESTION 2
Explain the importance of the following as causes of the revolution in Russia in 1917:
(a)   Tsarist dictatorship
(b)   The land problem and peasant unrest
(c)   Living and working conditions in Petrograd
(d)   World War I
(e)   The ideas of Karl Marx.

(25 marks) (NEAB)

QUESTION 3
You are a factory worker in Petrograd and you became involved in the events that led to the fall of Tsar Nicholas.
(a)   Explain why you were opposed to the tsar and welcomed the setting up of the provisional government.
(b)   Why, by the autumn of 1917, had you become an opponent of the provisional government and a strong supporter of the Bolsheviks?

(SEG)

OUTLINE ANSWERS

ANSWER 1
The first question is 'open-ended', allowing the candidate to answer it and to explain the causes of the two revolutions in his own way. It is not, however, a factual recall question. It is designed to test your understanding of causality, one of the skills specifically requested in the GCSE examination. Therefore answers which contain a narrative of events in Russia in 1917 which has been memorized from your notes will score relatively little unless this narrative is linked with suggested causes. An answer could be along the general lines of 'There were two revolutions because developments showed that one was not enough', dealing with the causes of the first revolution, and then going on to show how the first revolution failed and created a situation in which a second revolution was likely to follow. Alternatively, your answer could have as its central focus the idea that these were two very different kinds of revolution; the first a political revolution which changed the regime, but brought to power a new government which in a number of ways was similar to the original; the second a more profound type of revolution which aimed to change the whole social system of the country. Such an answer would then deal with the question of causes along more ideological lines. The sort of answer which left the examiner to infer for himself the likely causes from the historical outline you had provided would not score as highly as the answer which dealt explicitly with causes.

ANSWER 2
The second question, marked out of 25, will allow approximately 5 marks for each of the five parts of the question. In writing an answer, you should group your his-

torical material under these five headings, clearly marking each of the five sections with the appropriate letter, (a) to (e). Explanation rather than description is required in each part. The deceptive simplicity of the multi-part question should not delude you into thinking of this as a 'short-note' question; it requires assessment and you must use your factual historical knowledge to explain the importance of what is under discussion. Thus, under (c), a mere catalogue of points, or a simple description of living and working conditions in Petrograd, will not be credited so highly as it would if it were specifically angled to causes of revolution; the relevance of the points you are making may seem obvious to you, but the examiner may feel you are asking him to do the question for you unless you make the connection quite explicit. Some of your explanations, such as the uneven distribution of land holdings, and the grievances and poverty of the peasantry, you will probably think it best to fit under only one heading, (b); others, like graft and corruption, could fit either under (a), if the shortcomings of the Russian bureaucracy were under consideration, or under (d), if the embezzlement or theft of war supplies were being discussed. Also, the relative importance of (a), (b), (c), etc. in causing the revolution should be indicated. Some you may find more clearly relevant than others. In (e), for example, it could be argued that outside the ranks of a small number of party faithful the ideas of Karl Marx exercised very little influence at all on the majority of those connected with the revolution – though even here it would still be necessary to discuss how influential the members of the minority group were, and what impact these ideas had on the actions of those who were familiar with them.

ANSWER 3

The third question, of course, is an empathetic question. To assume the role of a Petrograd factory worker, you have to know something about his physical surroundings and his day-to-day life as well as something about his ideas and beliefs. You have to imagine what such a worker would be likely to have felt at the time the provisional government was set up after the first revolution, and how by the autumn of that year he might have been disillusioned with this government and come to the conclusion that he might get a better deal from the Bolsheviks. All this must be done against as authentic a background – poor living conditions, hard factory life and the tensions of wartime – as you can conjure up. In this question the use of the word 'I' will give some realism to your treatment of the two parts of the question, but whether your answer ultimately is very convincing will depend on how well you use your historical knowledge of the period, how good your background understanding of the situation in Petrograd during 1917 is, and how well you think yourself into the life of a Russian worker at that time. Flights of imaginative fancy will not be credible unless they are supported by an authentic knowledge of the place and the period.

SUGGESTIONS FOR FURTHER WORK

1. How and why was the unreformed Russian calendar different from the western calendar? Did you notice any discrepancy in the dates of the two revolutions? How can you find out more about this? Tip: you might begin by looking in any encyclopaedia, under the heading 'Calendar'.
2. Find out the details of the 1917 April Theses. How do these help to explain the appeal of Bolshevism for the ordinary Russian? Tip: begin by looking at the notes on Map 20 in Brian Catchpole, *A Map History of Russia*, Heinemann, page 45. In what book do you think you might find a fuller statement?

3. Study the two proclamations, the first from the Bolshevik revolutionary committee, the second from the provisional government, both dated 7 November 1917, and show what light they cast on the October revolution of 1917. Tip: the two proclamations appear on page 38 of J. Quinn, *The Russian Revolution*, UTP.

4. Collect material from the books listed in this chapter, and from any others to which you have access, so as to write a life of Lenin. How does this material help you to explain why Russians regard him as such a great man?

5. Draw maps illustrating a) the provisions of the Treaty of Brest-Litovsk and b) the events of the civil wars and the wars of intervention.

6. Write a week's entries in the diary of a Russian school child at the time of the civil wars and the great famine of 1920. In attempting this exercise, you should remember:

(a) What you are writing is a diary, which usually consists of brief entries made day by day. Important events figure in such a diary, but some of the material may be personal. You should remember that diarists have no way of looking into the future; things may happen for them quite unexpectedly.

(b) The author of the diary is supposed to be a school child. You would therefore expect the contents to be different from those of the diary of an adult person. You could perhaps refer to the way that the Whites rounded up parents for questioning, or how the Bolsheviks stationed Red Army troops in the school house as they were marching through in pursuit of their enemies.

(c) The events of the famine and civil war are spread over time. You should therefore not try to squash all the crucial events of the period into seven days. Remember, too, that you would not have first-hand knowledge of many of these events; there may be many events in other areas of which you have only heard rumours, or of which you have heard nothing at all. At the same time, you should not write a diary that is a flight of unsupported fancy. If you exclude all your historical knowledge from it, on the grounds that a child would not know much about it and would probably misunderstand what he did know, you will deprive yourself of the chance to score marks for relevant historical information. You ought to be aware, for example, that the worst of the famine experiences took place during the winter months, and credit will be offered to you for showing that you appreciate how the problems of hunger were aggravated by winter conditions. To choose for your seven days a time in late summer when your small harvest was being gathered will prevent you from making a number of telling points about the famine. Your diary entries, too, might find some space for accounts of bands of Red Army soldiers attempting to squeeze requisitions of foodstuffs from the barren countryside, or perhaps some mention of deserters from one side or the other trying to flee from the conflict. Would the Reds be more or less likely to desert than the Whites, do you think? What explanations can you offer for their behaviour? Which of the two sides behaved more brutally towards the villagers, and why? What did the village priest do at this time? Did he provide an inspiring example to the community, or was he only interested in saving his own skin? These are the kind of points through which you could reveal some genuine understanding of what was happening in Russia at this time.

STUDENT'S ANSWER – EXAMINER'S COMMENTS

Question

In 1917 Lenin promised the people of Russia 'Peace, Bread and Land'. Did Lenin's government keep these promises? Give reasons for your answer.

(NICCEA, Summer 1991)

This paragraph is the greater part of the essay, but is entirely irrelevant to this question.

'Lenin' is repeatedly misspelt, in spite of being written on the question paper. There are other basic errors of spelling and style.

'Peace, bread and land' are mentioned in this truncated paragraph, but little understanding is shown of their real significance.

No mention of the Treaty of Brest Litovsk with the Germans, or of the redistribution of the land to the Russian peasantry.

Question says 'Give reasons for your answer', but the reasons are flimsy and misplaced.

Vladimir Ulyanov, known as Lennin, was born at Simbirsk on the Volga in 1870 and was the son of a schools inspector. He was a clever youth who was expelled from Kazan University at the age of 17 for being involved in revolutionsary activity, and witnessed the hanging of his elder brother for taking part in a plot on the life of Alexander III. He later moved to St Petersburg where he took a brilliant first in law but he did not make any money because he fought the peasants' cases without taking any money for it. He began to study Marxism and in 1895 was arrested and spent over three years in exile in Siberia. He married his jailer's daughter Krupskaya. During his imprisonment he wrote an important work 'The Development of Capitalism in Russia' and when he returned he launched a revolutionary newspaper called 'Iskra' (The Spark). Persecution by the Tsarist authorities made him leave Russia and go to live in Switzerland where one of his followers said he ate, slept and dreamt the revolution, though he himself began to think he would not live to see the day arrive. On the outbreak of war in 1914 Lennin denounced all those socialists who supported their governments in a capitalist war.

Unrest continued to grow in Russia and in 1917 revolution broke out. The German Government allowed Lennin to leave Switzerland in a sealed train, for they knew he was determined to bring Russia out of the First World War. Under his skilful guidance the Bolsheviks took control of the Soviets and Lennin began to lay his plans for the next stage of the revolution. He promised the people 'Peace, Bread and Land', and he had a number of other slogans such as 'Little but Good' referring to Bolshevism. He promised the people bread because there was a severe shortage in the capital at the time, and the trouble had first broken out in the food queues when the regular army simpathised with the rioters. He did not give them peace, because civil war soon broke out in the Russian provinces when the people there refused to except Bolshevik rule. All the same he did give them land, because at the end of the sivil war Kolchak the White leader was shot along with the Tsar and all the lands of Russia were brought back again under Lennin's control.

THE
WEIMAR
REPUBLIC

G E T T I N G   S T A R T E D

The Weimar Republic did not arise out of the goodwill and democratic intentions of the German people; it was directly the result of defeat in war and the abdication of an emperor. The democratic institutions it established were new and untried and to many people unpopular, and they certainly were too superficial to withstand the social and economic problems arising from 1929 onwards. The Weimar politicians failed to retain the support of the population at large, who turned to the more extreme political groups. The parties loyal to Weimar were too weak, disunited and lacking in powerful political personalities to provide acceptable alternatives to Hitler.

HISTORICAL DEVELOPMENTS

In November 1918 the German empire came to an end. Defeat in war had led to the abdication and flight into exile of Kaiser Wilhelm II; a republic was declared; and a right-wing socialist, Ebert, headed a new government. Elections were held in 1919 specifically to choose a constituent assembly to devise a new constitution. Its meeting place in February 1919 was the small town of Weimar, over 100 miles to the south west of Berlin, chosen because the major cities of Germany, especially Berlin, had suffered outbreaks of disorder involving extremists of both right and left. It was never intended that the republic's capital should remain at Weimar, and in fact it was changed to Berlin in 1920, but by then the town of Weimar had already given the republic its name.

❝Germany was more free than ever before.❞

Germany had not been a democracy before 1919. Its elected parliament was always subject to the authority of the Emperor and the Chancellor. Yet the constitution drawn up and accepted by a large majority in the summer of 1919 was one of the most democratic of all written constitutions. The various German states retained their local independence and thus Germany remained federal in organization. But for national issues there was to be an elected lower house, the Reichstag, chosen by universal suffrage, secret ballot and proportional representation; 60,000 votes nationally were sufficient to secure a seat for any political party. The government was to be responsible to the Reichstag. The head of the government was the Chancellor, who would thus need a majority for his party in the Reichstag. General elections every four years kept the Reichstag in close touch with the people. The Chancellor was to be appointed by a President directly elected by the people every seven years. Although intended largely to be a figure-head, the President was allowed wide powers in the event of a national emergency, powers which, as the 1930s were to show, could be used unscrupulously.

The German states sent representatives to the Reichsrat, an upper house with the right of delaying legislation, but this house proved to be insignificant in power compared with the Reichstag. Although on paper the constitution looked ideal, much depended on German enthusiasm to try to make democracy work, and many Germans preferred, even at this early stage, more authoritarian forms of government: either a return to the monarchy or a communist revolution. Moreover, the electoral system tended to provide seats for a large number of political parties: the number of votes secured was directly proportional to the number of seats obtained and in the 1930s up to twenty eight parties contested for the available seats. Thus it was difficult for one party to obtain an absolute majority; compromise and coalition became inevitable, and compromise and coalition are not necessarily ideal in times of national crisis.

The Weimar Republic had a stormy beginning. Ebert and the National Assembly faced the difficulties of making peace, the problem of drawing up a new constitution and the need to maintain law and order, and had to deal on the one hand with those who looked for a Bolshevik revolution and on the other those like the Bavarian separatists who would wreck German unity. The Spartacist rebellion in Berlin in January 1919 which forced the republic to move its capital to Weimar was led by the communists Karl Liebknecht and Rosa Luxemburg. Their powerful leadership was of no avail against the irregular troops led by ex-officers of the Kaiser's army. An attempt to set up a socialist state in Bavaria was also suppressed. The signing of the Versailles treaty in June infuriated the nationalists who wanted a strong Germany and who believed that Germany's surrender in November 1918 had been the work of 'November criminals'. In large numbers they joined the Frei Korps, a civilian army of law and order which regarded communism as its main enemy. In 1920 the Frei Korps helped to suppress a left-wing rising in the Ruhr, and was itself emboldened to attempt to seize power in Berlin, where it was frustrated by a strike of the city workers and by the refusal of the army to give support. Its leader, Dr Kapp, was imprisoned, but already the Weimar Republic was beginning to gain a reputation for handling right-wing law breakers with much less severity than those of the left. It was already being whispered that Weimar was the tool of right-wing politicians and generals.

However, by 1921, although violence continued intermittently, the Weimar government could be said to have established shaky control. Yet the prospect of excessive reparations payments and lack of budgetary and economic planning pointed towards disaster. Only in foreign affairs was there any relief in the gloom. Germany gained some revenge for the diplomatic isolation imposed on her by the allied powers by signing the Treaty of Rapallo in 1922 with the other major European outcast, Soviet Russia. Germany became the first major power to recognize the Bolshevik state, and there was some limited military and commercial co-operation, but the practical benefits of the treaty were disappointingly limited.

 **Germany was troubled by renewed violence.... and by confetti money.**

4 ▷ REPARATIONS, RUHR AND INFLATION

The coalition governments which had been in power since 1919 had done little to restore Germany's economy. In a period of post-war shortages prices rose generally in Europe, but much faster in Germany. The allied committee which had been set up to decide on the amount of reparations Germany must pay eventually fixed on £6,600m: less than France had demanded but more than Germany expected. Germany could only make reparation payments from a profitable export trade and from coal and coke deliveries, but by 1922 the post-war shortages had largely disappeared and exports were becoming more difficult to sell. Coal and coke deliveries, moreover, fell below target. Germany found it increasingly necessary to rely on foreign loans if reparation payments were to be met at all. Hardly had reparation payments begun in 1922 when Germany announced in 1923 that she could no longer pay. France decided to compensate herself for the loss of reparation payments by seizing, in collaboration with the Belgians, the vital industrial area of the Ruhr, and by confiscating the Ruhr's industrial production. The German Ruhr workers, encouraged by the Weimar government, offered passive resistance to the French and Belgian invaders. France replied with largescale arrests, threatening saboteurs with execution (Schlageter, the only one who was executed, was regarded by the German people as a martyr), and cutting off the Ruhr economically from the rest of Germany.

France gained little benefit from her occupation of the Ruhr, but Germany was paralysed by it. Exports virtually ceased. The value of the mark on the foreign exchanges fell alarmingly. The German government's expenditure far exceeded its income, but it was reluctant to add to the hardships of the people by increasing taxes. So it resorted to meeting its needs by printing money. An expanding paper currency at a time when the economy was almost at a standstill led to rapid inflation. In 1914 the pound was worth 15 German marks, in 1919 50 marks, in 1921 nearly 300 marks, in August 1923 15.5 million marks, and in November 1923 15 million million marks. By then the German currency was almost worthless. Price changes were recorded hourly. Workers were released from their factories twice a day to make purchases before their marks depreciated further. Huge quantities of bank notes were required for even the smallest transaction. Property owners benefited in that they held real assets rather than worthless money. Those who owed money gained by paying off debts that had originally been substantial in paper money that had virtually no purchasing power. The government delayed taking steps to deal with the crisis it had itself created. And indeed inflation virtually wiped out Germany's internal debt, thus reducing the need for higher taxation. But there was a heavy cost. The working classes did not suffer excessively as mostly their wages rose rapidly and kept to some degree in pace with inflation. Those on fixed incomes were not so lucky; their few marks could hardly buy a postage stamp. Those dependent upon savings saw the value of their savings wiped out; a man who had patriotically lent the government 100,000 marks during the war to help the war effort had been a man of substance, but his 100,000 marks in the summer of 1923 would be worth merely a few pence and by November 1923 they would be valueless. The middle classes were the savers; they were the ones who lived on fixed incomes. Their commitment to the Weimar Republic was badly shaken and their enthusiasm for democracy much diminished. Their fear of a renewal of inflation and their lack of trust in the Weimar Republic weakened the republic and strengthened support for the extremist parties. Even though a miraculous economic recovery was about to begin, nothing could be done to compensate those who had lost everything during the great inflation, and bitter memories were to remain for a long time.

5 > STRESEMANN

In August 1923 Gustav Stresemann agreed to form a government with the intention of dealing with the combined problems of the Ruhr and the economy. He persuaded the French to leave the Ruhr by promising to resume reparation payments, and the ease with which the Munich *putsch* (see the chapter on Hitler) was suppressed suggested that Stresemann would be strong on law and order. In 1924 the old worthless mark was replaced by the Rentenmark and an independent Reichsbank was created to control the currency and inspire public confidence in it. At the beginning of 1924 Stresemann had given up the chancellorship and became foreign minister, but he was to be the most important and influential figure in the German government during the next five years.

The new confidence inspired by Stresemann and the determination of the government to tackle problems head on led to economic recovery. Small firms tended to merge and large industrial giants developed. American loans financed a revival of German industry and the Dawes Plan of 1924 produced a more sensible system of reparations based on Germany's ability to pay. In 1925 by the Locarno treaties Germany accepted the permanence of the German frontier in the west and agreed not to use force to disturb her frontiers in the east. Germany was no longer a diplomatic outcast and it seemed sensible that Germany was allowed to join the League of Nations in 1926.

Meanwhile in 1925, following the death of Ebert, the first president, elections for a new president resulted in the choice of former Field Marshal Hindenburg. His sympathy with right-wing nationalists tended to restrain nationalist opposition to the republic and to give to the republic a greater air of permanence. Even so, the republic still did not command universal respect. When the Old Soldiers' League publicly proclaimed 'We hate with all our soul the existing state system and everything it stands for' it was committing its wide membership to dissatisfaction with Weimar, and one of its national figures, Stresemann himself, felt obliged to resign his membership. The vast majority of its members, however, remained loyal to the league rather than to the republic.

Yet despite such opposition, the late 1920s were the heady years of Weimar's success. Stresemann's diplomatic achievements continued with the signing of the Kellogg Pact, in which Germany was one of sixty five states to renounce war as an instrument of policy. In 1929 the Young Plan cut reparations by more than a half and spread their payment over fifty nine years. Economic recovery seemed set to continue, with unemployment down to just over one million, when two events in October 1929 put all that had been gained at risk: Streseman died, and the Wall Street crash hit America.

6 > THE GREAT DEPRESSION AND THE RISE OF EXTREMISM

The death of Stresemann removed the republic's ablest politician; the Wall Street crash wrecked Germany's economic revival. American investment in Germany ceased, American loans were recalled, overseas demand for German goods dried up, the new Reichsbank got into difficulties and there were fears (ungrounded as it turned out) for the Reichsmark. But the main problem was unemployment: the number out of work rose from 1.3 million in September 1929 to over six million in January 1933. The government of Chancellor Brüning had, early in 1930, proposed to meet the situation by cutting expenditure, particularly on the social services. But this policy could only be carried through by the use of the president's emergency powers. Both the policy and the method of enforcing it were unpopular in the country, and this unpopularity weakened the republic and provided opportunity for the extremist parties to exploit the situation.

The communists made no secret of their aim to overthrow the republic and to set up a Bolshevik state. They took to the streets and resorted to violence to intimidate their opponents. But in this they were outdone by the Nazis (the National Socialist German Workers' Party); their violence was better organized, and their brownshirted, jackbooted SA (the Sturmabteilung, storm troopers or brownshirts) proved more than a match in most street battles with the left. An eyewitness, Kurt Ludecke, reported:

> Brownshirts were everywhere in evidence,...and now four private armies, equipped at the very least with jack-knives and revolvers, daggers and knuckle-dusters, were shouting in the squares and rampaging through the towns. Processions and meetings, demonstrations and protests, festivals and funerals, all wore the same face but a different uniform – except that the SS and SA of the Nazis and the Red Front of the Communists marched more defiantly, the Sozi (Social Democrat) Reichsbanner more fatly, the Stahlhelmer more sedately. The Reichswehr (the army) was least in evidence....

> Everywhere the swing was towards the radical wings. Thousands of Sozis flocked to the communists, thousands of nationalists joined the Nazis. Among the private armies, the enmity between those Marxist brothers, the Sozis and the communists, grew more deadly; the hypocritical truce between those hostile brethren, the Nazis and the nationalists, was about to end. The parties were all at each others' throats.

❝The great slump and the decline of the Weimar Republic.❞

Law and order was giving way to anarchy. The Stresemann era had seen the Nazi Party reduced to a mere twelve seats in the Reichstag, but the crisis of 1929 was the party's opportunity. Fear of communism gave the Nazis the backing of a number of important industrialists and a growing voice in the press. The middle class, too, feared communism, distrusted the republic and did not want savings again to be wiped out by inflation. The foreign banking failures of 1929 and 1930 had suggested that inflation might reappear, yet although there was no inflation during the great depression of 1929–33, the memory of it and the fear of it gave the Nazis a valuable propaganda asset. Their main platform, however, was the nationalist one of denouncing German's ill-treatment at Versailles, a treaty they asserted was a 'diktat', i.e. imposed on Germany against her will. And Germany's problems they blamed on foreigners, Jews, weak politicians, communists and, by implication, the Weimar political system. The Nazis promised to end reparations and to solve the problem of unemployment. To the German voters the moderate parties and support for the republic seemed less important than a strong government to deal with the crisis.

Both Nazis and communists, therefore, gained in the elections of 1930, the Nazis securing 107 seats in the Reichstag and the communists 77. Brüning's government, increasingly unpopular and dependent on the use of emergency powers, lasted until the end of May 1932, when he gave way to the nationalist leader, von Papen. The Nazi leader, Hitler, had already caused widespread excitement when he secured over thirteen million votes against Hindenburg's nineteen million in the presidential election of April 1932. Hindenburg was re-elected, but his and von Papen's authority was undermined, and when von Papen attempted to strengthen his position by another general election in July 1932, the Nazis with 230 seats became the largest single party in the Reichstag. Another election in November 1932 reduced the Nazis to 196 seats, making them still the largest party, and the election failed again to provide von Papen with the majority he had looked for. In December he gave way to von Schleicher, but von Schleicher had no more success than von Papen, and even toyed with the idea of establishing a military dictatorship; the republic no longer commanded the respect of its own politicians. Von Schleicher seemed too dangerous to be allowed to stay in office, and it was von Papen who by promising Hindenburg that he could control the Nazi leader, secured Hitler's appointment as chancellor in January 1933.

With Hitler's appointment the Weimar Republic was virtually at an end. The republic's death throes were short-lived; another general election in March 1933, preceded by the Reichstag fire, of great propaganda value to the Nazis in their fight against communism, gave the Nazis and their nationalist allies a majority in the Reichstag. By persecuting the left and cajoling the deputies of the centre, Hitler was able to win the two-thirds majority needed for his Enabling Act, which gave the Nazi government full powers to rule by emergency decree for four years. In effect the republic was now dead; any doubts on this point were dispelled when Hitler combined the chancellorship with the presidency on Hindenburg's death in August 1934.

7 ▷ REASONS FOR THE FAILURE OF THE WEIMAR REPUBLIC

❝Distinguish carefully between reasons and events.❞

The Germans were not used to democracy and they had too short a time to gain the necessary experience in the working of democracy. Many Germans never fully accepted the regime, and the lack of democratic tradition and of a firm popular base were to be exploited by Hitler, who had great political flair and a shrewd perception of how to turn situations to his advantage. It was unfortunate that from the start the new republic was saddled with the responsibility for accepting the unpopular Treaty of Versailles with its losses of German territory to France, Belgium, Denmark and Poland. And while the two economic crises of 1923 and 1929–33 were not initially of the republic's making, inflation, almost adopted as a policy in 1923, destroyed much of the republic's credibility, and in 1929 the government lacked both the economic knowledge of how to deal with unemployment and the political stability from which to tackle problems with confidence. Its weakness was shown in its unwillingness, except for a short time in 1932, to ban para-military organizations such as the Nazi SA. Apart from Stresemann, the republic produced no politician of outstanding quality, and even he was bitterly attacked by his rivals and a suspicious public. The multiplicity of parties made it difficult to sustain a stable government for long; politicians engaged in squalid infighting, while some of them, including even the president, Hindenburg, hankered for some more authoritarian form of government. It is no wonder that when the republic faced both the storm of economic recession and the threat of a popular and well-organized Nazi Party committed to its overthrow, it had little chance of survival.

IDEAS AND PRINCIPLES

LEFT WING AND RIGHT WING

Generally, left-wing politicians are those committed to major and rapid change in politics and society, and right-wing politicians are those who wish to preserve existing society and institutions with change and reform only when it is absolutely necessary. Extremists of the left want revolutionary change and are usually identifiable as communists or their close allies. Extremists of the right want a capitalist and authoritarian state, and are usually labelled as fascists.

In Germany during the 1920s and 1930s the description 'right-wing' was given to those who wanted authoritarian government, the restoration of the monarchy and the maintenance of the capitalist system. The right wing's main group was the nationalists, but after some wavering the national socialists committed themselves to capitalism and secured the support of a section of 'big business', so that in the early 1930s the extreme right was dominated by the Nazis.

The German left wing was the extreme socialists and communists who worked for the overthrow of capitalism. Both left wing and right wing, during Weimar, had it in common that they resorted to violent methods and that they both wanted an end to the Weimar Republic.

THE SPARTACISTS

The Spartacists were extreme left-wing revolutionaries, taking their name from a famous slave rebellion in ancient Rome. Their leaders were Rosa Luxemburg and Karl Liebknecht. They were powerful and effective agitators and they aimed to turn Germany into a Soviet republic – in effect the Spartacist movement was indistinguishable from a Bolshevik movement. Right-wing action, mainly by the Frei

Korps in January 1919, destroyed the Spartacists and Rosa and Karl were murdered by officers of the Guard Cavalry Division on their way to prison.

THE NATIONALISTS

The Nationalist Party was a German right-wing party which secured forty-four seats in the election of January 1919. They strongly supported capitalism, most of them wanted the return of the monarchy, they resented Germany's defeat in 1918 and they opposed the Treaty of Versailles. While they paid lip-service to the new republic, their true beliefs were better shown by the fact that they absented themselves from the Reichstag when Ebert was sworn in as the first president. The German army (Reichswehr) was largely nationalist in sympathy and so was Hindenburg, the president elected in 1925. The nationalists were outbid for votes by the Nazi Party in the elections of the 1930s, and their leaders Hugenburg and von Papen, by eventually agreeing to give the Nazis nationalist support, paved the way for the end of the Weimar Republic.

THE NATIONAL SOCIALISTS – NAZIS

This party was founded soon after the end of the First World War. Its early combination of nationalism and socialism seems somewhat contradictory, and it was soon to outdo the Nationalist Party both in right-wing extremism and in ruthless organization, using propaganda and violence as its principal methods of gaining support. Its socialist aims soon faded, and its early socialist background (lingering on amongst the leadership and membership of the SA) became something of an embarrassment during and after the successful Nazi bid for power (see Chapter 6).

APPLIED MATERIALS

Texts

R. Grunberger, *Germany, 1918–45*, Batsford, 1966
J.W. Hiden, *The Weimar Republic*, Longman, 1987
John Martell, *The Twentieth-Century World*, Harrap, 1980; Chapter 6
John and Gwenneth Stokes, *Europe and the Modern World*, Longman, 1973; Chapter 19

Documentary

J.F. Corkery and R.J.C. Stone, *Weimar Germany*, Heinemann, 1982
G.A. Cranfield, B.J. Dalton and F.G. Stambrook, *Select Documents*, McGraw-Hill, 1966
L.L. Snyder, *The Weimar Republic*, Anvil, 1966

EXAMINATION QUESTIONS

QUESTION 1

Show to what extent the Weimar Republic was successful during the 1920s in dealing with
(a) inflation
(b) reparations
(c) unemployment
(d) political extremism.

(20 marks)

QUESTION 2

Why did the Weimar Republic survive during the 1920s but collapse during the early 1930s?

(20 marks)

QUESTION 3

It is 1932 and the scene is a German beer cellar. A heated argument has broken out between Nazi supporters, who are urging the drinkers to vote Nazi, and others who from various different political viewpoints oppose the Nazis.
Give an account of the discussion.

(20 marks)

OUTLINE ANSWERS

ANSWER 1

Question 1 assumes an approximately equal division of the marks between the four parts. A description of each of the four themes will obviously be inadequate, because you are asked to measure (i.e. to assess) Weimar's success in dealing with each of the four problems. Thus in (a) you may well criticize the almost criminal responsibility of the republic for the accelerating inflation of the early 1920s, but you will show the effective tackling of inflation with the new Reichsmark at the end of 1923. It will be valuable to point out that the success was maintained throughout the rest of the 1920s and inflation was not a feature of the depression. Even so, the government might be able to create a new strong currency but it could not easily repair the economic, social and political damage brought about by the collapse of the old currency. In dealing with reparations it is easy to be led into lengthy accounts of such events as the occupation of the Ruhr: keep to the reparations theme – the early difficulties, the Dawes Plan and the Young Plan – and show that by the end of 1929 the reparations problem had been reduced but not eliminated. Note that in (c) your main theme will be economic recovery after the crisis of 1923, and that the unemployment following the Wall Street crash is relevant to the 1930s but hardly to the 1920s. Again, in (d) your main theme will be the handling of the extremists of 1919–21 and the Munich *putsch* of 1923, with the success story of the later 1920s when extremism was at its lowest ebb. As with (c), you should avoid trespassing into the 1930s, although it would be worth pointing out that the rapid resurgence of extremism in the 1930s shows that the extremists in 1926–9 were quiescent rather than moribund.

ANSWER 2

Question 2 has two parts and implies a historical contrast. The second part of the question is summarized at the end of the section 'Getting started', and this will provide a good basis which you can supplement with examples and material from your reading. The first part requires you to analyse the reasons for Weimar's survival in the 1920s and you should select a coherent list of points from your knowledge of the period. Thus a narrative will be weak: it will ask the examiner to identify relevant points. You will have to show why the extremist challenge was overcome in the years 1919–21 and you will refer to the Frei Korps, the use of the regular army, the strike of Berlin workers, the failure of left and right to achieve widespread sympathy or support, and then, of course, Stresemann and the period of Weimar success 1924–29.

ANSWER 3

Question 3 is an empathy question. Note that it asks for an account of a discussion and not an account of a brawl, so keep to varied arguments and do not let the discussion degenerate into a punch-up. The various Nazi arguments can be put forward, but remember that it is 1932, when the Nazis were still apparently willing to work within the Weimar constitution; the Nazis were not at that time openly calling for an end to Weimar. The opponents will undoubtedly criticize Nazi aims and methods, but remember to allow them to put forward positive aims and proposals of their own; your opponents could include social democrats, Centre Party and communists, and the first two, at least, ought to attempt some defence of the achievements of Weimar.

SUGGESTIONS FOR FURTHER WORK

1. Use the documentary sources which have been recommended to study details of the Weimar constitution. In what ways does the constitution deserve to be described as 'very democratic'?
2. Find out as much as you can about Stresemann and in particular his services to the Weimar Republic 1919–29. Tip: if you can't find a biography of Stresemann the major encyclopaedias will usually contain quite a lot of useful information on him.
3. Show how the inflation of 1923 affected the German people in different ways. Tip: it would be useful to select such people as i) a retired businessman living on income from his savings, ii) a farmer, iii) a factory worker and iv) a manufacturer with a very large mortgage on his business. This will enable you to show how some gained and some lost from the inflation. Try to find out how daily life was affected by the inflation, and make your description as vivid and realistic as possible.
4. Compile the Reichstag election statistics for the years 1930–33. How do these figures help to explain the collapse of the Weimar Republic? The figures can be found graphically displayed in the *Penguin Atlas of World History*, Vol.II, pages 148, 150 and 192.

TUTOR'S QUESTION AND ANSWER

1 ⟩ QUESTION Study Sources A–E below and then answer all parts of the questions which follow. When referring to sources in your answer you should refer to them by letter.

Source A

The Stage of the National Theatre was festively decorated with the new (black, red and gold) colours of the Reich and with plants and flowers... The House was packed with the exception of the Nationalists' and Independent Socialists' benches which remained ostentatiously empty. After an organ prelude Ebert, short, broad-shouldered, in dark morning dress and wearing gold-rimmed glasses, appeared on the stage, followed by the Cabinet also in black.

Inauguration of President Ebert, 21 August, 1919.

Source B

Dogs and Frenchmen forbidden.

Notice in a Ruhr café, 1924.

Source C

The Weimar politicians urged passive resistance to the French because they were too weak to find a political or economic solution. It was easy for the politicians to pose as patriots, but it was the workers of the Ruhr who actually confronted the French troops. While the country faced economic ruin the politicians paid off the country's national debt by reckless printing of paper money. Germany rid itself of the internal burden of war by ruining those who had lent money to pay for it, and at the same time whined so much about the external burden of war that the allies developed a guilty conscience and the Americans came to the rescue.

A historian's comment on 1923.

Source D

Election of a party man, representing one-sided extremist views, who would subsequently have the majority of the people against him, would expose the Fatherland to serious disturbance whose outcome would be incalculable. Duty commanded me to prevent this...If I am defeated, I shall at least not have incurred the reproach that of my own accord I deserted my post in an hour of crisis...I ask for no votes from those who do not wish to vote for me.

Election radio broadcast by Hindenburg, 10 March, 1932.

Source E

Hindenburg replied that because of the tense situation he could not in good conscience risk transferring the power of government to a new party such as the National Socialists, which did not command a majority and which was intolerant, noisy and undisciplined.

At this point, Hindenburg, with a certain show of excitement, referred to several recent occurrences – clashes between the Nazis and the police, acts of violence committed by Hitler's followers against those who were of a different opinion, excesses against Jews and other illegal acts. All these incidents had strengthened him in his conviction that there were numerous wild elements in the Party beyond control...After extended discussion Hindenburg proposed to Hitler that he should declare himself ready to co-operate with the other parties, particularly with the Right and Centre, and that he should give up the one-sided idea that he must have complete power. In co-operating with other parties, Hindenburg declared, he would show what he could achieve and improve upon. If he could show positive results, he would acquire increasing and even dominating influence even in a coalition government. Hindenburg stated that this also would be the best way to eliminate the widespread fear that a National Socialist government would make ill use of its power and would suppress all other viewpoints and would gradually eliminate them.

Report of a meeting between Hitler and Hindenburg, 13 August, 1932.

(a)   What weaknesses in the Weimar Republic are suggested in Source A?(3 marks)

(b)   i)   What does Source B suggest about the attitude of the inhabitants of the Ruhr to the French occupation? (2 marks)

ii)   How does Source C help to explain this attitude? (2 marks)

(c)   How effective an appeal for votes would you regard Source D? Give reasons for your answer. (3 marks)

(d)   i)   Give two reasons from Source E why Hindenburg would not give power to the Nazis. (2 marks)

ii)   Hindenburg's loyalty to the Weimar Republic has sometimes been questioned. How far does the evidence of Sources D and F confirm or deny that Hindenburg was a loyal servant of Weimar? (4 marks)

(e)   How far do Sources A and C appear to be biased? (4 marks)

2 ▷ ANSWER

(a) The specific weakness is the deliberate absence of the nationalists and independent socialists on the occasion of the president's inauguration, an event which should have been above party. But there is also a faint tone of ridicule in the description, which suggests an overall lack of confidence on the part of the writer.

(b) i) The inhabitants of the Ruhr equate Frenchmen with dogs, a deliberate insult against the occupying forces.

ii) Source C suggests that the defiance in the Ruhr was an attitude encouraged by Germany's politicians.

(c) Source D shows Hindenburg pointing out the danger of voting for a party man, and implying the need for a man above party if civil strife is to be avoided. Hindenburg poses as a man of honour committed to doing his duty, rather than a power seeker, which by implication his opponent is.

(d) i) Because the party lacked a majority and was committed to violence.

ii) In his broadcast Hindenburg certainly seems to equate extremism with a threat to the fatherland, and he feels it is his duty not to surrender to extremism but to continue in office as president. In the meeting, Source E, he shows reluctance to transfer power to a party that is irresponsible, and he seems concerned to give Hitler the opportunity to show that his party will, in effect, work within the constitution. Thus Hindenburg seems in both instances to be working to defend and sustain Weimar rather than to overthrow it.

(e) Source A is not specifically biased, but the concentration on trivia – plants and flowers, organ prelude, Ebert's gold-rimmed spectacles, etc. – gives something of a comic air to the description and belittles the importance of so historic an occasion. Source C is obviously hostile to the Weimar politicians – it describes them as weak, and it uses emotive words such as 'reckless' and 'whined'. Its reference to 'pose as patriots' even casts doubt on the patriotism of the politicians and the rest of the sentence queries their courage. The whole tone of the passage is much more hostile to its subject than Source A.

STUDENT'S ANSWER – EXAMINER'S COMMENT

Question

Why did the Weimar Republic survive during the 1920s?

> **The paragraph is a 'narrative', i.e. a description which makes no attempt to analyse the material being offered. It cannot score highly unless some attempt is made to explain the 'causality', i.e. the reasons why the Republic survived.**

```
    During the 1920s the Weimar republic survived for many
reasons. After the Kizer abdicated and the German people were
faced with much political disorder and chaos. There were
revolusheneries everywhere and a lot of street fiting. Before
a new form of government could be drawn up the Spartakists,
sort of communists, led by Rosie Luxemburg and her friend
Karl tried to (org) bring about a rebelion. But they were
defeeted by the Fry Corps who had once ben soldiers in the
Kyser's army. People were so pleased that the communists
leaders had been killed that the free Corps became too
important and self-satisfide. They tried to take over, first
in the Ruer and then in Berlin. But the Berlin workers went
on strike and the Fry Corps was (discr) weekened in its
influence.
    When France and Belgum occuped the Ruer and the value of
the German mark collapsed it seemed that Germany could not
survive. But survival was due to Streserman.
```

❝ The spelling here leaves much to be desired, and it is not even consistent. Poor spelling creates a bad impression, especially when words that are given on the question paper itself are mis-spelt, e.g. Weimar. Words attempted by the candidate but abandoned half-way through because of spelling uncertainty are given in brackets.. **❞**

He was only Chancellor for a few months, but during that time he restored public confidence and people's faith in the govenment. A new mark was issued to replace the old one, and inflation came to an end. By that time Streserman had become foren minister, and in this post he was able to (negot) perswade the French to leave the Ruer and the Americans, by the Doors Plan to reduce reparations. As this period coincided with a world economic recovery, extremist agitation in Germany died down. As unemployment fell and prosperity developped, so the number of Communists and nazis in the Riechstag fell.

Streserman negotiated with other countries on equal terms, signing the Geneva Protocol in 1925, and joining the League of Nations in 1926. This made many Germans feel that as Germany was now internationally acceptable, so Germany's form of government, the Wimar Republic, was now nationally acceptable.

❝ This is a useful point. **❞**

❝ The spelling has not improved, but the material here is being used more effectively and reasons are emerging. **❞**

HITLER
AND
GERMANY

GETTING STARTED

Hitler was born in 1889 in Austria, close to the German frontier, where his father was a minor customs official. His father died whilst he was at school in Linz. As a youth he drifted into Vienna where he lived in poor circumstances between 1908 and 1914, trying to launch himself as an artist. Already imbued by his history teacher with a passionate sense of nationalism, he now learned also to hate the Jews. In 1913 he moved to Munich and on the outbreak of the First World War he volunteered for service in the German army. He enjoyed the discipline, the security and the regular life, and though he never progressed beyond the rank of corporal he was twice wounded and was decorated for bravery. At the end of the war he was in hospital recovering from the effects of a gas attack near Ypres. He returned in 1919 to Munich and took up a minor appointment with army intelligence, keeping an eye on the many radical political movements which flourished in the city at that time. It was whilst he was engaged in spying on it that he decided to join the German Workers' Party in 1919, where he became member no. 7 of the party's committee.

Germany was in a state of turmoil at this time. Extremist groups, anti-liberal, anti-democratic, anti-socialist and anti-Semitic, were flourishing. Communists were increasingly strident and the German middle classes were rapidly losing the respectable position in society that they had once occupied. For the Weimar Republic there was little but contempt and hatred. Gradually there was emerging a simple but passionate form of folkish nationalism – 'a kind of Peter Pan ideology for a society which did not seem to want to grow up'.

HISTORICAL DEVELOPMENTS

1 ❯ A NEW PARTY

In 1920 Hitler became the leader of the new party and changed its name to the National Socialist German Workers' Party, or Nazi Party. In the early days he was very much impressed by the masterful character of Ernst Röhm, who was very influential amongst ex-servicemen in Munich and helped to recruit members of the Frei Korps and the Stahlhelm into the movement as well as students and workers. Hitler issued the party's first programme in 1920, with promises that were as much socialist as they were nationalist. They built up their own band of storm-troopers or brownshirts (the Sturm Abteilung or SA), who were used at first as hall guards during party meetings but later developed into a fully-fledged para-military organization.

In November 1923, with the support of people as respectable as General Ludendorff, Hitler attempted a coup in Munich, attempting a march on Berlin that seemed to be vaguely modelled on Mussolini's march on Rome. His followers were easily dispersed by regular troops, and Hitler suffered a dislocated arm and was carried off under arrest. Brought to trial before a rather sympathetic court, he turned the tables on his prosecutors by eloquently pouring scorn on the government and the other traitors who had betrayed his country. The court sent him to prison for five years, of which he served rather less than nine months. During this time he was shut up in conditions of some comfort in Landsberg Prison, where he spent much of his time dictating *Mein Kampf* to his friend and fellow-prisoner Rudolf Hess. The book, shapeless and almost unreadable, became the bible of the Nazi movement.

> **The rise of the 'great dictator'**

When Hitler came out of prison in December 1924 the Nazi Party had disintegrated, and he set about the difficult task of rebuilding it. He enlisted the co-operation of the fighter ace Hermann Goering and of Josef Goebbels, who was put in charge of propaganda. He began to develop the storm-troopers as his private army. He eked out his limited supply of cash as best he could, struggling to run a newspaper in order to spread his views more widely.

At first the Nazis made little impression. After the great inflation of 1923 the country was now settling down to conditions of some prosperity under respected figures like Hindenburg and Stresemann. Internationally, attempts were being made to rehabilitate Germany. The Locarno treaties were signed in 1925 and in the following year Germany was admitted to the League of Nations. The Dawes Plan seemed to be working well. Industrial recovery was progressing, and as discontent diminished few people were inclined to listen to Hitler's brand of hysterical extremism. In the mid-1920s there were only fourteen Nazi members of the Reichstag, and after 1928 only twelve.

Hitler's opportunity came with the onset of the great depression in 1929. For some time in 1928–29 US funds, earlier lent to Germany, had been making their way home so as to take advantage of high profits on the American stock market. In the autumn of 1929 the Wall Street crash and the consequent collapse of large areas of the US banking system led to even heavier withdrawals of US funds from European banks. As the crisis became more widespread, trade ground to a halt, and Germany, with a millstone of reparations debt around its neck, found itself faced with a financial crisis and over six million unemployed. In 1930 the Nazi Party was able to win 107 seats in the Reichstag. Brüning attempted policies of mild inflation, but these enabled Hitler to play on middle-class fears that if such policies were allowed to continue unchecked runaway inflation like that of 1923 might be the result. Discontent spread across many classes in Germany. The Nazis were able to get support from a wide range of disaffected groups by skilful use of publicity and by playing on well-established fears and prejudices – particularly the belief that Germany had been betrayed in 1919. Ex-servicemen and unemployed flocked to Hitler's banner, as did many middle-class professional people who feared that their savings might become worthless. Even big businessmen such as Thyssen and Hugenberg rallied to his cause, fearing that the advance of communism might lead to a loss of business profits and even violent revolution in Germany. Such men put at Hitler's disposal large funds to establish more newspapers and finance his political campaign.

By 1932 Hitler's influence was felt the length and breadth of Germany. Propaganda built up a picture of a party that was youthful, radical, patriotic and vigorous; one which, though anti-Jewish and anti-Marxist, was warmly sympathetic to the ordinary German and to the small businessman, without being simultaneously hostile to the industrial magnates and landlords.

Hindenburg's first term of office expired in 1932 and Hitler chose to oppose him at the presidential election in March. (See Chapter 5 for details of the working of the Weimar constitution). The field marshal was re-elected, but Hitler took thirteen million votes as against his nineteen million. Brüning was now forced to resign his Chancellorship and was replaced by von Papen, who imagined that he could manipulate the machinery of the republic with sufficient skill to build up a coalition of parties which he could then control. He even imagined that he could keep Hitler under control – he said 'I'll push him so far into the corner that he'll be squeaking.' He offered Hitler the vice-chancellorship, provided that he would accept his leadership. Hitler contemptuously rejected the offer. Then there was a general election in July 1932 in which Hitler once more increased Nazi representation in the Reichstag; he now had 230 members, and when the new chamber met, Goering became its president. Von Papen shortly afterwards resigned, and when Hitler refused Hindenburg's offer – this time of the chancellorship – because of the number of strings he attached, the post passed to von Schleicher in the autumn. Another election in November saw Hitler's representation fall back. Many people, thinking that the worst of the danger was past, were glad. Others feared that though Hitler now had only 196 members, the masses were turning to the communists instead. Nevertheless in January 1933 Hindenburg offered the Chancellorship to Hitler unconditionally, and he accepted it. In his first cabinet, however, apart from himself Hitler could manage only three appointments; the others were divided between the nationalists and the smaller parties.

REIGN OF TERROR

The first thing that Hitler did was to insist on yet more elections. In the lead-up to them the Nazis carried out their preparations ruthlessly. His henchman, Goering, reinforced the police with 50,000 men from the SA and the SS (the blackshirts, a specially selected corps which formed Hitler's personal bodyguard), and these began what was little short of a reign of terror to intimidate opponents. Then on 27 February the Reichstag building burned down, a crime for which the Nazis immediately blamed their communist rivals. A half-crazed Dutch communist, Cornelius van der Lubbe, was convicted of the offence and executed, but the leading communists who were supposed to be his accomplices were acquitted. Nevertheless, the fire served its purpose. Frick, Reichsminister of the interior, took advantage of it to push through a law empowering the government to detain suspects at will, search private houses, censor the post and take a number of other steps for 'the restoration of public security'. At the elections the Nazi Party won 288 seats with a 44 per cent share of the poll; but, with the support of their nationalist allies, managed to push their share over the 50 per cent mark, thus entitling them to claim that they were a genuine majority government.

The new Reichstag was opened on 21 March in the Kroll Opera House and at once set about the adoption of the Enabling Bill, the aim of which was to transfer to the chancellor full powers for a period of four years. This involved a major change in the constitution and was thus supposed to have a two-thirds majority in the chamber. Hitler simplified his task by arresting the eighty-one communist deputies and striking bargains with the other parties. The nationalists were persuaded to join with him on the issue, whilst the Catholic Centre Party agreed to support him if he promised them a concordat with the pope and proper respect towards the Catholic Church. In the end, only the social democrats voted against the proposal. Thus the Reichstag signed its own death warrant and the Nazi Party established complete authority.

CONSOLIDATION

Hitler now set about consolidating his own position. Apart from the presidency, the army and the churches, everything was brought under Nazi control by the Co-ordination Law. State Diets were swept away and their powers transferred to Berlin. Nazis were appointed to all leading positions in the country. Labour leaders and political opponents were arrested, beaten up and often put into concentration camps. Jews were excluded from the civil service in the first of a series of brutal steps which were finally to remove them from public life altogether. Political parties other than the Nazis were banned. Left-wing organizations were generally outlawed, whilst right-wing ones such as the civilian Peasants Organization and the Stahlhelm were incorporated into the Nazi system.

Hitler was not yet, however, fully master of Germany. Amongst the socialist wing of the Nazi Party there were still some like Gregor Strasser and Röhm, the chief of the SA, who were more socialist than nationalist, and were dissatisfied with the way they thought Hitler had sold out to the ruling classes. Of course, the SA had been useful in bringing Hitler to power, but now he felt they were too ill-disciplined and ambitious to be tolerated any longer. Hitler preferred the SS, an élite drawn largely from the middle classes, who were implicitly reliable. The army too feared a challenge from the SA; they were also rather doubtful about Hitler himself until he had shown them some token of good faith. First Hitler tried to buy off Röhm by giving him a cabinet appointment to quieten him. He still continued to intrigue against Hitler, however, demanding for himself and his colleagues senior appointments in the Wehrmacht and elsewhere in the civil administration. The showdown came in June with what became known as the Night of the Long Knives. Röhm and perhaps as many as 400 others were seized and murdered. The challenge from the SA was at an end, and no more was heard of the social revolution.

In August 1934 Hindenburg died, and Hitler declared himself simultaneously President, Chancellor and Commander-in-Chief of the army, with the title of Führer. A plebiscite followed in which nearly 96 per cent of a 90 per cent poll gave the stamp of legality to his actions.

3   NAZI POLITICAL AND SOCIAL POLICY

Hitler's government was fundamentally a dictatorship. It gave great power to the Führer and to his high-ranking supporters in the movement. It based itself, at least in the beginning, on the will of the people, since it sought the nation's approval in plebiscites. But because it was based on no clear constitutional foundation it operated in an arbitrary fashion. Hitler was invested with almost godlike authority; the SS and its political wing, the Gestapo, operated free from any legal restraint, and the party in power could not be challenged in the courts. The state extended its tentacles into areas of life where previously it had never ventured.

RACIALIST PHILOSOPHY

The ideas of Nazism

At the root of Nazism lay its racialist philosophy: the view that the Nordic Germans (or Aryans) were the master race, and all others to a greater or lesser degree were inferior. At the top, victors in the unrelenting struggle, were the Aryans, blond, athletic and beautiful; near neighbours such as the Swedes were a little below them in the hierarchy; then the English and then the Latin races; and finally, at the bottom, the contemptible non-people such as the gypsies and the Jews. This theory was as dangerous as it was ridiculous, and though buttressed by the findings of pseudo-science it was basically unsound. Linked with this racialism went a quest for territory. The Nazis laid claim to what they called the 'empty' lands to the east peopled only by the Slavs, which they could put to better use as living space (or *lebensraum*) for the chosen people. It was the destiny of the chosen *Volk* to conquer and to rule the world. A lot of Germans were flattered into believing this seductive nonsense; those who did not usually thought it better to keep their doubts to themselves.

THE JEWS

It was the Jews who felt the brunt of Nazi policies. Regarded as the scapegoats for all Germany's ills, they were driven from public life. Many of the professional classes in Germany – the doctors, the lawyers, university teachers, scientists and financiers – were Jewish, and there were many Germans who were happy to see them removed in order that they could walk into their jobs. Julius Streicher, the notorious 'Jew-baiter', built his career out of hounding them, and in 1935 the Nuremburg Laws were passed which effectively deprived them of their civil rights and turned them into non-citizens. Those in trade were deprived of their department stores and shops; manufacturers were not allowed to employ non-Jewish labour, since it was not fitting that a Jew should be the master of an Aryan; finally Jewish families were not even allowed to employ German girls as housemaids. In the end, thousands of Jews were rounded up and carted off to concentration camps where they perished through neglect or else were pitilessly exterminated.

THE CHURCHES

The churches also came into conflict with the Nazis. In 1933 Hitler signed a concordat with the papacy in the hope of appeasing opinion in the Catholic parts of the country, but his racialism upset the pope and in 1937 Pius XI condemned Hitler's actions in his encyclical 'Mit brennender sorge' ('With burning anguish'). The Lutheran Church was also alienated, part of it rallying behind the ex-submarine commander Pastor Niemöller in condemning the party's behaviour. Niemöller himself was sent to a concentration camp, and the rest of his Church was cowed into silence. Hitler had only one willing supporter, Pastor Müller, who was made evangelical bishop of the Reich in 1933. He adapted the Church's teachings to the Nazi philosophy and claimed to find racialism in the scriptures. Church observance continued within the Reich, but its role was strictly subordinated to the state.

THE YOUNG

Hitler attached great importance to the young, many of whom were more fanatical than their parents. Children could join the Little Fellows at 6 and the *Jungvolk* at 10 and could graduate to the Hitler Youth at 14. The girls joined the League of German Maidens, revering motherhood as the highest aim to which they could aspire. Formed in 1926, the Hitler Youth by 1934 numbered six million boys and many girls besides. Great emphasis was laid on outdoor activities and physical fitness, with summer camps, drilling and learning Nazi doctrines. On leaving school, boys did six months' compulsory labour service for the good of the Reich, followed in most cases by two years in the army. Some later joined the SS or the Gestapo. Nazis had an instinctive revulsion against intellectuals, whose independent habits of thought they distrusted and feared. Under Hitler, education became a vehicle of state propaganda, just as did the radio and the newspapers. Critics found themselves arrested and detained, and publications hostile to the Reich and even works of genuine scholarship were burned on bonfires.

Machine or morass?

Nevertheless, Nazi Germany was far from being a truly totalitarian state. It had a frightening apparatus of detection – concealed microphones, sophisticated interrogation techniques and so on – but these were often only spasmodically applied. The much-vaunted state control was also rather patchy. Vast vested interests went unchallenged by the state, and there were many private empires of influence from which the ruling Nazis averted their eyes. Nazi economic controls were a hit-and-miss affair, in which favouritism and jobbery were rampant and business malpractice almost routine. With the SS and the Gestapo free of political controls, government operations resembled much more closely the manoeuvrings of the gangster underworld than any systematic tyranny. It was the frivolous caprice of the Nazi regime at least as much as its premeditated brutality which struck terror into the hearts of those who observed it.

4 ▷ NAZI ECONOMIC AND FINANCIAL POLICY

Though Hitler had broad general aims when he came to power, he did not have a blueprint ready to put into effect. In detail the Nazis actually adopted the policies put earlier by the civil servants to Brüning, but rejected at that time because of the cost. Clearly one of Hitler's main aims was to remedy the grave unemployment problem existing in Germany when the Nazis came to power. To a large extent his efforts were successful. Many people found jobs in the huge new Nazi bureaucracy and in organizations such as the Hitler Youth. Others were able to take over from displaced Jews. A large number remained in jobs where they were really redundant, kept there by government orders; yet others went into the forces or went into arms factories as rearmament progressed. The government drafted young people into compulsory labour service, where they lived in camps and worked for a little pocket money as a demonstration of their patriotic devotion. By the end of the 1930s, unemployment had shrunk to little more than 250,000.

The main source of new jobs, however, was in public works and in rearmament. Many massive new public buildings were put up, slums cleared and housing constructed, and great motorways (or *autobahnen*) brought into being. Simultaneously, guns, tanks, aircraft, ships and submarines were constructed in great numbers. Whilst this was going on the Nazis gave the German working classes much of what they demanded: food prices and rents were controlled, health services were improved and cheap cars were put on the market. Trade union members were not allowed to complain even if they wanted to; a new organization known as the Labour Front was set up in 1934 under Dr Ley, and was joined both by employers and employees, the officers and other ranks of the army of industry. This organization exercised very wide powers: it provided sports and recreational facilities, and offered cheap family holidays to the masses.

66 'The economics of the madhouse'? 99

Hitler had been from the beginning aware that the main danger to his programme would be inflation. If the government succumbed to the temptation to print money as it had in 1923, a flood of paper similar to the one which had swamped Germany earlier might threaten the country again. This was avoided in various ways. One was strict controls over wages. Though earnings increased, they were not permitted to rise as far or as fast as they would have done without controls, and the men were generally too glad to be in work and assured of a minimal level of price increases to make much fuss. Budget deficits were avoided by raising loans from people with money to invest, relying on the confidence which such people felt in the government. But those who benefited most from low tax levels and modest wage increases were the employers, who were made to pay for the privilege. Corporation taxes were increased so that companies had to help to pay for the schemes they were working on. Furthermore, the government issued new bonds, in which any saver could invest and towards which commercial banks were forced to contribute; in these bonds manufacturers were paid for the contracts on which they worked, and they could either be cashed immediately by the Reichsbank or they could be held until maturity with interest received on them for up to five years.

One consequence of job creation was the greatly increased consumer demand, resulting in a steep rise in imports. But since much of the work being done was for rearmament and construction work at home, Germany found itself with relatively little to export in exchange. Thus the Third Reich soon found itself in a balance of payments crisis. The task of dealing with this fell to Dr Schacht, president of the Reichsbank. His aim was to boost exports and to restrict imports. One method was to pay for imports by exporting part of Germany's output of armaments, but his customers were not always interested in buying these – though if they bought guns they would certainly need ammunition later. Another method was to arrange deliveries of foodstuffs and raw materials and then to delay paying for them for as long as possible, and then in the end to pay with credits which could only be spent in Germany. Most complex of all was a fiendishly ingenious system whereby Schacht maintained over 250 different exchange values for the German mark at the same time, blocking off all the country's external trade into a series of nontransferrable bilateral deals at different rates of exchange.

Efforts were made too to render Germany self-sufficient, so that the need for imports would be less. The objective of self-sufficiency was said to be *autarky* (or economic independence). The plan involved the widespread use of synthetics. These substitute commodities were known as ersatz goods. A not unpalatable type of coffee could be made from acorns or from dandelion roots, whilst in industry plastics and even a sort of artificial wool could be made from the by products of the chemical industry. German industry also synthesized oil and petrol from coal and made a tough sort of synthetic rubber which was employed for vehicle tyres. Generally, however, synthetics were expensive to produce and inferior in quality. Goering's ambitious Four Year Plan, introduced in 1936, was supposed to make Germany entirely independent of imports, but in fact it produced only limited results.

The end of the 1930s, therefore, saw German trade becoming more and more unbalanced. Schacht was driven from cabinet office in 1937 and had to resign from the Reichsbank in 1939, his 'system' in ruins about him. The Nazi economic system was fundamentally unsound, since those responsible for it were unable or unwilling to trade with their neighbours in the usual way. Having failed to trade with them they tried to cheat them; then, having failed to do that effectively, they were increasingly driven to the position of having to exploit them by conquest.

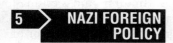

5 NAZI FOREIGN POLICY

Hitler's motives on coming to power were clear. He wished to remove the stigma of the Versailles treaty, repudiate the reparations burden, reject the notion of war guilt and set about the restoration of Germany's self-esteem. In particular, he did not intend to be bound by the disarmament clauses, and he was determined to recover the territories taken from the Reich in 1919 as well as to establish control over any lands where there was a German population living. 'One blood demands one Reich' was the phrase he used to describe his foreign policy objectives.

❝Design or drift?❞

The question is still debated whether Hitler had – as many historians have believed – some 'grand design', a carefully worked out programme of expansion and if need be war; or whether he was purely an opportunist with broad but flexible objectives, exploiting the weaknesses and fears of other powers. Some see him as a lucky gambler who came up on so many bets that he began to think he couldn't lose.

Originally, however, he had only limited success, for Mussolini – a man whom Hitler much admired and respected at first – blocked his designs on Austria. He was forced hastily to disavow his attempted take-over of that country and to try to shift the blame to the Austrian Nazi Party. In 1934 he was not yet strong enough to cope with opposition.

In January 1935, however, he was victorious in a plebiscite held in the Saarland, which voted by more than 95 per cent to be once more incorporated into the Reich. This was quite in accordance with the terms of the treaty, though France had some misgivings that it involved the start of Germany's westwards expansion. A few weeks afterwards, in March, Hitler went on to repudiate the Versailles disarmament clauses and to set about the building of a peacetime army of thirty-six divisions, or about 550,000 men. His actions passed almost unchallenged. Indeed, in 1936, Britain even signed a naval treaty with Germany signifying its willingness to allow Germany to reconstruct its navy, provided that its total strength at no time exceeded 35 per cent of the British navy.

In March 1936 Hitler struck again. Whilst Italian troops were engaging the world's attention by invading Abyssinia, Hitler repudiated the Locarno agreements and marched his troops into the Rhineland to remilitarize it. It was an act of considerable daring, since only three battalions of troops, many of them on motor-bicycles, actually crossed the Rhine. If the western powers had resisted, Hitler would almost certainly have been compelled to withdraw again. But neither Britain nor France moved, and though for a time the air was thick with paper protest, Hitler was allowed to get away with his defiance.

When war broke out in Spain in the summer of 1936, Hitler took advantage of it to sign a number of alliances with sympathetic powers. A vague, but quite important, alliance was signed in October with Mussolini; it was known as the Rome–Berlin Axis. Later that year, Germany and Japan, both feeling themselves threatened by Soviet Russia, signed the Anti-Comintern Pact, and Italy also became a member in 1937.

All this prepared the way in the spring of 1938 for an *Anschluss* with Austria. In February the Austrian Chancellor Schuschnigg was summoned to Berlin and there browbeaten into making concessions to the Austrian Nazis. Nazis such as Seyss-Inquart were promoted to key positions, and in March, after stirring up trouble in the country, they provided Hitler with an excuse to march his troops in and take over. The western powers again did very little. Many people thought that after all the Austrians were German and there was nothing very wrong in uniting them all under the same government. In the end, all that Britain and France did was to remove Austria's name from the membership list of the League of Nations.

Czechoslovakia was now exposed to pressure from three sides, and later that year Hitler made his next move. The German population of the Sudetenland, led by Konrad Henlein, claimed they were being persecuted by the Czechs. Chamberlain, trying to resolve the problem by peaceful methods, sent the Runciman Mission to the country in order to investigate the grievances. Then, in September, he flew to Germany three times in an effort to produce a just solution. In the end, at Munich, the western powers agreed to hand over the Sudetenland to the Germans, and Czechoslovakia was forced to accept these humiliating terms. It was little more than six months before Hitler moved to take over the whole of Czechoslovakia.

Also in 1939, Hitler presented an ultimatum to Lithuania and occupied Memelland where a considerable number of other Germans lived. Next it was Danzig's turn. Hitler demanded not only that Albert Forster, the Nazi gauleiter of Danzig, should be left free to manage the affairs of German residents without interference from the Poles, but also that the Nazis had the right to open up a strategic route by road and rail across the 'corridor', thus connecting Germany with east Prussia via the city of Danzig. The Poles rejected these demands, encouraged in their defiance of Hitler by an Anglo–French declaration that they would defend the country from a German attack. In August, however, Hitler pulled off his most brilliant coup. Molotov and Ribbentrop, whose officials had been negotiating in Moscow since May, produced a Russo–German non-aggression pact, with secret clauses agreeing to the partition of Poland between the two. On 1 September, after carefully staged frontier incidents, Nazi forces invaded Poland and the Second World War began.

6 ▶ THE END OF HITLER

Though spectacularly successful in overrunning Norway, Denmark, Holland, Belgium, Luxemburg and much of France, Hitler, by invading the Soviet Union in 1941, eventually bit off more than he could chew. He seemed to think that the USSR could be speedily overrun – he said at the outset of the campaign 'You only have to kick in the door and the whole rotten structure will collapse' – but this turned out to be a serious miscalculation.

By the end of the war, he found himself faced with overwhelming odds. He was at war with Britain and the Commonwealth, and with the USSR and the USA, whose combined resources far outstripped his own. At sea he was beaten by the British and allied navies, and subjected to a crippling blockade. By 1943 the Nazis were penned into 'Fortress Europe' and most of their contacts with the outside world were severed. After the Battle of Britain and the blitz, the allies also achieved great superiority in the air. German towns, ports and industrial plants were mercilessly hammered. Thousand bomber raids took place by night and in the later stages of the war daytime raids proceeded almost incessantly. Local resistance movements also played their part in wearing the Germans down. Hitler also seriously overestimated the strength of his allies. He was frequently called on to support his Italian allies in north Africa and the Mediterranean area; whilst the Japanese, though brilliantly successful for a time, eventually ran out of steam in their efforts to dominate the Pacific.

Within Germany there was little organized resistance to the Führer's rule. Opposition groups took care to keep out of sight; like fugitive Jews they sometimes had to live in self-imposed imprisonment to survive. After 1943, furthermore, the Nazi leaders were increasingly hidden away from the public eye; no one was able to assassinate them even if they were willing to take the risk. Hitler hid himself in the Chancellery in Berlin, at Berchtesgaden or at his distant military HQ amid the forests of east Prussia; he moved from one to another unpredictably, and most people had no idea where he was at any given time. Few people ever came into regular contact with him, and those who did were never allowed to be armed; revolvers made the Führer nervous. Besides, every German soldier had taken a personal oath of loyalty to the Führer, and the vast majority would rather die than betray him. Nevertheless there were a few of the officer class who were prepared to take the risk. Two early attempts to kill him, one by handing over to him a bomb that was supposed to be a gift of bottles of brandy, the other by demonstrating to him a new type of army greatcoat with explosive charges hidden in the pockets, came to nothing in 1943. The Stauffenberg bomb plot of 1944 came the nearest to success, but the plot failed by accident and the hideous reprisals inflicted on the participants served as a sufficient deterrent to others thinking on the same lines.

By 1945 the Russians were at the gates of Berlin, having overrun Poland and most of eastern Europe. On 30 April, with the Red Army scarcely half a mile away, Hitler shot himself and his body was burned in the garden of the Chancellery. The Third Reich, which was to have lasted a thousand years, had perished in little more than ten.

APPLIED MATERIALS

Texts and Atlases

J. Brooman, *Hitler's Germany*, Longman, 1987

B. Catchpole, *Twentieth-Century Germany*, Oxford, 1965

J.F. Corkery and R.J.C. Stone, *Weimar Germany and the Third Reich*, Heinemann, 1986

B.J. Elliott, *Hitler and Germany*, Longman (Modern Times Series), 1966

Evidence and Empathy

J. Simkin, *Rise of Hitler*, Spartacus, 1986

J. Simkin, *Hitler's Germany*, Spartacus, 1986

Documentary Books

M. Berwick, *The Third Reich*, Wayland, 1971

T. Edwards, *Hitler and Germany, 1919–39*, Heinemann History Broadsheet, 1986

D.M. Phillips, *Hitler and the Rise of the Nazis*, Arnold, 1968

General Studies Project, *The Nazi Germany Collection,* Longman

Filmstrips, Records etc.

M. and P. Roberts, *Fascism, its Rise and Fall,* (4) VP

M. and P. Roberts, *Origins of World War II, Student Recording Ltd.*

Adolf Hitler , AVP 594

Audio learning, *Hitler and the Rise of the Nazis*, HM 0008

Audio learning, *Rise of Nazis and Nazi Seizure of Power*, HUA 008

EXAMINATION QUESTIONS

Candidates must answer Question 1 and either 2 or 3 or 4.

You should spend about 30 minutes on each question.

Study the sources below and answer the questions which follow:

Source A

'The meeting began at 7.30 and ended at 10.45. The lecturer gave a talk on Jewry. He showed that wherever one looks, one sees Jews. It is a scandal that the German workers.....let themselves be so harassed by the Jews. Of course the Jew has money in his hands. The Jew sits in government and swindles and smuggles..... Therefore, Germans, be united and fight against the Jews!'

A local party secretary describes one of Hitler's first speeches, 1919.

Source B

'Teachers are directed to instruct their pupils in the nature, causes and effects of all racial problems, to bring home to them the importance of race....to awaken pride in their membership of the German race.....and the will to co-operate in the racial purification of the German stock.'

     Order from the Reich minister of education, Dr Rust, January 1935.

Source C

'Berlin had (in 1933) 32% Jewish Chemists, 48% Jewish Doctors, 50% Jewish Lawyers, 8.5% Jewish Newspaper Editors....No people on earth with a vestige of pride in itself could put up with such domination of many professions by members of a completely alien race.'

     Dr Gross, Head of the Reich Bureau for Enlightenment on Population Policy and Racial Welfare – quoted in a book published for British readers by the German Embassy in London, 1938.

QUESTION 1

i)   (a)   What was the full title of the political party to which Hitler belonged in 1919? [1 mark]

         (b)   In Source A, what type of people was Hitler hoping to attract support from? [2 marks]

ii)   (a)   What point is Dr Gross making in Source C? [3 marks]

         (b)   What similar idea is found in Source A and Source C? [3 marks]

iii)   (a)   In your own words say what teachers are being told to do in Source B. [3 marks]

         (b)   What do you think is meant by the phrase 'racial purification of the German race'? [2 marks]

         (c)   Give one result which might have arisen from such an order to teachers. [2 marks]

iv)   (a)   How reliable is Source C in describing the position of Jews in Germany in 1933? [4 marks]

         (b)   Which of these sources do you think is the most useful in explaining why there was no large-scale opposition in Germany to the persecution of the Jews? Give reasons for your answer. [5 marks]

Answer either Question 2 or 3 or 4.

QUESTION 2

What do you think were the main differences in how Germany was ruled under the Weimar Republic and under the Nazis? [25 marks]

QUESTION 3

i)   What were the main aims of Hitler's foreign policy 1933–41?

ii)   Why was there no large scale opposition within Germany to Hitler's foreign policy? [25 marks]

QUESTION 4

Why was the Nazi Party able to gain so much support between 1919 and 1933? [25 marks]

                                                               (NICCEA)

QUESTION 5

Explain the importance in Hitler's rise to power of:

(a)   the Versailles treaty (1919);

(b)   the Munich *putsch* (1923);

(c)   the world economic depression (1929–33);
(d)   the Reichstag fire (1933);
(e)   the Night of the Long Knives (1934). [25 marks]

(WJEC)

QUESTION 6

What were Hitler's aims in foreign affairs? Which of these aims did he put into effect between 1938 and 39 in his relations with (a) Austria, (b) Czechoslovakia and (c) Poland?

(WJEC)

OUTLINE ANSWERS

ANSWER 1

Question 1 is largely document based. In part i), the answer to (a) is recall based, but (b) demands an understanding of Source A. Here the 'type of people' he was hoping to attract were those already half inclined to anti-Semitism; alternatively the appeal was to relatively uneducated working-class people who might easily be persuaded to accept this superficial analysis. In ii) (a), the speaker in Source C is suggesting not only that the Jews have taken all the top jobs for themselves, but also that they are in some sinister way 'completely alien'; whilst (b) requires the candidate to look for similar ideas, e.g. the supposed great influence and sinister activities of the Jews, or the need to be rid of them, in the other passages. In iii), (a) asks for comprehension and paraphrase, and (b) invites fuller explanation of the central idea; (c) is a semi-empathetic question, since it asks you to put yourself into the pupils' position and imagine the results which the teacher's work might have had. Part iv) invites evaluation of the reliability of Source C in terms of the actual situation of Jews inside Germany in 1933 in (a); whilst in (b), the heaviest weighted part of the question, comments are invited on the usefulness of the sources in explaining why anti-Semitism met so little resistance in Germany in the 1930s, and reasons are also asked for in relation to the evaluation offered. You should note that relatively little recall is required in this question, but that a considerable degree of understanding, analysis and evaluation is expected for high marks.

ANSWERS TO 2, 3 AND 4

Answers to the different parts of Question 1 lead on to an answer to one of the following questions, 2, 3 or 4. Question 2 requires a comparison between two methods of government; care must be taken here not simply to offer two distinct descriptions, of the Weimar Republic and the Third Reich, place them side-by-side and leave the examiner to make his own comparison – specific points of comparison must be made by you in the course of your answer. Question 3 has two components: the aims of Hitler's foreign policy and the reasons for the lack of resistance to it in Germany in the period 1933–41. Again, a purely descriptive account of the policy will not suffice to score more than a small proportion of the marks on offer; to deserve high marks, answers must deal specifically with aims and with reasons for lack of resistance. Question 4 is perhaps more straightforward and deals with the grounds for the support enjoyed by the Nazi Party between 1919 and 1933; a number of reasons for this support should be given and elaborated here. It is worth noting, however, that support for the Nazis was by no means constant throughout the period: in the mid-1920s, which was a period of relative stability and recovery in Germany, they had very little following; but with the coming of the great depression support rapidly built up.

ANSWER 5

Description in reply to Question 5 of the rise of Hitler will again suffice to secure only a limited number of the 25 marks on offer; rather more than half the mark allocation in each part will be reserved for material relating to the importance of the episodes dealt with. Thus, for instance, in (a) what is to be stressed is not the factual provisions of the treaty – although these of course are relevant – but how these treaty provisions provided Hitler with a series of grievances which he was cleverly able to exploit in the course of the next ten or twelve years. Likewise in (e), the Night of the Long Knives is important not on account of its ruthless methods or the total number of its casualties, but because it allowed Hitler to purge the internal resistance to his leadership within the party and to win over the dubious Wehrmacht to his side.

ANSWER 6

In answering the first part of Question 6, on Hitler's foreign policy, you must show some knowledge of the aims of his policy in foreign affairs. He wanted to reverse the various aspects of the Versailles treaty which were unpopular in Germany, to bring all German-speaking peoples within the one German state, to acquire more living space for the Aryan race and to restore the country's pride and self-respect. In demonstrating the link between aims and events, you should go on to demonstrate how far the aims you have mentioned in the first part of your answer are borne out in the cases of (a) Austria, (b) Czechoslovakia and (c) Poland. In writing about how Hitler fulfilled his aims, you should be prepared to admit that two different interpretations are possible: Hitler may have deliberately planned his foreign policy so that one step led to the next in a campaign to restore Germany to its rightful position in Europe, or alternatively he may have taken advantage of the various episodes as they occurred to further his objectives in an opportunistic fashion. The best answers must show that the notion that Hitler was hell-bent on war from the beginning is rather implausible.

SUGGESTIONS FOR FURTHER WORK

1. Collect election figures under the Weimar Republic (votes cast and seats won) and build up graphs or charts to show how well the various political parties fared during these years. Tip: see how this kind of material is presented in Volume 2 of the *Penguin Atlas of World History,* on pages 148, 150 and 192.
2. Look at a translation of *Mein Kampf* by Adolf Hitler, or selected extracts from it, and write paragraphs on it to show what it reveals of Hitler's thinking. Why do you suppose the book was so popular?
3. Write a week's entries in the diary of a school pupil in the mid-1930s, telling of your everyday life and of how it was affected by the Nazi government. NB: include the part you played in the various Nazi Youth movements.
4. Collect photographs of Nazi marches, rallies and meetings during the 1930s. What do these photographs reveal about the nature of the Nazi regime?
5. As a historical adviser to a television series on Hitler's Germany, what materials would you select for inclusion, and why?

STUDENT'S ANSWER – EXAMINER'S COMMENTS

Question

Explain the importance in Hitler's rise to power of
(a) the Versailles Treaty (1919);
(b) the Munich Putsch (1923).

> **This paragraph is not relevant to the question and will not score any marks.**

> **You should learn to spell terms such as armistice, Versailles and Czechoslovakia.**

> **It would help to give more detail here, such as Alsace-Lorraine lost to France, Northern Schleswig to Denmark, etc.**

> **Much of this paragraph is a narrative account of the Treaty of Versailles and does not explain the main features of the Treaty which so enraged Hitler and many Germans.**

Hitler was born in Austria in 1889, his father was a minor customs official on the border of the old Austrian Empire. Adolf's mother has a great influence over him, often spoiling him, and she died in 1908. He did not do well at school and failed to get into art college though for a time he made a living by selling postcards, leading the life of a down and out in Vienna. In 1913 he went to live in Munich in Germany and in the First World War served in the German army where he became a corporal and rose to the rank of being decorated for his bravery by getting the iron cross second class.

He was in hospital recovering from the effects of a gas attack when the news of the armistise came. He was bitterly dissappointed, he thought that Germany had been betrayed by Jews and Communists. In Munich he joined the Nazi Party as member number 7 and rose to be its leader. He hated the Treaty of Versaile. Under this treaty Germany lost land to France, to Belgium, to Denmark, to Poland and to Checkoslovakia. Also all her colonies to the allies to be divided up into mandates. She was not allowed to link up with Austria and was not allowed in the League of Nations. Germany's rivers and canals were made international and there was to be an army of occupation in the Rhineland for many years.

When French troops occupied the Ruhr in 1923 Hitler tried to take over power in Bavaria in the Munich Putsch. It was not successful. After the Putsch Hitler was imprisoned in Landsberg Prison where he shared a cell with his good friend Rudolf Hess and he dictated to him his famous work Mein Kampf. He only served in prison for about nine months in spite of being sentenced for much longer. This was often because the authorities were kinder to right-wingers, though they were tough on left-wingers and communists.

> **There is relatively little information here about the Putsch itself; this response concentrates on what happened afterwards.**

> **This answer is not satisfactorily subdivided. (a) and (b) should be inserted.**

STALIN

GETTING STARTED

Stalin was effectively ruler of Russia from 1926 to 1953. During that time Soviet industry made spectacular advances, agriculture was collectivized, the Bolshevik revolution consolidated and Stalin led his people triumphantly through the Second World War. Yet collectivization had been a near fiasco and led to widespread famine, the purges had terrorized the whole nation and major errors in foreign policy from 1938 to 1941 had been followed by a disastrous opening to the war. None of Stalin's successors would have maintained political power in face of any one of the blunders he committed, yet he survived and at the time of his death his political power still seemed unshakeable.

HISTORICAL DEVELOPMENTS

Joseph Djugashvili was born in 1879 in the Caucasian province of Georgia in the Russian empire. Although his parents were poor – he was to be one of the few Bolshevik leaders to come from the working class – he went to a Tiflis seminary to train for the priesthood, and it was there that he fell under the influence of Marxism. His political activities and lack of religious commitment led to his expulsion from the seminary and to trouble with the Tsar's police. Like most other leading revolutionaries he adopted a shorter, and in his case a less non-Russian, name, Stalin, and spent some time (a total of seven years) in jails and labour camps before 1917. These formative years gave him plenty of experience as a dedicated revolutionary, distributing propaganda, holding secret meetings and organizing demonstrations. He even planned a remarkable bank robbery in 1907, but its success was marred by the fact that the bank notes were traceable and therefore unusable.

By 1917 he was a well-known revolutionary figure in his native province of Georgia, and although he was in exile in Siberia when the February revolution broke out he was soon liberated and returned to European Russia to support the policy of co-operation with other socialist parties. He gained valuable experience as co-editor of *Pravda,* the Bolshevik newspaper. But when Lenin arrived in Russia in April and found his plans opposed by the majority of the Bolsheviks, Stalin became one of his early converts, won over by Lenin's persuasive arguments.

Stalin works his way to the top

After the Bolshevik coup Lenin rewarded Stalin by appointing him Peoples' Commissar for Nationalities, a post for which he was particularly suited as one of the few non-Russian Bolshevik leaders. During the civil war he gave useful service as a military commissar, although he did not always see eye to eye with Trotsky. When, in 1919, he took charge of the workers' and peasants' inspectorate, he acquired the right to intervene in the functioning of all government departments. But his most important appointment was in 1922 when the Politburo appointed him to the newly-created post of party general secretary. It may be that the party leaders thought that this new post would tie down Stalin in administration while they dealt with important matters such as party policy and decision making. But Stalin used his new post to appoint loyal followers and dismiss those he could not implicitly trust. Through the secretariat Stalin created a civil service loyal to himself which provided information and draw up agendas for the Politburo and the government. That Stalin was building up enormous power did not go unnoticed. In December 1922, only a few months after approving Stalin's appointment, Lenin wrote of him: 'Comrade Stalin, having become General Secretary, has concentrated unlimited authority in his own hands, and I am not sure whether he will always be capable of using that authority with sufficient caution.'

Lenin's doubts led to distrust and only two weeks later he was criticizing Stalin further and suggesting that the central committee should 'consider ways of removing Stalin from his post and replacing him by someone more patient, more loyal, more polite, more considerate to comrades...'

But Lenin suffered a severe stroke soon afterwards and was never able subsequently to follow through his denunciation of Stalin by getting him dismissed. Trotsky, who agreed with Lenin about Stalin, seemed unwilling to attack him while Lenin still lived. For the moment Trotsky seemed anxious to avoid splitting the party.

Lenin's illness rendered him virtually helpless for a year, and when he died in January 1924 his would-be successors embarked on a struggle for power. Stalin's genius lay in reducing to their simplest elements issues which seemed complex to others, in encouraging his rivals to make mistakes and in controlling the votes in the central committee, which he had carefully filled with his own nominees. His main rival, Trotsky, was on shaky ground: he wanted world revolution to take priority over socialism in Russia, but hopes of world revolution, high in 1918–19, had faded by 1924. Most Bolsheviks, like Stalin, wanted to leave the world to its own devices and concentrate on the revolution within Russia, even if this meant continuing with the NEP. Stalin used Zinoviev and Kamenev to isolate and defeat Trotsky. The central committee ignored Lenin's last testament in which he expressed serious reservations against Stalin. By 1926 Zinoviev and Kamenev realized that Stalin had merely made use of them in the power struggle: they decided to throw in their lot with Trotsky. But it was too late: Stalin controlled *Pravda* and thus the press, *Pravda's* articles and innuendoes could not be contradicted in print, and since 1924 Stalin had taken steps to fill vacant posts with his own supporters. Thus Stalin made sure that Trotsky and his supporters were consistently outvoted in the fourteenth party congress of 1925–6 and in the central committee. So few dared to support the opposition that Stalin was able to expel Trotsky and Zinoviev first from the central committee and then from the party in 1927. Zinoviev's admission of his 'errors' allowed him temporarily to rejoin the party, but Trotsky refused to admit that he was in error. In 1928 he was exiled to Alma Ata, wearing only his pyjamas; his hurried night arrest was a foretaste of things to come. In 1929 Stalin felt strong enough to expel Trotsky from the USSR. He eventually settled in Mexico, where he was murdered in 1940 by an alleged Stalinist agent wielding an ice-pick.

3 ▷ INDUSTRIAL ADVANCE AND AGRICULTURAL CHAOS

> 66 You must master the details of the transformation of Russia 99

Lenin had never intended that the NEP should be a policy for the long term, but the power struggle delayed industrial decisions. Gosplan, the state planning commission, had existed since 1921, but had very little to plan. Capital for industrialization was scarce and seemed likely only to come from agriculture by paying poor prices for agricultural products and charging the peasants high prices for industrial goods. During the years 1925–28 the private and commercial activities of the Nepmen (those who had done well out of the NEP) were increasingly restricted; in 1927 the Dnieper hydro-electric scheme and the Stalingrad tractor plant were begun, and the last link on the Trans-Siberian railway complex was completed. In 1929 the first Five Year Plan (starting in fact in 1928) was presented to the sixteenth party conference. It proposed to double industrial production within five years, it set production targets and it rewarded success and penalized failure. But enthusiasm was no substitute for capital. Although the emphasis was on producing goods to lead to further production – fuels, electricity, cement, timber and metals – rather than goods for immediate consumption, and grain was to be sold abroad in exchange for machine tools, nevertheless output fell short of what was planned. Yet the figures show that there had been a considerable achievement.

	Coal (in million tons)	Oil (in million tons)	Pig iron (in million tons)
Actual annual output 1927–8	35	12	3
Planned annual output 1932–33	75	22	10
Actual annual output 1932–33	64	21	6

The plan of 1933 resulted in Stakhanovites, honoured workers who in their own ways had done their best to follow in the footsteps of the miner Stakhanov who cut over 100 tons of coal in a single shift. But while the plan failed to fulfil its promise of consumer goods, the years of the second plan saw the completion of the Dnieper dam and the opening of the tractor stations, huge steel works arose at Magnitogorsk and Russia's chemical industry rapidly expanded. Moreover if material rewards were limited, illiteracy was being effectively tackled, health services developed and welfare benefits and old age pensions were made widely available.

Industrial advance was not matched by agricultural progress. A bad harvest in 1928 led to the reimposition of bread rationing. The elimination of private grain traders in 1929 led to inefficiency in the purchase and storage of grain. Attempts to overcome the shortages by confiscating grain led to peasant riots. Stalin decided to meet the crisis by forcible collectivization; the peasant farmers were to be compelled to join collective farms in which land, resources and profits would be pooled and in which there was no private ownership. The more successful peasants, known as kulaks, strenuously resisted. During the months of December 1929 to March 1930 millions were uprooted from their homes and farms and placed in concentration camps or deported to Siberia. In March 1930 Stalin could announce that 58 per cent of farmland had been collectivized. But the cost, in villages decimated of manpower, in burning resentment against the government and in cattle and other farm animals killed to avoid confiscation, was such as to persuade even Stalin to call a halt. He blamed excesses on over-zealous officials and abandoned compulsory collectivization. By June 1930 collectivization had fallen back to a mere 24 per cent. A revival of forcible persuasion, combined with the offer of tractors from the new tractor stations meant that collectivization was virtually complete by 1941. The disruption of 1930, however, led to famine in 1932–3. No official news of this famine reached the outside world, no appeal for foreign help was made at this time by Stalin, although Lenin had welcomed foreign aid in 1921, and this famine was probably equally as bad as that in Lenin's time. Stalin had thus destroyed the kulaks, almost destroyed agriculture and precipitated a famine of horrific proportions. His collectivization policy may have succeeded, but in 1940 grain production was still thirteen million tons below that of 1913.

4 ▷   THE PURGES

By 1929 opposition to Stalin within the Communist Party had largely been eliminated, and Stalin was virtually dictator of Russia. Even those of the 'left' who had opposed Stalin over the NEP and industrialization (demanding immediate industrialization and the abandonment of the NEP) were thrown into confusion when Stalin adopted their policies. In 1929–30 many party members, especially in the countryside, were denounced as 'rightists' (too favourable to kulaks and Nepmen) and lost their party membership. Stalin filled the vacant ranks with white-collar workers, some of whose loyalty was suspect and whose motives for joining the party were questionable. Some of these were expelled in 1933–4, but it was the murder of Kirov in 1934 which provoked the reign of terror that was to follow. Kirov, the leader of the party in Leningrad, was young and popular and was known to oppose Stalin's aim to escalate political persecution. His mysterious death and the faked accident to the chief witness of his death have inclined many to believe Stalin to have been an accessory to his murder. But Stalin chose to use the murder to justify secret trials and mass executions. At first the purge was directed against those outside the party. But in 1935 leading communists such as Kamenev and Zinoviev were put on trial. The purge intensified in 1936. Stalin was obsessed with fear of opposition; unity was needed to consolidate the revolution, divisions menaced his leadership. As he told the party: 'These comrades did not always confine themselves to criticism and passive resistance, they threatened to raise revolt in the party, ...More, they threatened some of us with bullets.'

Stalin's fears had some substance in that Trotsky was publishing from abroad information that could only have come directly from one of Stalin's colleagues in government. Stalin eyed all his associates with suspicion.

❝Stalin uses terror to guarantee progress❞

For the ordinary Russian the false denunciation, the arrest in the dead of night, the slow death in a labour camp or quick despatch by firing squad without a trial became the nightmare too often turned to reality. For the senior party member there was the spotlight of publicity; after arrest there was physical but more often psychological torture – confession was wrung from the confused or those fearful for the safety of their families. There was the humiliation of the court and the denunciation by the chief prosecutor, Vyshinsky; no one was more devoted to Stalin's cause than this man, who had narrowly escaped 'purging' himself in the 1920s. As he said, 'This trial has uncovered and demonstrated the stupid obstinacy, the reptilian cold-bloodedness, the cold calculation of professional criminals, shown by the Trotskyist bandits in their struggle against the USSR...'

After this it is not surprising to hear that no attempt was made to give the accused a fair trial and that Vyshinsky usually ended his denunciation of the accused with a typical request: 'I demand that the mad dogs be shot, every one of them'. And they usually were! Above all Stalin feared the power of the army: he was convinced that it was planning his overthrow, and his influence over appointments and promotions in the army had been much less than it had been with government and party. In January 1937 Stalin reshuffled the senior commands, removing troops from commanders to whom they were loyal. The Red Army chief, Marshal Tukhachevsky, compromised by documents probably forged by the Germans, was charged with treason and shot. Two-thirds of the generals were eliminated in the trials that followed. The damage to the senior command was to be all too obvious in the Finnish campaign of 1939–40 and in the early months of the German invasion of 1941.

Well into 1938 the purge increased in intensity, but when it seemed to be accelerating out of control Stalin, blaming his subordinates for over-enthusiasm, deliberately slowed down the rate of arrests, and the worst of the purge was over. It did not stop, however, and not until after 1953 could an ordinary Russian who had not committed a crime, and who had not taken part in dissident politics, feel safe from the security forces and secret police.

At the time of the show trials of 1936–8 it was believed inside Russia and by many foreign observers that the accused, having confessed, must indeed be guilty. Few suspected the physical and mental torture that had forced people to confess. Historians unfavourable to Stalin have alleged that ten million people died directly or indirectly as a consequence of collectivization and purges. Khrushchev admitted after 1956 to two million; the truth probably lies somewhere between the two. The killings were not part of communist ideology; Lenin killed because he believed it necessary to do so, Stalin killed because of fear and paranoia. The purges were symptomatic of totalitarianism rather than communism. Even in his final illness Stalin could believe that eminent doctors, far from treating their patients, had been involved in a sinister conspiracy for political assassination. But by 'worship' of Stalin the personality cult had in part superseded the 'worship' of Bolshevism and Leninism, and Russia's totalitarianism was a personal dictatorship rather than a party dictatorship.

Against the purges must be seen the real progress that Russia was making, especially in industry, welfare and education. Added to these developments, a new constitution granted in 1936 seemed to promise liberty, justice and democracy. A parliament of two houses, the Supreme Soviet, was to be elected by secret ballot. The selection of candidates was under the strict control of the Communist Party and the Supreme Soviet had little if any real power. But at least, against the background of the purges, the new constitution gave a promise of better days to come.

5 > FROM PEACE TO WAR

Stalin inherited from Lenin and Trotsky the Comintern, with its aim of world revolution and international subversion, and certainly the Comintern soured relations between Russia and the western powers in the late 1920s. Britain even broke off diplomatic relations with Russia in 1927. But Stalin's aim was socialism in one country, not world revolution, and his foreign policy was defensive rather than menacing. He was prepared to seek agreements and even allies if these served the interests of Russia. Thus the USSR joined the League of Nations in 1934, and Litvinov, the Russian foreign minister, was keen to form alliances with other nations to check the growth of fascism.

The Spanish Civil War which broke out in 1936 gave Stalin a difficult problem. A fascist victory he certainly feared, but if the republicans, with their powerful communist backing, succeeded then France might be driven to seek an anti-communist alliance with Hitler. Stalin therefore intervened too little and too late. The fascist powers provided Franco with military and air support and the republican cause was lost by 1939. In 1936 the Anti-Comintern Pact between Germany and Japan threatened Russia with the danger of war on two fronts. Stalin distinctly felt the lack of allies, and when during the Munich crisis of 1938 Russia was virtually elbowed aside by Britain and France, Stalin concluded that these two powers were unreliable, had betrayed Czechoslovakia and would have no hesitation about leaving Russia to her fate at the hands of Germany and Japan. Although Litvinov continued negotiations for an alliance between Russia and the western powers, Stalin felt that time was running out. In April 1939 he dismissed the pro-western Litvinov and determined upon his own 'Munich' with Hitler. The new foreign minister, Molotov, continued to negotiate with Britain and France, while a treaty with Germany was secretly arrived at in August. The non-aggression treaty, known as the Ribbentrop–Molotov Pact, provided for a ten-year agreement to maintain peace between the two countries. It shocked communists both in Russia and elsewhere. The secret agreement to partition Poland would have shocked them still more had they known of it. Stalin had bought time; the question was whether he could make good use of it.

Remarkably enough for so cynical a politician, Stalin became a sincere ally of Germany. He took his promised gains in Poland in September 1939 and in the Baltic states in 1940, even though his attempt to coerce Finland in late 1939 led to the exposure of Russian military weakness and the expulsion of Russia from the League of Nations. The 'phoney war' in the west even enabled Britain and France to toy with the idea of giving Finland military aid, which could only have cemented the Russo-German alliance. The supplies of Russian oil and raw materials promised to Germany by Russia in 1939 were, as far as practicable, delivered in full: Russia was helping Germany build up her strength for the breach that was to come. Stalin's anti-western prejudices made him turn a deaf ear to British and US warnings about Hitler's intention; there is no evidence that he rejected them publicly and acted upon them secretly. He distrusted the west; and he trusted Germany (whose leader had so frequently in the past made it clear that communism was the chief enemy) in the hope rather than the belief that Hitler would not attack Russia. It was by accident rather than by design that Stalin complemented his non-aggression pact with Germany with a neutrality pact with Japan in 1941; Russian and Japanese forces had tangled in 1939, and the Japanese wanted to clear the decks for the forthcoming struggle with Britain and the USA. The Japanese treaty was well timed: in June 1941 German forces invaded Russia, taking Stalin and the Russian people completely by surprise.

Stalin as the 'little father of his country'

Until the very day of the German invasion Stalin had maintained a conciliatory attitude to his German ally despite provocation, and the initial disasters of the war suggested that Stalin was losing his grip. But in July 1941 he made a radio broadcast to the Russian people in which the appeal was to patriotism rather than to party. As in 1919 the Russian people fought for their country, not their government. And so it became the great patriotic war. Stalin the tyrant became Stalin the father figure, exhorting his people to greater sacrifice and obscuring the terrible memories of collectivization and purges as he identified himself with the 'brothers and sisters' he formerly would have addressed as 'comrades'. Behind the scenes Stalin's undoubted administrative abilities were turned to war, and the German advance was halted in 1942–43, but at enormous cost.

Stalin's greatest war achievements, however, were as much diplomatic as military. The allies were grateful when in 1943 Stalin dissolved the Comintern. Perhaps they were lulled into a sense of false security. At Yalta and especially at Potsdam in 1945, Stalin won concessions that were to bring much of eastern Europe under his control and so give Russia that security in the west which she had lacked in the 1930s.

Ten million Russian civilians died in the war – 700,000 in Leningrad alone – and nearly seven million of the Russian armed forces. The economy was in virtual ruin; railway lines were twisted and tangled, bridges wrecked, factories destroyed, fields uncultivated. Not all was the work of the Germans; in part the devastation was due to the Russian 'scorched earth' policy. But what Stalin had helped to destroy it was now his task to rebuild, and it was his achievement to bequeath to his successors a superpower which Lenin and Trotsky might have dreamed of, but which would have seemed unthinkable during the dark days of the 1930s.

6 ▷ INTERNAL RE-CONSTRUCTION 1945-53

The war had once again equated communism with patriotism and Stalin received grudging respect and even admiration for his wartime leadership and achievements. It was unfortunate that Stalin did not cultivate this goodwill by some political relaxation and promise of material improvement. Instead his postwar rule was as harsh as it had been pre-war, and another major purge seemed imminent. The privations of war were to be continued in peacetime and while the fourth Five Year Plan was the first step towards post-war reconstruction, Stalin promised little by

**You should not ignore the career of Stalin in his later years.**

way of material rewards, and in fact warned that the next two Five Year Plans would be tough. The Russian people geared themselves in the peacetime battle for the economy in the same way that they had fought the wartime battle so single-mindedly against the German invader. Thus Russian industry achieved a remarkable revival within three years. The recovery was helped by reparations from East Germany and eastern European countries, the labour of two million prisoners of war and one-sided trading agreements with satellite countries. Good planning, so effective in the later stages of war, helped to overcome almost insuperable difficulties. There were, by the time of the Fifth Plan in 1950, some expensive prestige projects such as the Volga–Don canal, short on traffic but plentiful in statues of Stalin, and vast hydro-electric schemes which would take decades to make any contribution to the economy. But the pre-war industrial base had been largely restored by 1950, and might well have made a significant impact in raising living standards had not so high a proportion of industrial production been set aside for armaments.

Progress in agriculture was slower. Despite a poor harvest in 1946 and near famine conditions in some areas in 1947, agricultural revival was held back by low priority and by shortages of manpower and machines. Some agricultural policies of the period, such as the merging of smaller collectives into much larger ones, were largely irrelevant to production problems; and others, such as planting trees in areas where trees would not normally grow, were a damaging waste of resources. Agricultural production lagged well behind consumer requirements, and it was not until the time of Stalin's death in 1953 that production figures for most agricultural commodities had recovered to pre-war levels.

7 ▶ EXTERNAL EXPANSION 1945-53

If recovery seemed almost beyond reach in 1945 it should be remembered that a devastated Russia was part of a shattered Europe and an exhausted world. At least Russia had an enormous army and had used it in 1945 to occupy much of eastern Europe. Contrary to alarmist belief in the west, it is highly unlikely that Stalin had any aim to dominate Europe and certainly he did not aim to dominate the world. His aim was security – a security he had failed to achieve in the 1930s and which had led to his embarrassing pact with Hitler. Thus Stalin in 1945 incorporated the Baltic states into the Soviet Union; used his occupying forces to promote favourable regimes in Romania, Bulgaria and Hungary; and engineered a coup in Czechoslovakia when he feared that Czechoslovakia would come under American influence by accepting Marshall aid. In Poland Stalin resented and resisted western attempts to interfere. By 1948 these countries were communist in all but name, and Stalin intended to maintain control by directing these satellite communist states from Moscow. When Yugoslavia, whose communism was native grown and not imposed by Moscow, attempted to show its independence, Stalin used every tactic short of armed force in unsuccessful attempts to bring Tito, Yugoslavia's leader, to heel. Yet it should not be forgotten that Stalin made no attempt to impose communism upon defeated Finland; and he held back from direct intervention in Greece, so that the communists in the civil war there suffered defeat at the hands of a monarchist regime directly supported by British and later American military aid. He agreed in 1946 to withdraw his troops from Iran, thus reducing the Russian threat to Middle East oil and to India. And if Stalin had been intent on world domination he should have given much stronger support to Mao Tse-tung, the Chinese communist leader, in his struggle against the Chinese nationalists of Chiang Kai-shek. In fact Stalin's support was grudging and lukewarm, amounting to little more than allowing the contents of Japanese arms dumps in Manchuria to fall into Chinese communist hands.

Stalin's limited objectives were, however, less easy to judge at the time. The division of Europe brought about the Cold War (see Chapter 14). Stalin tried to counter Western efforts to reconstruct Germany by precipitating the Berlin crisis of 1948–9. The detonation of the first Russian atomic bomb in 1949, as much a tribute to Russian science as to Russian espionage, deepened the atmosphere of mistrust. NATO had been formed only six months earlier, confirming Stalin's belief that the West wanted to overthrow Russian communism by force. The appointment of Vyshinsky as foreign minister in 1949 meant that he transferred his abusive language, first seen in the courtrooms of the purges, to the arena of international relations. The Russian 'veto' became a diplomatic weapon at the UN. The Korean war, which was not of Stalin's making, brought East–West relations to a new low. Stalin died in March 1953 before an armistice in Korea caused some easing of international tension.

8 > ESTIMATE OF STALIN

Russian historians replaced unstinted praise of Stalin with harsh criticism of him in the late 1950s. It is true that as a mass killer of the twentieth century Stalin is second only to Hitler, but there are solid achievements to admire and it is possible to find excuses, but not justification, for his excesses. It could be argued that the purges were undertaken to impose discipline upon a party whose internal differences might cause it to lose control, and to stave off a real danger of a take-over by the Red Army. Possibly only he among the Russian political leaders had the determination to carry them through. Totalitarian rulers know no other means of maintaining themselves in power but force and repression. And if Stalin in the 1930s was suspicious of the West he had good reason. Western attitudes in the 1940s, particularly in keeping news of the atomic bomb secret from him until the last minute, convinced him that the West had not changed, and thus were sown the seeds of the Cold War. But the Russians had some cause to be grateful. Stalin's Five Year Plans transformed Russian industry although they fell short of target, and made possible effective Russian resistance to Germany in the Second World War. Stalin's leadership during the war years was not flawless, but he achieved order out of the early chaos, he personally directed the economic and military planning which led to victory and he provided the patriotic leadership which could unite most Russians behind the war effort. He was accorded both respect and fear; without the superhuman effort these inspired could Russia have survived the war and become a superpower?

IDEAS AND PRINCIPLES

COLLECTIVIZATION

The Bolsheviks had won peasant support by encouraging peasant seizure of land and the creation or enlargement of peasant smallholdings. Yet private land ownership was contrary to the anti-capitalist basis of communism, and once the Bolsheviks had consolidated power they expected peasants to grow food for the state without payment. The grain confiscations of war communism gave way to the compromise of the New Economic Policy which substituted tax payments for grain confiscation and allowed efficient peasants to prosper. Even so, in the mid- and late 1920s both Stalin and his 'opposition' were agreed on the eventual elimination of private land ownership, and differed only on the question of its timing. Collectivization on a voluntary basis had begun in the mid-1920s and it had its attractions for some of the poorer peasants; private ownership was abolished, farms were grouped into larger units, peasants pooled their livestock and implements, small plots were set aside for private cultivation and the work on the collective was shared among its peasant families. Profits from the collective farm, after the state had taken a substantial slice, were shared between those who worked on it. The collective farms were in fact peasant co-operatives, known as *kolkhozy*. After the failure of Stalin's enforced collectivization drive in 1929–30, the squeezing of private farmers by taxation and other methods and the attractions of collectives, mechanized largely at state expense, helped to complete the programme of collectivization by the outbreak of the Second World War.

Not all state lands were farmed as collectives. Lands seized by the state rather than individual peasants in the early days of the revolution were sometimes organized as state farms. Here the peasants were merely labourers, and as wage earners they had no entitlement to a share of the produce and profits. These state farms were called *sovkhozy*.

PARTY AND GOVERNMENT

The Bolshevik Party was renamed the Communist Party in 1918. It was always a minority party and membership of it was a privilege and not a right. A minimum of three members in a workshop or factory had the right to form a cell and to elect representatives to the local district committee. Through the local committees was chosen the party congress, meeting annually and delegating its continuous and routine administration to the central committee. This was normally too big to conduct business except on a formal basis, and immediate decisions were taken by the very senior members of the central committee. These men were known as the Politburo and could be as few as five in number. They were, in effect, a kind of Communist Party cabinet.

Side by side with the party was the government. It was headed by the Council of Peoples' Commissars, and its chairman was the prime minister. As he was also a member of the Politburo, and the higher government posts were all held by party members, the party was able to keep firm control of the government both at central level and at the lower levels of province and district. Elected soviets (councils) were responsible for local and central government, but in practice election to these was controlled by the party. Thus even after the new constitution of 1936 it was the central committee of the party and its power group, the Politburo, not the Supreme Soviet, which determined policy and ran the country.

THE SECRET POLICE

Lenin's dreaded Cheka was less active after the successful end to the civil war made the Bolsheviks more secure. But although the Cheka was abolished in 1922, its activities were merely transferred to the NKVD – the people's commissariat of the interior. Its headquarters in Moscow copied that of the Cheka in combining the functions of an administrative centre for the conduct of all Russian security, a prison, a court for secret trials and a busy execution centre. The OGPU or GPU was the secret police section of the NKVD and played a major part in conducting Stalin's purges in the 1930s.

APPLIED MATERIALS

Texts

P.D. Allan, *Russia and Eastern Europe*, Arnold, 1983 Chapters 4,5,6 and 8
S.E. Ayling, *Portraits of Power*, Harrap, 1965
T. Howarth, *Russia 1900–53*, Longman (History Series), 1970
J. Robottom, *Modern Russia*, Longman, 1970
Tamara Pimlott, *Stalin's Russia*, Macmillan (History in Depth), 1984

Map

B. Catchpole, *Map History of Russia*, Heinemann, 1974; Themes 4 and 5

Sources

F.W. Stacey, *Stalin and the Making of Modern Russia*, Hill and Fell (Archive Series), 1970

EXAMINATION QUESTIONS

QUESTION 1

Study Sources A,B,C and D and then answer questions (a) to (d) which follow:

Source A

line 1   The characteristic feature in the work of the Party during the past year is that we, as a Party, as the Soviet power, have developed an offensive along the whole front against capitalist elements in the Countryside. To launch an offensive against the Kulaks means that we must smash them, eliminate them as a class....Today we

line 5   have an adequate political base for us to strike, to break their resistance and to replace them by the output of the collective farms....

Source B

(from the writings of an opponent of Stalin)

line 1   Will it ever be known how terrible was the disorganization of agriculture that resulted? Rather than hand over their livestock to the *kolkhoz*, the peasants slaughter the beasts, sell the meat and make boots out of the leather. Through the destruction of the live-market...trainloads of deported peasants left for the icy

line 5   North...in seven years 1929-1936 over five million families disappeared...

Source C

Agricultur l statistics:

	1928	1929	1930	1931	1932	1933
Grain harvest *(millions of tons)*	73.3	71.7	83.5	69.5	68.6	68.4
Livestock-cattle *(million head)*	70.5	67.1	52.5	47.9	40.7	38.9
Grain taken by the state *(million tons)*	10.8	16.1	22.1	22.5	18.5	22.6

By 1931, 56 per cent of all farms were collectivized.
By 1932, 62 per cent of all farms were collectivized.

Source D

Industrial statistics:

	1928	1933	1940
Effective power *(billion kwts.)*	5.0	16.3	48.3
Crude Oil *(millions of tons)*	11.6	21.5	31.1
Coal *(millions of tons)*	35.5	76.3	165.9
Steel *(millions of tons)*	4.2	6.9	18.3
Locomotives *(units)*	479	948	928

(a)   What is the meaning of the following terms as used in Source A?
    i)   the *Party* (line 1). (1 mark)
    ii)   the *Kulaks* (line 4). (1 mark)

(b)   i)   Why did Stalin consider it necessary to *smash* and *eliminate* the Kulaks (Source A)? (3 marks)
    ii)   For what reasons does he suggest that at the time of this passage he was now ready to launch such an attack? (2 marks)

(c)   i)   With reference to the details given in Source B, explain why the state of disorganization (line 1) existed. (3 marks)
    ii)   In what ways do the statistics in Source C support the description of this disorganization? (3 marks)

(d)   i)   What name is usually applied to the system of improving Soviet industry during the years covered by the industrial statistics in Source D? (1 mark)
    ii)   Describe the main features of the working of this system. (2 marks)
    iii)   How do the industrial statistics (Source D) show some of the priorities in the system and the success that it achieved? (4 marks)

(ULEAC)

QUESTION 2

From 1928 major changes in agriculture and industry took place in the Soviet Union.

(a) Why were these changes introduced?

(b) How successful were these changes in the years up to 1941?

(c) How were the ordinary people of the Soviet Union affected by these changes?

(Total 30 marks) (SEG)

OUTLINE ANSWERS

ANSWER 1

In Question 1 (a) brief definitions are all that are required for a mark each: the party can be identified as the communist ruling party and the kulaks as the richer and more successful peasants. For 3 marks in 1 (b) (i) attention can be drawn to grain shortages, kulak resistance to forcible collectivization and the ideological problem of peasant land ownership. The answer to (b) (ii) lies only in the last sentence of the Stalin quotation; put it in your own words – basically what Stalin is saying is that only now are the communists strongly enough entrenched to tackle the kulak problem. Suitable references to livestock slaughter, food shortages and depopulated countryside will cope with 1 (c) (i), and the figures in Source C, while showing slight decline in grain production and marked decline in livestock, do not entirely support the 'disorganization' theory, especially as the state grain supplies rose except in 1932. In (d) the Five Year Plans and the incentives for success and penalties for failure will cope with (i) and (ii), while in (d) (iii) the industrial statistics should be used to show the priority given to heavy industry and capital goods, although it is worth pointing out that the question sources offer no figures for consumer goods for comparison. .

ANSWER 2

Question 2 does not provide a breakdown of the mark allocations for the subquestions. In such circumstances you will have to decide your own weighting, but a roughly even division of the marks is the safest. Part (a) requires reasons, and these should include the backward state of Russian industry in the 1920s, held back by war, civil war and lack of investment. For agriculture mention should be made of lack of mechanization, low production levels, unwillingness of farmers to sell to the state at artificially low prices and ideological objection to Nepmen, private landownership and capitalist methods of distribution. In (b) changes should not only be described but the degree of success assessed; thus use could be made of the figures quoted in Section 3 and in Question 1 to show that while great progress was made in electricity and coal, progress was less spectacular in oil, steel and machines. Lack of consumer goods, despite the intentions of the second and third plans, should be noted. In agriculture the collectivization problems of 1929-30 were followed by rapid collectivization from 1931, but this did not bring with it increased grain production – here management problems and lack of tractors could be mentioned. In (c) industrial change could be shown as providing a goal to aim for but shortages were hard work to cope with. The horrors of collectivization by compulsion and the famine of 1932–3 are one line of approach, but consideration should also be given to the adjustment necessary for the millions changing from private plots to working as part of a co-operative team on a collective.

SUGGESTIONS FOR FURTHER WORK

1. Collect statistics on the economy of the USSR during the Stalin period, and make your own analysis of growth, particularly comparing growth rates in industrial goods, consumer goods and agricultural products. Find as many reasons as you can for the varying rates of growth and decline. Tip: in addition to the statistics in this chapter, useful figures can be found in J.P. Nettl, *The Soviet Achievement*, Hudson, 1967, pages 272–3, and in J.N. Westwood, *Russian History 1812–1971*, OUP, pages 454–6 in the appendix.
2. Construct short biographies of *two* of Stalin's chief rivals in the 1920s, e.g. Trotsky, Zinoviev, Kamenev. Tip: encyclopaedias present this sort of information in a more immediately useful form than ordinary textbooks.
3. Write a short memorandum in which Stalin in 1938 explains to his closest colleagues why the purges were necessary. Write a reply from a bold colleague disputing Stalin's arguments and pointing out the damages the purges were doing and were likely to do to Russia.
4. How far does your study of Stalin show that he was just as ruthless and repressive in the post-war years (from 1945) as he was in the 1930s? How do you explain the continued repression in the post-war years?

STUDENT'S ANSWER – EXAMINER'S COMMENTS

Question

How was Stalin able to gain and retain power?

> **This is biographical, i.e. about the life of Stalin, rather than an explanation of how he was able to gain or retain power.**

> **The last two sentences need much further development to show Stalin building up his power base among his fellow revolutionaries.**

> **This is an effective explanation of Stalin's power and importance.**

Stalin was not really a Russian. He was born in Georgia of poor but religious parents who sent him to train as a priest. He soon showed more interest in politics than religion, and was expelled. He now moved among revolutionaries and gave up his Georgian name, and tried to lose his Georgian accent in order to impress the native Russians among his friends. But he was always something of an odd man out. Even so he worked very hard preparing pamphlets, arranging meetings, planning bank robberies - that is when he was not a guest of the Tsar in one of his labour camps or jails.

Stalin's importance grew because of his close links with Lenin; when other Bolsheviks questioned Lenin's plans to take over in October 1917, Stalin soon gave Lenin his backing, and Lenin came to trust him. Some important posts brought Stalin valuable experience and brought him into close contact with other Bolsheviks that he could now watch closely. As a military Commissar Stalin saw a good deal of Trotsky and did not always agree with him. But it was Stalin's appointment as General Secretary of the Communist Party which gave him his real opportunity: he was at the centre of politics, he knew the agenda of all the various committees, he promoted his friends, he passed over his enemies and even got them demoted or dismissed; there was no activity within the party that he

66 It was not necessary for the student to show his or her lack of knowledge in this way. Careful rewording could have helped hide the fact that the student had read about Ida Kaplan, but had forgotten her name. For example just take out 'by' in the second line. 99

was unaware of. Lenin's health never recovered from the attempt made on his life by ...., he had a stroke, was nursed carefully by his wife Krupskaya, but was no longer able to work hard. He suspected Stalin of being power-hungry, and although he put his reservations about Stalin in writing, this was hidden by the Politburo on Lenin's death. After all the Politburo did contain a majority of Stalin's men. Thus with the help of Kamenev and Zinoviev he fought off a challenge from Trotsky, and by 1928 so dominated the party that he was able to have Trotsky exiled.

66 Good general idea. Needs to be rather more devlopment of the power struggle. Excellent spelling and use of language throughout the answer. 99

APPEASEMENT

G E T T I N G   S T A R T E D

Europe in the 1920s was slowly recovering from the First World War. The slaughter and horrors of that conflict made all nations and their politicians determined that there should never be another world war. The League of Nations was established in the high hope that disputes between nations could be settled by compromise and negotiation, and certainly during the 1920s the League had success in a number of important international disputes. If cynics noted that these involved minor rather than major powers, the League's supporters might reply that the League's growing prestige ought to ensure that the major powers would eventually allow it to determine disputes between the great as well as the small. There were, in the 1920s, important problems as yet unsolved. It was generally agreed that the stockpiling of weapons and the maintenance of large armies increased rather than reduced the likelihood of war. All nations expressed an abhorrence of war (in the Kellogg Pact of 1928) and a willingness to discuss disarmament. But many countries were still suspicious of Germany; Britain feared for the loss of her naval supremacy and France would not disarm while a sullen and resentful Germany was just across the Rhine. Russia talked of disarmament but western intervention in the civil war had made Russia cautious and suspicious. Germany was full of grievances concerning Versailles, but the only way the Germans could compensate for their defeat in war was to wage a successful one. And although they appeared to have no such intention, their former conquerors were not willing to take the risk. France would only feel secure if the Versailles ban on German rearmament remained in force. The Germans would only agree to disarmament if they were allowed partially to rearm.

HISTORICAL DEVELOPMENTS

The situation was complicated by the rise of the totalitarian states. On the flimsiest of pretexts the Japanese overran Manchuria in 1931–2, and although Japanese aggression was condemned by the Lytton Commission of the League of Nations and the Japanese were ordered to withdraw from Manchuria, the Japanese instead withdrew from the League. Protests by the western powers were ignored. Japan also cancelled its naval agreements with Britain and the USA. In the face of such defiance the League could either persuade its members to support its decisions by force, or it could back down. It backed down!

Mussolini had gained power in Italy in 1922. His attitude towards the League and disarmament had generally been reassuring apart from his embarrassing seizure of Corfu in 1923. But since then he had become a major European statesman, and could surely be relied upon to join in the collective search for peace. The rise of Hitler in Germany coincided with the resumption of the disarmament talks. When the French would not agree to a programme of disarmament which would allow Germany to rearm, Germany withdrew from the talks and disarmament collapsed. Now that one route to peace had been closed attempts were made to find others.

COLLECTIVE SECURITY

Some pinned their faith in collective security – the belief that if enough powerful states were willing to band together to preserve peace, then would-be aggressors would be sufficiently deterred. Germany might rearm, but the combined might of Britain, France and Italy would keep Germany in check; it was unfortunate that the USA was still committed to isolationism.

But all seemed well when Mussolini raced his infantry divisions to the Brenner Pass to prevent a German takeover of Austria in 1934. At Stresa in 1935 Italy, Britain and France announced 'close and cordial collaboration' to ensure that treaties were adhered to, and they denounced German rearmament. Perhaps the Stresa front would provide the security Europe was seeking.

ABYSSINIA

It was not to be. Even while the three-nation meeting was taking place at Stresa, Italy and Abyssinia were already quarrelling about the oasis of Walwal, where hostilities had occurred in December 1934. The Abyssinian emperor, Haile Selassie, wanted the League of Nations to settle the dispute, but the League told the emperor to negotiate directly with Italy. Britain, who controlled the Suez Canal, must have been aware that the large numbers of Italian troops passing through the canal could hardly have been intended purely for defence. Yet Britain did not wish to offend Mussolini as the Stresa front relied on Mussolini to keep Hitler in check. When the Italians invaded Abyssinia in October 1935, the League of Nations denounced Italy as an aggressor and imposed economic sanctions (trade restrictions) upon Italy. Austria, Hungary and, very significantly, Germany refused to apply the sanctions. Even though the sanctions specifically did not apply to coal, oil and steel – the commodities of which Mussolini was in most desperate need – countries during the depressed 1930s were reluctant to accept the trade loss that would arise from banning trade with Italy. It was not surprising, therefore, that attempts to extend the sanctions to oil ran into difficulties with Britain and France. They did not want to lose valuable trade; even more they did not want to lose a valuable friend. Britain allowed Italy to pour her troops and raw materials through the Suez Canal. Britain and France did, however, take the initiative towards a compromise settlement by suggesting in the Hoare–Laval Plan that Italy, who had no justifiable claim on Abyssinia at all, should take two-thirds of it. The plan attracted almost universal condemnation and was such an embarrassment to Britain that Hoare, the foreign minister, resigned. But that did not save Abyssinia, whose capital, Addis Ababa, fell to the Italians in May 1936. The exiled emperor made an impassioned appeal to the League of Nations in person; he aroused much sympathy but no positive support. Abyssinia now had a new emperor, Victor Emanuel III of Italy.

COLLAPSE OF THE STRESA FRONT

The Abyssinian episode caused the collapse of the Stresa front and with it the failure of collective security. It also reinforced the impotence of the League of Nations. Mussolini now adjusted his attitude towards Hitler. Until 1936 the western powers, who had now virtually taken over from the League of Nations as guardians of the peace, had shown uncertainty about how to deal with the German dictator. He had made the return of the Saar in 1935 seem like a victory and a triumph, and had followed it by declaring Germany's intention to rearm and to introduce conscription. This was denounced at Stresa, but even so in June 1935 Britain's foreign minister, Hoare, signed an Anglo–German naval agreement which allowed Germany to build a fleet of up to 35 per cent of the tonnage of Britain's fleet. The agreement was just as much a breach of Versailles as conscription. The French were very angry and felt they had been betrayed by Britain. And as they reeled from the blow, Hitler broke the Treaty of Versailles by marching into the Rhineland in March 1936. Resistance by Britain and France would probably have forced Hitler to withdraw, but they did nothing. There was some sympathy in Britain for 'Germany's right to her native lands'. It was left to the League of Nations to make a protest, and Britain and France half-heartedly and shame-facedly attempted without success to negotiate after the seizure of the Rhineland what they might well have prevented had they acted immediately German troops crossed the Rhine.

> 66 **Hitler tests the thickness of the ice... and finds it supports him** 99

GERMAN–ITALIAN CO-OPERATION

Italy, grateful for Hitler's attitude over Abyssinia, failed to bolster the British and French reaction to the seizure of the Rhineland. The outbreak of the Spanish Civil War in the summer of 1936 saw co-operation between Germany and Italy to aid the nationalists against the republicans in Spain. Hitler and Mussolini cemented their new friendship by the Axis Pact in October 1936, joining soon after in the Anti-Comintern Pact with Japan. In view of this development it was hardly surprising that the western powers and the League could do nothing about the full-scale invasion of China by Japan in 1937. China's appeal to the League of Nations resulted in a sanctions recommendation which virtually all countries felt free to ignore.

By now Britain and France had begun to rearm while assuring their peoples that they were doing no such thing. In Britain a new prime minister, Neville Chamberlain, was prepared to do everything humanly possible to preserve peace against an international background that was growing steadily more menacing. Hitler, by the end of 1937, was convinced that with Italy now on his side, with Russia crippled by purges and the League of Nations powerless, he could pursue his expansionist aims unchallenged. He assumed that British sympathy over the Rhineland would extend to sympathy with his ambitions in Austria and even Czechoslovakia, and that Britain would not attempt to oppose him. In Britain the horrors of the Spanish Civil War and the dangers of aerial bombardment, demonstrated by the fate of Guernica, had made a profound impression. In 1933 the Oxford University Debating Union had passed the motion that 'This House will not fight for king or country', and there was no reason to suppose that the country's mood, in so far as this motion represented the mood of the country and many believed that it did, had changed now that war seemed much more imminent. So when in 1938 Hitler, in defiance of the Treaty of Versailles, seized Austria, declared the *Anschluss* – or union with Germany – and secured 99 per cent support for it in a plebiscite, neither Britain nor France was prepared to make a stand. After all, the Austrians were really German too, weren't they? And the plebiscite had shown that what Hitler had done was done with the approval of the vast majority of the Austrian people. But the seizure of Austria meant that Germany surrounded Czechoslovakia on three sides. Now that Britain was prepared to give way to Germany to keep the peace, and this is the popular view of what is meant by appeasement, it was a vital question whether Hitler's designs on Czechoslovakia would be regarded as a different case from that of merely taking over lands that were indisputably German in language and sympathy.

2 THE HIGH WATER MARK OF APPEASEMENT – MUNICH

You need to know the Munich episode in detail.

Like the Germans of Austria, the Germans of Czechoslovakia had never been part of pre-war Germany. What justifiable grievances the three million Germans of the Sudetenland had were certainly fostered and inflamed by Nazi propaganda. German pressure on Czechoslovakia began to build up from June 1938 and in August Chamberlain, Britain's prime minister, was so concerned that he sent Lord Runciman to Czechoslovakia to look at the problem at first hand. Lord Runciman wanted to give the Sudeten Germans self-government within the Czechoslovak state, but Hitler preferred more drastic solutions, encouraged violence in the Sudetenland and denounced Czechoslovakia as an 'artificial state'. In alarm Chamberlain went to see Hitler at Berchtesgaden. Hitler demanded the immediate granting of the Sudetenland to Germany. Chamberlain consulted the French government, and offered to cede to Germany all areas of Czechoslovakia where the German population exceeded 50 per cent. To this the Czechs had no alternative but to agree, even though they had not been consulted. The 50 per cent areas were to be determined by plebiscite, but Hitler, when Chamberlain met him for a second time at Godesburg a week later, demanded that German troops occupy the whole of the Sudetenland by 1 October, thus pre-empting any plebiscite results. Chamberlain was dismayed. He could hardly have been surprised when the Czechs rejected this new demand. France was prepared to honour her treaty obligations to help Czechoslovakia; Russia, too, was bound to help, but only if France moved first. In Britain the crisis set primary school children to filling sandbags and trying on gas-masks.

Chamberlain was convinced that the British people wanted peace at any price, and that they would not take up arms over 'a quarrel in a faraway country'. Moreover, although Britain's rearmament programme was under way, Chamberlain believed that Britain needed to buy time. A few more months, a year or so, and Britain would be, he believed, in a much stronger position to face up to Germany. Chamberlain also had a rather simple optimism about human nature; he believed that Hitler was basically a reasonable man who would respond to fair dealing. So Chamberlain made another attempt; with French prime minister, Daladier, and with Mussolini of Italy, he met Hitler for the third time, on this occasion at Munich. The Czechs and the Russians were not invited. It was there agreed that German armies should march into the Sudetenland with Hitler making the 'concession' that the occupation be completed by 15 October, rather than the 1 October date he had demanded at Godesburg. Parts of Czechoslovakia were to be ceded to Poland and Hungary, and final boundaries other than the Sudetenland (which would go to Germany completely) were to be decided later by plebiscite. Hitler also signed an agreement, the famous 'piece of paper' in which Britain and Germany pledged their joint commitment to peace. Chamberlain waved this paper about triumphantly as he got off the plane bringing him back from Munich. 'I believe it is peace in our time' he told the crowd of waiting officials and reporters. Perhaps it would have been if Hitler had been the reasonable man Chamberlain believed him to be. If so the price might have been worth paying. But Munich did not teach Hitler how to be reasonable; it taught him that ruthlessness pays. Czechoslovakia had been deserted by its allies and made defenceless by the loss of its munitions factories and frontier defences. Germany had been much strengthened and its prestige had soared. Britain and France had shown that they were unreliable as friends and allies, and that they had given in to threats of force. Some critics, including Churchill, believed that Munich was a humiliation, and that Hitler's bluff should have been called. It seemed unlikely to Churchill that Hitler would have dared attack a mobilized and powerful Czechoslovakia, especially a Czechoslovakia firmly backed by France, Britain and the USSR. As it was, Munich proved the high-water mark of appeasement; peace had been bought at high cost, but for the last time on a major issue, and the peace that remained could be measured only in months, not years.

3 ▶ THE ABANDONMENT OF APPEASEMENT

Hitler was now convinced that Britain and France were so committed to appeasement that they could be safely ignored. In March 1939 disorders in Czechoslovakia as the state began to fall apart gave Hitler the excuse to march into Prague and seize the rest of Czechoslovakia. Two days later Chamberlain, in a speech at Birmingham, felt obliged in the light of this latest development to defend his Munich policy:

> But I had another purpose, too, in going to Munich. That was to further the policy I have been pursuing ever since I have been in my present position – a policy which is sometimes called European appeasement, although I do not think myself that that is a very happy term or one which accurately describes its purpose. If that policy were to succeed, it is essential that no power should seek to obtain a general domination of Europe; but that each one should be contented to obtain reasonable facilities for developing its resources, securing its own share of international trade, and improving the condition of its own people. I felt that, although that might well mean a clash of interests between different states, nevertheless, by the exercise of mutual goodwill and understanding of what were the limits of the desires of others, it should be possible to resolve all the differences by discussion and without armed conflict. I hoped in going to Munich to find out by personal contact what was in Herr Hitler's mind, and whether it was likely that he would be willing to co-operate in a programme of that kind. Well, the atmosphere in which our discussions were conducted was not a very favourable one, because we were in the middle of an acute crisis; but, nevertheless, in the intervals between more official conversations I had some opportunities of talking with him and of hearing his views, and I thought that results were not altogether unsatisfactory. (HMSO)

❝ Try to understand Chamberlain's policies here. ❞

But this attempt to justify appeasement was almost immediately followed by an attempt to distance himself from it:

> (Six weeks ago) I pointed out that any attempt to dominate the world by force was one which the democracies must resist, and I added that I could not believe that such a challenge was intended, because no government with the interests of its own people at heart could expose them for such a claim to the horrors of world war.
>
> And, indeed, with the lessons of history for all to read, it seems incredible that we should see such a challenge. I feel bound to repeat that, while I am not prepared to engage this country by new unspecified commitments operating under conditions which cannot now be foreseen, yet no greater mistake could be made than to suppose that, because it believes war to be a senseless and cruel thing, this nation has so lost its fibre that it will not take part to the utmost of its power in resisting such a challenge if it ever were made. For that declaration I am convinced that I have not merely the support, the sympathy, the confidence of my fellow-countrymen and fellow country-women, but I shall also have the approval of the whole British Empire and of all other nations who value peace, indeed, but who value freedom even more. (HMSO)

If Chamberlain wondered whether Czechoslovakia was the last of Hitler's legitimate demands or the first of his steps towards world domination, Ribbentrop's brow-beating of the Lithuanian foreign minister, followed by the seizure of Memel a week after the fall of Prague, convinced him. Any hope that Mussolini would offer a voice of restraint was dashed when Mussolini used the Easter religious festival to launch a surprise attack on Albania. Chamberlain had already pledged Britain to defend Poland against attack. France renewed its alliance with Poland, and after the Albanian episode both Britain and France gave guarantees to Romania and Greece. Thus Chamberlain, who had in March declared against Britain engaging in 'unspecified commitments operating under conditions which cannot now be foreseen' had by April entered into three such commitments. Appeasement was over. Britain introduced conscription in May, and made some effort, despite ideological differences, to secure a promise of Soviet help in the defence of Poland. Stalin's purges made Chamberlain doubt the efficiency of the Red Army, so Chamberlain was not prepared to put pressure on Poland to allow Russia immediate access for her troops in the event of a German invasion of Poland. Litvinov had been replaced by Molotov as Soviet foreign minister in May and Russia began negotiations to secure a non-aggression pact with Germany, thus ensuring that if Germany went to war it would be war in the west, not war in the east. Throughout the summer of 1939 German pressure on Poland varied as the prospects of a Russo-German pact advanced or retreated. At one time it seemed that the Russians might well make an agreement with the west. But when in late August the Molotov-Ribbentrop Pact was signed, Poland's fate was sealed, and only the most abject appeasement would have enabled Britain and France, to escape their obligations to Poland. Hitler invaded Poland on 1 September 1939 knowing that by the pact Russia would not only give Poland no support but would actually take part in Poland's partition. Chamberlain tried at first to get Hitler to call off the invasion. Through a day of negotiations and feverish diplomatic activity he avoided presenting Germany with an ultimatum. He was not planning to leave Poland to her fate, but he was understandably reluctant to abandon the cause of peace for which he had struggled for so long. Inevitably, however, and with the backing of all parties in the House of Commons, an ultimatum was presented to Germany. Germany's failure to reply by the deadline meant that Britain and Germany were at war at 11a.m. on Sunday 3 September, 1939.

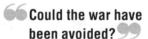

4 ⟩ **ASSESSMENT**

❝Could the war have been avoided?❞

Historians are divided as to whether appeasement did buy time for Britain and France to rearm, and on balance those who argue that it did not seem the more convincing. Had Czechoslovakia, with British, French and possibly Russian backing, resisted Hitler in 1938 then Hitler would have encountered serious military difficulties of a kind that he did not face in Poland a year later. An earlier opportunity to make a stand was over the Rhineland in 1936 when Hitler crossed the Rhine with a totally inadequate force and would have called off his venture had he met British and French resistance. It might have been difficult without the support of the USA to have done anything about the Japanese invasion of China in 1937, but co-operation with the USA over Manchuria in 1931 might well have worked and could at least have been tried. Even the League had persuaded Japan to withdraw from Shanghai in 1932. Appeasement was not solely a fear-ridden and guilt-ridden policy of giving in to brute force and naked aggression. Its supporters were honest men like Chamberlain, who believed that Germany had justifiable grievances for which it was not worth going to war, and which could be settled by compromise and negotiation. In the last resort the appeasers realized that the appetite of the dictators and Hitler in particular could not be satisfied by sacrifices, and that western freedom and democracy would have to be defended by force, not words.

APPLIED MATERIALS

Texts and Atlases
See books on Hitler in applied materials section for Chapter 6.
I. Richards, J. B. Goodson, and J.A. Morris, *A Sketchmap History of the Great Wars and After*, Harrap, 1965
W. R. Rock, *British Appeasement in the 1930s*, Arnold, 1977
R. Stone, *The Drift to War*, Heinemann, 1976

Documentary
R. Parkinson, *The Origins of World War II*, Wayland Documentary, 1970

Filmstrips, records, etc.
A. J. P. Taylor, *Chamberlain and Munich*, Discourses, DCL 1207
Audio Learning
Causes of the Second World War, HM 0009
British Appeasement, HEA 004
The Road to Munich, HUA 020 – Track One

IDEAS AND PRINCIPLES

COLLECTIVE SECURITY
It had been hoped in 1919 that would-be aggressors would be deterred by the collective membership and the moral force of the League of Nations acting to preserve world peace. Statesmen pinned their hopes on disarmament and the League, with an uncertain confidence that League membership conferred some kind of immunity from attack. By the 1930s these hopes had faded, but the supporters of collective security turned to the idea of strong alliances being powerful enough to preserve peace. The Stresa front seemed promising at first, but there was no fulfilment. In fact collective security was little more than a dream: the self-interest of individual states took precedence over the collective interests of Europe and the world. Many saw collective security as a substitute for rearmament. When collective security was seen to be unattainable, appeasement seemed the only short-term alternative while long-term plans were made for rearmament.

APPEASEMENT
By the 1930s, when the term came into general use, it meant the satisfying of the aims of the aggressive powers, and giving in to those aims by concession. Chamberlain, however, and other appeasers believed that what they were doing was recognizing the legitimate grievances of other powers and solving disputes with them by careful negotiation.

EXAMINATION QUESTIONS

QUESTION 1
(a) Describe Chamberlain's dealings with Hitler between 1937 and 1939.
(b) Explain why Chamberlain followed a policy of appeasement. (30 marks)

(SEG)

QUESTION 2
Chamberlain has just returned from Munich. You are a journalist and your editor has asked you to interview people in the street, asking their views on Munich and on appeasement generally. Give a report of two such interviews, chosen because of the differing views expressed. (25 marks)

OUTLINE ANSWERS

ANSWER 1
It will be unusual to be asked for descriptive answers in the GCSE because it will be difficult to assess the answers in terms of skills. Where such questions do crop up, as here, students would be wise to aim at more than descriptive coverage. The 1937 starting date in Question 1 (a) is the beginning of Chamberlain's prime ministership, so the Rhineland, Abyssinia and the Spanish Civil War are only of marginal introductory relevance. The main themes will be the *Anschluss*, the Munich crisis, the seizure of Czechoslovakia in March 1939 and the developing Polish crisis leading to war. The description should be bolstered with effective analysis, and change could be demonstrated in the move away from appeasement in 1939.

Analysis and change would take the description into the higher skills and enable the examiner to place it in the higher level of achievement.

The second part of the question requires reasons, and several should readily spring to mind: Chamberlain's overwhelming desire for peace and his horror of war, his belief that he was dealing with a reasonable man (Hitler) with justifiable grievances, his need to buy time to rearm and his belief that the British people were united in their opposition to war. Some attempt should be made to assess the relative importance of these reasons if you are aiming at the highest level and thus the highest marks. Was Chamberlain taken in by Hitler? Did he really believe that a signature on a piece of paper would be a reliable guarantee of peace? Was Chamberlain just playing for time?

ANSWER 2

When answering Question 2 remember that at the time Chamberlain's successful mission was greeted with almost universal relief that the horrors of war had been avoided. Few (of whom Churchill was one) criticized him at the time, and a major shift in public opinion did not occur until several weeks later. You could therefore choose for one of your views the Churchillian line that Czechoslovakia had been betrayed, that Hitler was a greedy dictator with an insatiable appetite, that paper guarantees were worthless and would soon prove to be so, and that what we needed were strong allies, massive rearmament and resolution. The alternative would be to make your interviewee relieved at the continuation of peace but uneasy in conscience about Czechoslovakia. More typically your Chamberlain supporter would enthuse about Chamberlain's mission, believe that justice had been done both to Czechoslovakia and to Hitler's just claims, welcome the paper guarantee and be naïvely optimistic about the future. It would be unhistorical for anyone in September 1938 to have suggested that Chamberlain was cynically buying time, so this line should be avoided.

SUGGESTIONS FOR FURTHER WORK

1. Study the two extracts from the speech by Chamberlain given in this chapter. How effective a defence of appeasement does Chamberlain offer in the first extract? In what ways is he moving away from appeasement in the second extract?
2. What arguments were used against Chamberlain by the critics of appeasement in 1938? Tip: find extracts from Churchill's speeches either in biographies or in books of documents such as J.H. Bettey, *English Historical Documents 1906–39*, Routledge.
3. Find out the attitude of the Liberal and Labour Parties to the policy of appeasement in the years 1937–39. Did they have any constructive alternative policies to it?
4. France was the other main power which supported appeasement in the 1930s. How were French reasons for appeasement different from or similar to those of Britain?

STUDENT'S ANSWER – EXAMINER'S COMMENT

Question

(a) Why were Britain and Russia unable to reach an agreement in 1939?
(b) Why was Germany anxious to conclude a pact?
(c) Why did Stalin agree to the Nazi-Soviet Pact?

> **This is a good point, as the initiative for the Nazi-Soviet pact came from Russia rather than Germany.**

(a) There was little trust between Britain and Russia. The Russians had not forgotten Britain's part in the Civil War, and Britain's Conservative government was very afraid of Communism. Stalin knew that Hitler wanted to destroy Communism, and thus feared a German attack on Russia, and he believed that Britain was holding back an agreement in the hope that Hitler would attack Russia rather than France. So he dismissed his foreign minister Litvinov, who seemed to want a Western alliance, and replaced him with Molotov, who was prepared to buy time from the Germans. The Germans were only too pleased to respond to the Russians, because they did not want to fight a war on two fronts. Russia believed that Britain was just playing for time and did not seriously want a Russian alliance. This belief was strengthened by the fact that Britain refused to put Poland under pressure to agree to allow the passage of Russian troops in the event of war.

> **This is a useful explanation and is well developed; but the candidate had not read the question right through, as some of the answer overlaps with (b).**

(b) Germany was afraid that a pact between Britain and Russia would mean that Germany would have to fight a war on two fronts. As Germany was now committed to the invasion of Poland the prospect of a combined British and Russian defence of Poland was viewed with alarm in Germany. But if Germany made a pact with Russia it was likely that, as at Munich when the West abandoned Czechoslovakia, so Britain was unlikely to undertake the defence of Poland on her own, and so there would be another Munich.

> **This is quite effectively done and would certainly reach one of the higher assessment levels.**

(c) Stalin was afraid that Britain and France would leave Russia to fight Germany without assistance. He did not trust the western powers, and with his army crippled by the purges, needed to buy time to prepare for war. If Britain and France had no intention of defending Poland then some kind of agreement with Hitler was vital for Russian security. If by any chance Britain and France did defend Poland they would only be defending Russian interests anyway. Stalin used the time gained by the Nazi-Soviet pact to build up Russian strength, he remained on the alert, aware that Germany could and would attack Russia at any time.

> **This section continues the high level set in the previous sections, developing argument rather than just relying on description (i.e. narrative). Excellent spelling and use of language throughout the answer.**

> **The last sentence is historically dubious as the German attack in 1941 took Russia by surprise. But it is also an unnecessary sentence, as there is no need to go beyond 1939.**

THE SECOND WORLD WAR

GETTING STARTED

The determination of most European states after 1919 to avoid war at all costs gave a great advantage to those powers which were willing to risk war for national advantage. The weakness of the League of Nations made 'collective security' unattainable. And although Britain and France looked for firm alliances in the 1930s they ignored Soviet Russia (e.g. at Munich) until it was too late. If the Versailles treaty had any defects these ought to have been dealt with by international negotiation. Instead the defects were magnified into enormous grievances; and from the invasion of Manchuria in 1931 Japan, Italy and Germany embarked upon a series of aggressive acts which could only have been stopped by a war which no one was willing to undertake. When Britain and France finally decided to make a stand in support of Poland, a country they were incapable of defending, the Second World War began. Britain and France can be blamed for lack of preparedness, the USA for isolationism and the Soviet Union for the non-aggression pact which removed Hitler's fear of fighting on two fronts. But weakness and short-sightedness can be excusable: it is impossible to defend or excuse Hitler's policy of expansion and aggression, and Germany's leaders must accept the major responsibility for the war.

HISTORICAL DEVELOPMENTS

German troops invaded Poland on 1 September 1939; Britain and France honoured their obligations to Poland by going to war with Germany, but they could do little to help Poland. Tactics soon to be repeated in the campaigns of 1940 and 1941 crushed Polish resistance: the German airforce (Luftwaffe) pounded Poland's airfields and destroyed Poland's airforce on the ground; it then had a free hand to attack railways, roads, troop concentrations and other strategic targets. Mobile army units moved rapidly forward, followed by heavily armoured tanks, against which the Polish cavalry fought bravely but in vain. This 'blitzkrieg' (lightning war) in western Poland was supported by a Soviet invasion from the east on 19 September. By early October virtually all Polish resistance was at an end.

Meanwhile the British and French in the Maginot Line and the Germans in the Siegfried Line faced each other along the Franco–German border. Both sides seemed confident that their line was impregnable; both sides expected to overwhelm the other with a tremendous offensive and avoid the trench stalemate of the First World War. Along the Belgian frontier, however, French defences were primitive and incomplete. While the war at sea provided plenty of sensations during the first six months of hostilities, the western front provided none. The mood of complacency and over-optimism was reinforced among the British public when at Christmas 1939 Gracie Fields's broadcast home from 'somewhere in France' included the popular song 'We're going to hang out the washing on the Siegfried line if the Siegfried line's still there'. By the spring of 1940 the inactivity had given the war its description of the 'phoney war'.

When Finland refused the Soviet demand for bases in November 1939, a winter war began which contrasted with the calm of the western front. The defence of their country by the determined Finns excited western admiration, and plans were even discussed to help the Finns by sending aid through Norway and Sweden, a scheme blocked by the determination of the Swedes to maintain their neutrality. Norway's neutrality was compromised by allied mine laying, but the Russo–Finnish War ended with Finland's defeat in March 1940, and the allies were taken by surprise when Germany attacked Denmark and Norway on 9 April. Denmark was easily overrun, but the Norwegians put up a tougher resistance. British attempts to establish a foothold in central and northern Norway were weakened by lack of air support, but severe damage was inflicted on the German fleet. Before the last resistance in Norway ended in early June, the Germans had invaded the Low Countries on 10 May. On that day British misfortunes in Norway had helped to cause the replacement of Chamberlain's government by a coalition government led by Winston Churchill.

> ❝ Churchill replaces Chamberlain at this point. ❞

The blitzkrieg was repeated in Holland, Belgium and France. Much of Rotterdam was obliterated by German air attack. The Dutch had no answer to the Luftwaffe and the Panzer divisions and Holland was overrun in five days. The Belgians surrendered in a little more than a fortnight, just as the British and French troops sent to help were being cut off by a German drive to the Channel ports to the south of them. The British air force gave the trapped troops some cover, while the British navy organized during six days the evacuation of nearly 340,000 British and allied troops from Dunkirk. Whether Hitler's interference had slowed down the German advance or not, the Dunkirk 'miracle' was also a disaster which saw the loss of all the British Expeditionary Force's guns and transport, and inflicted on British Fighter Command heavy losses of aircraft. Desperate French pleas for Spitfires were turned down by the British, and with France on the verge of collapse Britain prepared to defend itself against attack.

Despite Churchill's offer of a political union with France to bolster flagging French resistance, France signed an armistice with Germany on 22 June 1940 and Germany came into possession of all France's Channel and Atlantic coasts. Churchill inspired the British people with speeches, but the British army lacked numbers and equipment and the navy could not defend Britain without air cover. Only the British air force could save the country from the fate of France – mercifully, unknown to the Germans, it was equipped with radar, a recently invented tracking device which enormously increased its strength.

Italy's entry into the war in June 1940 seemed to Britain at first an irrelevance. The main issue was whether Germany could win sufficient mastery in the air over Britain to mount a successful invasion. The battle of Britain – the contest in the air – lasted from July until the end of September. The fine summer made it a grandstand spectacle for those living in the counties of the south east: for six weeks children in some areas slept in air raid shelters rather than in their own beds. Historians have argued that the Germans, by attacking RAF airfields, came close to victory, but their temporary switch to bombing raids on London in early September gave the sorely pressed RAF a breathing-space and a time to recuperate. By mid-September the Germans were getting the worst of it; the air battle was called off, and the invasion was postponed. While Britain stood alone the possibility of invasion always remained, but the removal of the immediate threat coincided with the development of a serious menace to Britain's lifeline in the Mediterranean. Much shipping used the Suez Canal route, and Britain's oil supplies reached her from the Middle East via the Mediterranean. When Italy joined the war on Germany's side, Britain's vital communications were threatened. The British garrison and dockyard in Malta was very close to Sicily and the Italian troops in Libya were dangerously close to the Suez Canal. The Italian attack on Egypt from Libya might have achieved more but for Italy's embarrassingly unsuccessful invasion of Greece, begun in October. By December the British were able to counter-attack, clear the Italians out of Egypt and overrun eastern Libya. The Italian navy suffered such losses at British hands at the battle of Matapan that it was forced to stay in its harbours. Italy's humiliation was further enforced by the defeat of her armies in Abyssinia in April 1941 and the restoration of Emperor Haile Selassie.

> **Britain now faces Germany alone.**

Italy's weakness was a source of irritation to Hitler, and its defeats made it a liability. In the autumn of 1940 Romania and Hungary had signed what amounted to treaties of alliance with Germany. Bulgaria followed in March 1941. Once the adhesion of Yugoslavia had been secured, the Balkans would be effectively in German hands and Mussolini could be rescued from the Greeks. Hitler was in a hurry as he was already planning Operation Barbarossa – his invasion of Russia. But he was forced to delay it for six weeks: Yugoslavia decided to resist. It took two weeks for Yugoslavia to be crushed and another month for Greece to be overrun. The British thinned their troops in north Africa to send aid to Greece, and they gave the German parachutists some bad moments in Crete in May 1941; but by the end of that month the Germans and Italians controlled almost all of south-east Europe, and the Italians with German help had recaptured all their lost territory in Libya and once again invaded Egypt. Only Tobruk held out behind their lines, until it surrendered in June 1942.

3 ⟩ RUSSIA ON THE DEFENSIVE

Russia's alliance with Germany in August 1939 had been an odd marriage of convenience. The Nazi leader, whose followers had fought the communists in the German streets and whose hatred of communism fills many pages of *Mein Kampf*, had merely postponed his quarrel with Russia in order to avoid a war on two fronts by dealing first with Britain and France. Stalin thought he had bought time. But such was his suspicious nature that he ignored western warnings that a German attack was imminent, believing them to be designed to drag Russia into the war. His own intelligence services seem to have underestimated the German preparations, for the German attack on 22 June 1941 took the Russians completely by surprise. One Red Army unit radioed 'We are being fired on. What shall we do?' The answer came back from headquarters 'You must be mad. And why is your signal not in code?' It is not surprising then that in the confusion bridges were captured intact, hundreds of Russian planes were destroyed on the ground and no concerted defence was attempted.

Lack of preparedness, the 1930s purges of high-ranking officers and the precision of the German attack cost the Russians heavily in the first few weeks. The swiftness of the German advance trapped Soviet armies well behind the German lines: 650,000 Russian prisoners were taken by October, and 700,000 Russians were encircled at Kiev. While Hitler and his generals haggled about their objectives – to seize the coal and industry of the Don basin and move on to capture the oil fields of the Caucasus, or to make an all-out effort to take Moscow – the German forces reached the outskirts of the Russian capital and 450 miles to the north west began a siege of Leningrad that was to last nearly three years. The onset of winter gave the Russians their first real respite. In many areas the Germans had overreached themselves: they lacked suitable airfields and had to fight without air cover. Moreover, the expected anti-Bolshevik uprising never came: Soviet citizens, communist and non-communist alike, accepted Stalin's leadership and turned the German invasion into the great patriotic war. The Russians transferred their factories east beyond the Urals, and began to build up their strength for the following year.

With spring came the renewal of the German advance. German forces pushed towards the Volga River and the Caucasus, and in August 1942 came up against Stalingrad, a city the Russians decided to turn into a fortress to stem the German advance. As the Germans seemed poised for victory, the Russians counter-attacked and cut the German communications, and the German attackers were trapped. A breakout and withdrawal from the city would probably have saved the bulk of the German Sixth Army at an early stage, but Hitler would not hear of it. Through the intensifying winter cold the surrounded Germans fought hopeless street battles. The last remnants of a German army originally numbering nearly 300,000 men surrendered on 2 February 1943. Perhaps not everyone realized it yet, but Russia was no longer on the defensive.

4 ▷ JAPAN ON THE ATTACK

 **The war now becomes a world war.**

It has been argued that the Second World War began not in the west in 1939, but in the Far East in China in 1937. Japan had a controlling grip on nearly all China's coastal provinces by 1939. In 1940 Japan took advantage of the fall of France and Holland to seize Indo-China and the Dutch East Indies. The Japanese were short of resources and wary of the Soviet Union, with whom Japan had fought briefly and unsuccessfully in 1939 in a short military encounter. But in April 1941 Japan was relieved of a possible Russian attack when the two countries signed a neutrality pact. Japan's plans to create a co-prosperity sphere and bring all south-east Asia under her economic and political control could now be developed. But one obstacle remained – the USA. The Japanese suffered a US trade embargo in order to prevent the Japanese using American supplies in the war against China. The Burma road, which provided a trade route between India and China, had been closed by the British in 1940 under pressure from Japan, but the road was soon reopened and increased supplies of war materials were reaching China by the summer of 1941. To the Japanese the situation was becoming intolerable. They decided to break out of the trade stranglehold by making a surprise and devastating attack upon the USA. It was odd that the simultaneous departure of most Japanese merchant vessels for their home ports, and the sudden radio silence they now observed, passed almost unnoticed. In the unexpected attack on Pearl Harbor, the US Hawaiian naval base, the US Pacific fleet was severely crippled. At the same time the US air bases in the Philippines were attacked. For the time being US power was paralysed and, seizing the advantage, the Japanese won a series of spectacular successes. British Hong Kong was soon captured. Malaya soon followed, and there the loss of the British warships the *Prince of Wales* and the *Repulse* taught Britain how defenceless the navy was without air cover. During 1942 the Americans lost the Philippine Islands, the Japanese overran Burma and threatened India, and the Japanese invasion of New Guinea posed a direct threat to Australia. For a time the Japanese seemed invincible.

5 ▷ THE CIVILIAN WAR

The Second World War had a more direct effect on the civilian populations than the war of 1914–18. Blitzkrieg attacks devastated cities and caused heavy civilian casualties. Systematic air raids made necessary the creation of elaborate communications systems, effective fire-fighting organizations and first aid and hospital facilities for the injured. In Britain the worst of the air raids were during 1940–2, generally known as the period of the blitz. London suffered heavily and so did major cities such as Coventry, Plymouth, Liverpool, Manchester, Southampton and Portsmouth. The pilotless aircraft, the V1s, did some damage in the southern counties and in London in 1944, and the V2 rockets, against which there was no defence, might have become a serious threat to the morale of London had not their launching sites in Europe been overrun by allied armies. Altogether over 50,000 British civilians died from enemy air attack during the war, but this figure was considerably lower than the number killed in German air raids on Polish cities in 1939, Dutch cities in 1940 and Russian cities in 1941. It was also low compared with the number killed in German cities from 1942 onwards. Some had been bombed before then, but with American planes and supplies pouring in the allies intensified their air offensive. Thousand-bomber raids became commonplace in 1944. Berlin suffered severely, but the raid on Dresden in February 1945, devastating most of the city and creating a great fire storm from which there was no escape, was the most dramatic and according to some critics the most unnecessary, coming as it did when the war was virtually over. Churchill's threat in 1940 to retaliate for German air attacks had been carried out: Germany lost ten times more civilians from air attack than did Britain.

EVACUATION

Some attempt had been made in Britain in 1939 to avoid unnecessary bombing casualties: town children, often pale and undernourished, and clutching gas-masks, which as it turned out were never needed, were removed for safety to foster-homes in the countryside. Many evacuees returned to the cities during the 'phoney war', only to be involved in new evacuation schemes organized when German air raids started in earnest in the autumn of 1940. The black-out – the rigorous banning of all artificial lighting in the open (vehicles in Britain moved at night with dimmed lights) – made night travel a hazard in all countries which were at war, and was even enforced after December 1941 in vulnerable coastal states of the USA.

FEMALE WORK

The insatiable demand for men for the armed forces made it necessary for most women to take up some form of work, at least part time. Oddly enough, even in Germany's greatest time of need in 1944 and 1945 fewer women were in war work there than in Britain. This is partly accounted for by Germany's importation of thousands of foreigners as forced labour. The demands of factories and mines took precedence over other needs. But it was necessary to maintain food production, even though the supply of consumer goods dried up. In Britain an effectively enforced system of rationing food was introduced in January 1940, as U-boat attacks on British shipping lanes began to bite. Spare plots of land were dug up and planted. 'Dig for victory' was a slogan persistently presented to the public throughout the war. Although there were anxious moments for Britain's food supplies during 1941, the British people were adequately fed during the war, and the physical fitness of the civilian population, especially children, showed a marked improvement over that in the 1930s. This was not the case in occupied Europe, drained of its food supplies to feed Germany. Rationing was severe, and malnutrition was common – especially in the major cities where people had little means of access to the resources of the countryside. Military operations interrupted food distribution in areas of hostilities such as western Russia; anyway, priority was for the troops. Thousands died of starvation. In contrast, the German people, cushioned by food imports from other areas of Europe, were adequately provided for until the last stages of the war. Allied servicemen crossing from occupied Holland into Germany were struck with the contrast between the gaunt half-starving Dutch civilians and the well-fed Germans.

HOME GUARD

❝Effects of the war in
Britain.❞

In Britain the invasion danger of 1940 led to the revival of the Local Defence Volunteers, soon to be renamed the Home Guard. All able-bodied male civilians except children and pensioners had to serve in it, unless they were engaged in other war work, in order to assist in the defence of the country against invasion. Subsequent generations may have laughed at their fictionalized exploits in *Dad's Army*, but at the time they were taken very seriously, although they would have had little chance against invading Panzer divisions, no matter how great their patriotism and fighting spirit.

CENSORSHIP

All countries at war censored the news and selected the information which the public should be given. Much censorship was necessary for obvious security reasons. In Britain posters constantly reminded the population that 'Careless talk costs lives'. Even so, propaganda news broadcasts from Germany could be listened to without fear of prosecution. 'Lord Haw-Haw' gained a large radio following in Britain without undermining British morale. His technique of using accurate pieces of information gleaned from pre-war guide-books ('Trinity church clock is two minutes slow') added a convincing touch to his much more questionable comments on the war. In Europe, however, listening to allied broadcasts was an offence which in occupied territories was usually punishable by death. Nevertheless, broadcasts from London were listened to by many. They gave some comfort to those suffering German occupation and encouragement to the resistance movements which increasingly plagued the Germans in many countries from 1942 onwards.

TRAVEL RESTRICTIONS

Restrictions on news were accompanied by restrictions on travel. Railways and roads were needed for troop movements; civilian travel was discouraged and trains and buses were infrequent, uncomfortable and invariably overcrowded. In Britain the arrival of American forces in increasing numbers made security of vital importance. Above the low cloud on the day of the Dieppe raid (August 1942), planes, mostly German, could be heard but on the ground near the south-east coast there seemed little activity. But from late 1943 activity was unmistakable: roads were marked with yellow parking lots for tanks and armoured vehicles. Civilians living within ten miles of the coast in the south east were forbidden to cross county boundaries except on urgent business. But nothing could prevent the locals seeing the huge concentration of weapons and equipment building up on the roads in May and early June 1944, and the sight of gliders moving across the coast at dusk on 5 June merely confirmed what everyone had known for some weeks: the invasion of Europe was imminent. Troop concentrations on a lesser scale must have been a common sight in many areas throughout the war.

CIVILIAN HARDSHIP

In Britain the hardship and suffering of war was bearable, as it was in Germany until the final days of chaos and destruction in 1945. The Japanese expansion in south-east Asia often brought death, destruction and atrocity in China, and Europeans falling into Japanese hands suffered unendurable privations in notorious prisoner-of-war camps. But other nationalities avoided undue hardship if they collaborated with the Japanese. In occupied Europe it was a different story. Collaboration did not mean the absence of privation, and as resistance movements grew German retaliation against civilian populations reached heights of barbarity such as the obliteration of the Czech village of Lidice and the French village of Oradour-sur-Glane. In both cases there were few survivors.

THE HOLOCAUST

The Germans reserved their most unspeakable inhumanity for the Jewish population. Anti-Jewish measures culminated in 1941 with 'the final solution'. Jews were rounded up, taken to special concentration camps and there systematically exterminated in gas chambers. In Russia execution squads despatched hundreds of thousands. There were acts of heroism and sacrifice by those who tried to protect and save Jewish lives. Nevertheless, in this appalling Holocaust six million Jews died, probably accounting for about half of all the civilian deaths of the Second World War.

6 > RUSSIA ON THE ATTACK

❝The turning of the tide.❞

After Stalingrad the Germans were never again able to mount a major offensive in the east. For the first two summers, 1941 and 1942, the Russians had defended themselves, turning to the offensive only in winter. But in the summer of 1943 the Russians hit back. After destroying the massed German tanks at the battle of Kursk, they recaptured large areas of the Ukraine and White Russia and overran the Crimea. The British and the Americans sent limited but useful supplies along the long and hazardous sea-lane to Murmansk. Stalin and communists in the west demanded the opening of a second front, conveniently undervaluing allied activity in north Africa and Italy, but Russian sacrifices had been heavy and Stalin was anxious for any respite that would ease the strain. In January 1944 Russian forces entered Poland, but they concentrated in the early part of 1944 on liberating Romania, Bulgaria and Hungary from German occupation. Although the Russians were close to Warsaw in the summer of 1944, a rising of Polish patriots proved to be premature. In crushing it the Germans did the Russians an unexpected and uncalled-for service in destroying much of the anti-communist leadership in the city.

After a brief pause the Russians moved on again in January 1945, occupying east Prussia and reaching the River Oder. They fought their way against stiff German resistance to the outskirts of Berlin, while to the south they liberated Austria and Czechoslovakia. Russian and American forces linked up in Germany on 25 April 1945. Within a few days Hitler had committed suicide and Germany had surrendered.

7 > THE INVASION OF EUROPE

The Germans had taken over control of the campaign in north Africa in 1942, and in September, at the first battle of El Alamein, General Rommel, their commander, tried but failed to break through towards the Nile Delta. In October the British Eighth Army led by General Montgomery attacked the Germans with overpowering superiority, both on the ground and in the air, and the Germans were forced into retreat. Surprise allied landings in Morocco and Algeria threatened Rommel's rear and communications; he abandoned Libya in order to concentrate on the defence of Tunisia and on his communications with Italy. German reinforcements delayed the inevitable but swelled to 160,000 the German army that surrendered in May 1943. Within two months the first invasion of Europe had occurred: the allies landed in Sicily and crossed to the mainland of Italy. Although Mussolini's government fell and Italy soon surrendered, the allies in the confusion that followed missed the opportunity to seize Rome. The Germans took political control of most of the country, establishing a powerful defensive position in the south. Heavy fighting followed, particularly around the monastery of Monte Cassino, but not until June 1944 did the allies enter Rome.

When Churchill and Roosevelt met at Casablanca in January 1943 they had agreed on the timing of an invasion of France, and further details were discussed when they met Stalin at Teheran in November. Supreme command was entrusted to the American General Eisenhower, and the enormous problem of moving men and supplies was recognized and given priority. The actual invasion took place, after a brief postponement caused by the weather, on 6 June, D-Day. The Germans had expected the attack nearer Calais, with its advantage of a shorter sea crossing, and the attack on the Normandy coast took them by surprise. Speed and secrecy, superiority in the air and the use of parachute troops – essentials to German success in 1940 – guaranteed success to the allies now. An oil pipeline, Pluto, kept allied vehicles refuelled with less need for cross-Channel tankers which would be exposed to U-boat attack. Within a month German resistance crumbled. Once Normandy was cleared of German resistance the allied advance was rapid. Paris was captured on 25 August, and the Rhine in Holland was reached in September. Temporary German resistance in the Ardennes was overcome in December. Once the allies crossed the Rhine in March 1945 German resistance in the west virtually ended.

8 ▷ JAPAN ON THE DEFENSIVE

The Japanese fell short of their objectives in 1942. China remained undefeated; India was still in British hands; Australia lay unconquered to the south and the American Pacific fleet was crippled but not put out of action. Although Japan's enemies decided to concentrate on the European war, their reserves were growing at a faster rate than those of Japan, which were greatly overstretched to hold the vast empire just acquired. The Japanese loss of four aircraft carriers at the battle of Midway in June 1942 was a serious blow, for the Pacific war was to become largely a battle for air supremacy based on such carriers. The Americans, led by General MacArthur, turned to the offensive and captured the island of Guadalcanal, after a bitter six-month battle, in February 1943. The island-hopping tactics of the Americans, by which they captured one island and bypassed the next, took them ever closer to Japan and brought Tokyo within range of American air attack. The naval battle of Leyte Gulf paved the way for the Americans to begin the reconquest of the Philippines in October 1944. The Japanese were driven out of their foothold in India, most of Burma was back in British hands by January 1945 and in February the Americans captured Iwojima. The Japanese fought tenaciously to hold the islands; the Americans lost 4,000 men at Iwojima and 12,000 at Okinawa in June. Air attacks by the 'kamikaze' suicide pilots against American ships and bases caused further heavy losses. Although the Japanese were everywhere in retreat, and Tokyo itself suffered appalling air raids, the Americans were alarmed that the Japanese would defend every inch of their territory to the last, and that there would be casualties of catastrophic proportions when an invasion of Japan was attempted. So it was decided to drop the atomic bombs on Japan, the first at Hiroshima on 6 August, the other at Nagasaki on 9 August. These forced the Japanese to surrender unconditionally. Argument still rages as to whether the use of nuclear weapons was necessary and whether the Japanese were ready to abandon a hopeless war before the bombs were dropped.

9 ▷ THE WAR AT SEA

For Britain at war the sea is always of vital importance; for other countries which do not depend on the sea for their food and oil its importance is more limited. At the very beginning of the war the U-boats resumed the campaign they had been forced to abandon in 1918. But this time there was no argument about convoys: merchant ships were organized in convoys almost from the beginning although this did not prevent crippling losses. By early 1941 Britain was losing more shipping than could be replaced in its shipyards. But the US entry into the war eased the situation; improved detection systems combined with the use of air cover led to decreasing loss of merchant shipping and increased loss of U-boats. In 1944 U-boat losses had become so serious that the U-boat campaign was temporarily suspended. The battle of the Atlantic had been won. During these years the German surface fleet made no serious attempt to challenge British naval supremacy: it had lost too many ships in the Norwegian campaign of 1940 to make it worth the risk. But there were moments of tension when German pocket battleships made isolated attempts to run the gauntlet of the watching Royal Navy: two, the *Scharnhorst* and the *Gneisenau* actually passed unmolested through the Straits of Dover in 1942. In the Mediterranean, the Italian fleet posed a threat to British routes, but it was largely destroyed from the air.

Only in the Pacific were there any decisive naval battles, and these were battles in which the contesting navies were often unable to see the ships they were supposed to be fighting. Coral Sea, Midway Island and Leyte Gulf were really air battles fought from the moving sea bases of aircraft carriers. The traditional battle of the fighting ships was already outdated, and there was no major one of these in the Second World War.

10 ▷ WHY THE AXIS POWERS WERE DEFEATED

Both Germany and Japan had aims that were to prove to be beyond their power to achieve. Germany's attempt to dominate Europe and Russia demanded a succession of campaigns and an availability of resources that put Germany under enormous strain. Japan's expansionist policy in south-east Asia, while still bogged down in the war with China, proved in the end to be too much. Thus the Axis

> **In building up your notes, always include some analysis of this sort.**

powers underestimated both the nature of the task they had taken on, and the strength of the opposition that they had to face. Germany was also handicapped by its ally, Italy, which had to be rescued in north Africa and Greece, diverting German resources which were needed elsewhere. Germany failed to end British resistance in 1940 because of its inability to secure command of the sea, and although it came near to success its U-boat campaign was eventually a failure. The Axis powers, in challenging Russia and the USA, found themselves inferior in manpower and supplies. The world's resources were at the disposal of the allies, but Germany and Japan drained their occupied territories dry; and then had no further sources to turn to. Resistance movements sprang up in Europe and in some of Japan's conquests; and, in Europe especially, resistance movements made a significant contribution to the allied war effort. The allies had learnt much from the early German and Japanese successes: in the later stages of the war air power, either from land bases or aircraft carriers, was vital; the speed of the Panzers in 1940 was more than matched by the speed of the allied push through France in August 1944. It may be argued that Hitler's personal decisions weakened his own side: for instance, his indifference to the Mediterranean war until it was too late and his frequent refusal to allow strategic withdrawal in time (Stalingrad and Normandy). But Germany and Japan had taken on virtually the whole world – surely a contest they could not ultimately hope to win.

IDEAS AND PRINCIPLES

BATTLE OF THE ATLANTIC

This was the battle to keep open the Atlantic shipping lanes. These carried supplies from the USA, both as a friendly neutral from 1939 to 1941 and as a powerful ally of Britain from December 1941 onwards. The German U-boats inflicted much damage; but especially equipped destroyers, radar and convoys were well on the way to winning the battle by the end of 1943.

BATTLE OF BRITAIN

From July to September 1940 an aerial battle was waged over southern Britain to secure air superiority in British skies. The German failure to win meant that the invasion of Britain planned for the autumn of 1940 had to be cancelled.

BLITZ

This German word for lightning has come to mean concentrated bombing from the air; it was first used in connection with the German air attacks on Britain cities from late 1940 to early 1942.

BLITZKRIEG

This literally means a lightning war. It is the name given to the tactics used by Germany in Poland in 1939, and in Holland, Belgium and France in 1940. Dive-bombers attacked strategic targets and destroyed opposing aircraft on the ground. Lightly armoured Panzer units advanced rapidly, followed by tanks and heavy armour. Surprise, speed, technological superiority and precision planning ensured success.

CO-PROSPERITY SPHERE

This is the Japanese equivalent of the German *lebensraum*. Japan's aim was to bring south-east Asia under economic (and political) domination, and it was temporarily achieved by the Japanese at the height of their military power in 1942.

HOLOCAUST

The policy of systematic extermination of European Jews carried out by Germany during the years 1941–5; six million Jews lost their lives.

PHONEY WAR

This name is popularly given to the war on the western front from 3 September 1939 to 10 May 1940, when the opposing armies sat tight in the Maginot and Siegfried lines, and the only skirmishes were those between reconnaissance patrols.

APPLIED MATERIALS

Texts and Atlases

C. Bayne-Jardine, *World War Two*, Longman (Modern Times Series), 1968
D. Evans, *Second World War*, Arnold, 1987
Sir Basil Liddell Hart, *History of the Second World War*, Purnell, 1968; six volumes
M.J.A. Mortimore, *The Second World War*, UTP (Two Centuries Series), 1974
P.J. O'Brien, *Britain at War*, Allen & Unwin, (Britain and the 20th Century World, 4), 1975

Documentary

J. Ray, *The Second World War*, Heinemann, 1977
M. Yass, *Hiroshima*, Wayland Pictorial, 1970
M. Yass, *The Home Front*, Wayland Pictorial, 1971

Audio-visual

Audio Learning, *World War II – the War in the Pacific*, HM 0014
Audio Learning, *World War II – the War in Europe*, HM 0015
Audio Learning, *The Second World War: Strategic Issues*, HUA 040
Audio Learning, *The Second World War*, 39/B2/12
Audio Learning, *The Second World War: British Involvement*, ED/1008/12
Audio Learning, *The Second World War: the Propaganda War*, FD/1257/24
Audio Learning, *The Second World War: Campaigns, Arms and Armaments*, FD/1255/24
Audio Learning, *The Second World War: Occupation, Collaboration and Resistance*, FD/1256/24

EXAMINATION QUESTIONS

QUESTION 1

Describe two of the following battles or campaigns of the Second World War and in each case show how it contributed to the eventual defeat of Germany:
(a)   the Battle of Britain;
(b)   the battle of the Atlantic;
(c)   the battle of Stalingrad;
(d)   the Normandy landings.

(Total 30 marks) (SEG)

QUESTION 2

'For Germany 1940 was the most successful year of the war.'
(a)   In what sense was there a 'phoney war' from October 1939 to April 1940?
(b)   Describe and account for Germany's successes during 1940.
(c)   Why, despite these successes, was Germany unable to overcome Britain in 1940?

(Total 30 marks) (SEG)

OUTLINE ANSWERS

ANSWER 1

The first question asks for description but the descriptive elements will not take you beyond the lowest level of assessment. You must, if you are to achieve a reasonable mark, be prepared to show how the battle or campaign chosen contributed to Germany's defeat. It will not be enough simply to say that the Battle of Britain thwarted German invasion plans or that the battle of Stalingrad prevented the Germans from reaching the Caucasus oil. It will be expected (and, for the highest marks, required) that not only are the consequences of the battle or campaign clearly brought out, but that each must be shown in the overall context of the war and of the effectiveness of its contribution to Germany's ultimate defeat. So the Battle of Britain meant the survival of Britain, and without Britain's survival there would have been no European base for the USA and no second front, and Russia would have had to have fought single handed or given up the struggle. The battle of Stalingrad saw the collapse of the last major German summer offensive in Russia. Stalingrad destroyed the myth of German invincibility, forced the Germans on to the defensive and ended their dreams of conquest. It was the first major step towards their ultimate defeat. Arguments on similar lines can be advanced for (b) and (d).

ANSWER 2

The second question focuses on 1940. In (a) it would be insufficient to describe the war on the western front. Its quietness and its absence of major battles and major incident help to justify its name and 'phoney' implies its unreality. But remember that the war at sea was real enough, long before the phoney war ended. In (b) description again will be rewarded only at the lower level. Do not presume that adequate reasons will emerge from your narrative: identify reasons as allied unpreparedness, blitzkrieg methods, German technological superiority, careful planning, etc. and be prepared to develop these reasons with further material. Similarly in (c) developed reasons are required – the skill and bravery of the RAF, German tactical errors, radar, Churchill's leadership, etc., and these reasons should be treated as interlinking rather than as separate and complete in themselves.

SUGGESTIONS FOR FURTHER WORK

1. Choose six major events of the war and write diary entries for each by (a) a London housewife, (b) a Berlin pensioner and (c) a French resistance leader.
2. Construct and label maps of the campaign in Russia and Eastern Europe, 1941–5. Compare the strategy of the Germans during 1941–2 with that followed by the Russians in 1943–5.
3. Collect information about the Holocaust. What have been its most important consequences?
4. Interview older members of the family and their friends about their memories and experiences of the Second World War. Tape-record their replies if possible, otherwise make an accurate written record of them. Compare these interviews with the standard historical treatment of the events as described in the textbooks. Try to explain any points of difference you have found.
5. Attempt an eyewitness account of events in Hiroshima for the week beginning a few minutes before the dropping of the atomic bomb in August 1945.

6. (a) Explain why, as a French farmer in 1943, you have decided to join a local resistance group.
   (b) Explain why, as an Indonesian businessman in 1943, you are collaborating with the Japanese.

STUDENT'S ANSWER – EXAMINER'S COMMENT

Question

'Hitler's greatest mistake was the invasion of the Soviet Union in 1941.'

(a) Why did Hitler invade the Soviet Union?   (8 marks)
(b) For what reasons did the invasion turn out to be a disaster for Hitler and Germany?   (10 marks)
(c) Choose two other wartime 'mistakes' made by Hitler and show why they were costly for Germany.   (12 marks)

SEG (1988)

> **This is about Russian weakness – what about other reasons for Hitler's attack: ideological, strategic, supplies and oil, and 'lebensraum'?**

> **Some exaggeration here.**

> **This is very disjointed: it needs a well-knit and coherent argument; some points e.g. Stalin's leadership, need to be developed.**

> **Useful on the Battle of Britain, but the second mistake is vague (it might have been better to avoid Russia) and the references need to be explained.**

(a) Hitler believed that the Russians would be easy to beat. He had lulled them into a sense of false security by the Molotov-Ribbentrop Pact and he knew that Stalin regarded British warnings of a German attack on Russia as ploys to get Russia into the war. Hitler knew the Russian army was in chaos; Stalin had shot most of his officers, and the Russian army had disgraced itself in the war against Finland.

(b) The weather was colder than expected and the diesel oil froze, immobilising Hitler's tanks. The Germans had not been equipped for winter campaigning and the Russians were - their Cossack horses could deal with the cold better than the German mechanised transport. Stalin was a great leader. The British and Americans gave Russia very little help, but the Japanese did not help the Germans either. Russia is a very big country. There was much partisan resistance to the German invaders.

(c) Two mistakes are switching tactics during the battle of Britain in 1940, and refusing to allow his generals to retreat. In the first Hitler ordered his airforce to switch their attacks from British airfields to British cities as a reprisal for a British air-raid on Berlin. This enabled the RAF to recover and to secure eventual victory, thus making a German invasion of Britain impossible as the Germans had not won control of the air. The other mistake occurred at Stalingrad, in North Africa and at other places in Russia in 1943-44. Hitler had become power-crazy and lost the war single-handed.

> **Overall the answers avoid narrative and try to present reasons and explanation, but the arguments require greater precision, and clearer and more logical presentation.**

CHINA
TO 1949

CHINA IN 1911
CHINA UNDER THE
KUOMINTANG
JAPANESE ATTACKS
ON CHINA
THE COMMUNIST
VICTORY
1945–49

GETTING STARTED

China under the Manchu dynasty had long been the victim of powerful and ambitious foreign states. One of these, Russia, had nibbled at China's borders from the west and had sought to extend Russian influence in border regions such as Mongolia and Manchuria. Others, like Britain, France and Germany, had infiltrated the country at points along the eastern seaboard. They had secured treaty ports like Shanghai and Kaiochow, where they were granted extra-territorial rights and could act independently of the Chinese authorities, draining off the country's trade to their own profit. Even China's Far Eastern neighbour, Japan, was able to prove its strength by winning a war against China in 1895 and imposing its will on its much larger neighbour. The Chinese, who in any case had a deep distrust of outside influences, seemed to be powerless to prevent the country's exploitation by these imperialist invaders.

HISTORICAL DEVELOPMENTS

1 > CHINA IN 1911

Deep resentment existed at the presence of the 'foreign devils' in China, and from time to time there were outbreaks of popular violence against them, such as occurred at the time of the Boxer rising in 1900. Indignation was also shown towards the Manchu government, bureaucratic and incompetent, which turned out to be putty in the foreigners' hands. The old Empress T'zu-hsi, her court and ministers disdainfully regarded the westerners as 'barbarians', but in terms of power the 'superior' Chinese were no match for the resources and cunning of the imperialists. Attempts were made by a handful of reformers to bring the empire up to date, but the conservatism of the dynasty proved in the end to be too much for them. Meanwhile the mass of the Chinese peasantry lived under the heel of autocratic feudal landlords in conditions of grinding poverty, scratching a bare living from the soil and always at the mercy of famine and flood. Heavily taxed, ignorant, oppressed, their womenfolk scarcely more highly valued than the cattle in the fields, the Chinese peasantry were the prey of the local gentry and of imperial officials who were equally corrupt and selfish. Foreign big business was another source of exploitation by industrialists and traders who were interested only in making as much profit out of the peasants as they could.

**Some knowledge of the old order in China is useful.**

A minority of middle-class Chinese, many of them educated overseas, were deeply ashamed at the depths to which their once-proud country had fallen, and seized the opportunity of the death of the old empress in 1908 to press for reforms for the people. Many were attracted to the western ideas of self-determination and democracy, and some even claimed to be socialists. But they recognized that their chances were slight, for the bulk of government officials were unwilling to share power with anyone and were doing too nicely out of the existing system to want to change it. Their resistance to change brought about the final overthrow of the dynasty in 1911, when a number of popular revolutions in the main Chinese cities sent the new boy emperor, Pu-yi, and his court scurrying into exile, their luggage loaded with the country's treasures. Overnight the rotten pyramid of officialdom collapsed. Dr Sun Yat-sen, one of the bright hopes of the budding republican movement, returned from the USA, where he had been on a lecture tour, to become the first president. He was rightly respected as an intellectual, a statesman and a revolutionary, and aimed, with the support of the masses, to purify and modernize his country. His dream was to realize a new way of life for China based on his 'three principles' of democracy, nationalism and the people's welfare.

2 > CHINA UNDER THE KUOMINTANG

For some years after 1911 Dr Sun was overshadowed by the former Manchu general, Yuan Shi-kai; though Yuan was nominally a supporter of the new regime, he actually aimed to make himself emperor. Sun was a politician rather than a soldier, and Yuan, with his powerful connections, did not find it too difficult to get his own way. He refused to be a constitutional head of state, rejected Sun's advice, banned his party, the Kuomintang, and dissolved the Chinese parliament. The republic was saved from overthrow only by the death of Yuan in 1916, as was said at the time, 'from a fit of pure displeasure.' The Kuomintang, meanwhile, had established itself in the southern city of Canton, but its troubles were far from over, and the whole country seemed about to be plunged into anarchy. Much of the north was under the control of scheming and ambitious barons warring amongst themselves, carving out their little empires and mercilessly repressing and exploiting their peasant subjects. The official government in Peking seemed quite incapable of bringing China to order under civilian rule.

The European powers at this time were much too busy with the First World War to profit from China's weakness, but the Japanese were closer at hand and more ruthless. In 1915, just before Yuan's death, Japan presented the Chinese government with the Twenty-One Demands, which, had they been fully enforced, would have virtually put an end to Chinese independence. A number of the demands were rejected, but enough were granted to strengthen Japan's grip on

China. In 1917 China was persuaded to join the allies in the war, but at the 1919 peace conference it was Japan which chiefly benefited by Germany's defeat. The Fourth of May Movement in China in 1919, organized mainly by the Kuomintang, registered nationalist protests against the offhand way in which the Chinese had been treated, but few people paid much attention to it and it enjoyed little success.

For as long as he lived Dr Sun never managed to get very far in his plans for China. He never fully gained control over the army, and he lacked many of the basic tools for a social revolution. He appealed hopefully to the western democracies for support, but got little response. In their disillusionment the Kuomintang turned to the Soviet Union for help. In 1921 the Chinese Communist Party was founded under Mao Tse-tung and Chou En-lai, and Sun, though himself a moderate parliamentary socialist distrustful of Bolshevism, was eventually prevailed upon to accept Soviet help. A young soldier called Chiang Kai-shek was trained in the Soviet Union to become the head of the new Military Academy at Whampoa, and the Kuomintang itself was reorganized along Bolshevik lines by a Comintern agent, Michael Borodin.

"Dr. Sun and his contemporaries are worth biographical treatment."

CHIANG KAI-SHEK

The alliance between the two wings of Dr Sun's party remained shaky, and in 1925 he died. His successor was Chiang Kai-shek, whose suspicions of communism were never very far below the surface. In 1926 he formed a 'united front' between the right- and the left-wing groups, and embarked on a successful attack against the northern war-lords; but he could not help noticing the radicalism of some of his allies; as they advanced they purged the landlords in the countryside, redistributing their estates amongst their peasants, whilst in the towns they turned their hostility against the propertied upper classes and the representatives of foreign companies. Militarily Chiang's campaign enjoyed great success. He soon took Hankow and laid siege to Nanking and Shanghai. What he did not at first fully realize was that one of the forces which underlay his success was the very radicalism that he found so distasteful.

By April 1927 Chiang had come to the conclusion that his allies were more dangerous than his enemies. Whilst he was engaged on the siege of Shanghai he was approached by representatives of the business and banking groups there, who offered him their help if he crushed the communists. Suddenly, therefore, he turned on them and in a bloody purge eliminated many of them. Though some of their leaders managed to escape, they were rounded up, and about 5,000 of them were shot in large batches. Soon afterwards he allied himself even more closely with the propertied and banking classes by marrying Soong Mei Ling, sister-in-law of Sun Yat-sen and sister of the Chinese minister of finance, in a Christian ceremony. Relations with Russia were now broken off and Borodin was sent packing back to Moscow.

By 1928 Chiang's northern campaign was brought to a successful conclusion. By a variety of methods – force, threats, diplomacy, intrigue and even poison – the war-lords were subdued and Peking was occupied. Once again China had a strong central government. The communists were driven to the south, where they set about the task of building up bases of their own. Believing that the grip of the Kuomintang in the towns was too strong, Mao concentrated on the Chinese peasantry, educating them and organizing them into collectives so as to prepare the foundations of his later revolution. By 1930 Kuomintang influence tended to be confined to the larger towns of the east coast of China, with the capital at Nanking. The communists retreated into the mountain areas of the west and south, chiefly in Kiangsi and Hunan; but though they built up quite a following amongst the peasants, their position was far from strong. They had few weapons, and there was little food or protection in the inhospitable areas in which they lived. All the same, they had the talents of a capable soldier in Chu Teh, who built up the Kiangsi Red Army in preparation for the forthcoming struggle. It was during this time that he and Mao evolved the principles of guerrilla conflict so that their men could win the war when it came.

THE LONG MARCH

In the period 1930–4 the Kuomintang launched one attack after another in efforts to 'exterminate' or 'encircle' their communist enemies. With their situation daily becoming more difficult, Mao eventually decided in October 1934 to break out and move into safer territories.

The Long March is very important but should not be over-emphasized.

The original aim of the Long March, which began with 100,000 supporters and finished with little more than one-fifth of that number, was to move Mao's headquarters only about 100 miles to the west, where the danger from Chiang's nationalists would be less. But so intense were the attacks made upon them that the marchers were forced to continue westwards to the borders of Tibet, and then northwards towards Yenan in Shensi. The march was to become part of Chinese mythology. The marchers were continually harassed by Chiang, local war-lords and hostile tribesmen; and confronted by swamps, steep ravines and scorching deserts. Their journey was one of over 2000 miles, and it took a year and a half to complete. As the marchers proceeded on their way through eleven different provinces, they gathered new recruits and set up local soviets. Nevertheless, when they arrived at their destination they were in a very battered condition as well as being sadly depleted in numbers. But the foundations of the future communist regime in China had been well and truly laid.

3 ▷ JAPANESE ATTACKS ON CHINA

The Japanese had already secured considerable advantages in China under the Versailles treaty, securing control of many of the areas where the Germans had earlier established themselves. They secured Kaiochow and much of the important silk-producing province of Shantung. They also extended their special rights in northern China, penetrating and gradually taking over Manchuria. In the 1920s the legal position of this province seemed uncertain. The Soviet Union regarded it as being within their sphere of influence, but the Japanese disagreed. They controlled much of the east and south, and were bringing the central industrial regions into their grasp. They had already gained the right to set up garrisons there under the peace arrangements. The local war-lord tried to counter the Japanese, but he was murdered in 1928; his son's efforts to recover the position only increased the Japanese determination to annex the province.

In September 1931 the Japanese staged an incident on the South Manchurian Railway near the capital, Mukden, and within a short time took over the whole province. Chiang Kai-shek offered them very little resistance, not least because he preferred a Japanese to a Russian occupation of Manchuria. There was some sporadic fighting in 1932, but otherwise Japan was hardly opposed. A League of Nations commission sent to Manchuria condemned Japanese aggression, but its recommendations were ignored and Japan left the league. Manchuria was renamed Manchukuo and Pu-yi, the boy Emperor deposed in 1911, was made Japanese puppet Emperor there.

Chiang Kai-shek faces a very difficult choice.

Early in 1933 the Japanese continued their expansion southwards from Manchukuo. In May of that year there followed a brief truce, but the Japanese paid little attention to it and went on fortifying Manchukuo as their main base, continuing their efforts to probe Chinese weakness whenever they found it. Chiang's attitude throughout this time was one of appeasement: he thought that it was only after establishing his power over the communists that he could expect to win a full-scale war against Japan. He therefore concentrated his efforts against Mao, ignoring the communists' call for a patriotic war.

THE SIAN PACT

At the end of 1936 Chiang went to Sian in southern Shensi to organize a massive attack against his enemies there, but his army, composed largely of men from the area round Manchuria and much influenced by communist propaganda, refused to fight. Chiang was kidnapped by his own troops and forced to agree to a new united front with the communists. At first he refused, but Mao sent Chou En-lai, one of his foreign affairs experts, to confer with him, and Chiang at length agreed. Mao found a double advantage in this: not only did he secure himself against nationalist attacks in the future, but he was now also part of the official patriotic struggle against the Japanese, in the course of which he intended to show the Chinese peasantry who their real friends were.

Time was to show, however, that Chiang was never very loyal to the Sian Pact; in practice he continued to spend much of his time plotting against his allies. At least the pact provided a chance for many ordinary Chinese to unite their efforts in the struggle against the national foe.

FULL-SCALE WAR

Full-scale war between China and Japan began with the Marco Polo Bridge incident in July 1937. Within a month the Japanese had seized Peking and Tientsin. Soon the whole of north-eastern China was in their hands as far as Nanking. The forces of the nationalists were easily defeated, and Chiang had to move his capital to the mountain stronghold of Chungking. Here he prepared to sit out the war with Japan, leaving the fighting to the much more patriotic communists, who used their limited resources to their best effect so as to hinder the Japanese advance. From 1937 the Kuomintang received increasing help from the Russians, Stalin appearing to think that Chiang was his only effective ally against Japanese imperialism and an important nationalist symbol against capitalist infiltrators. Especially after Chiang made his agreement with Mao, Stalin thought it best to supply the Kuomintang with a trickle of arms and supplies.

With the attack on Pearl Harbor in 1941, the Sino–Japanese War merged into the Second World War, and soon the other western allies began sending supplies to the nationalists. The Japanese air force cut the Burma road which connected Chungking with the outside world, but the United States instead began to fly in masses of supplies by heavy transport aircraft across the Himalayas. Little positive resulted from it. Partly because his supporters were getting ever more greedy and ruthless, his whole government steadily sinking deeper into corruption, and partly because Chiang's main idea seemed to be to stockpile whatever resources he could get his hands on to renew his attack on the communists when the war was over, the Western allies saw little return for their efforts. The US government in particular became increasingly irritated and at one point actually contemplated switching their aid to the communists instead. Their natural caution came to their minds, and the Chungking regime continued to be the main beneficiary. At least they could console themselves that Chiang was keeping an eye on the communists, and at the same time tying down a large number of Japanese troops who otherwise would be fighting in the Pacific theatre of the war.

In contrast, Mao's fighters were much more active and successful in their struggles. They employed their guerrilla tactics with good effect and soon had Japanese troops virtually prisoners in the towns they occupied. They built up their hold most successfully in the rural areas and soon came to control a large area of the north in which something like a hundred million people lived. They rarely risked open conflict, but their persistence steadily frayed the nerves of the scattered Japanese garrisons, and they soon felt themselves to be on top.

4 ▷ THE COMMUNIST VICTORY 1945-9

66 Pick out the main points of the analysis here and develop them. 99

In August 1945 two atom bombs were dropped on Japanese cities, and within a few days the Japanese surrendered. The struggle now began in earnest for the future control of China. By this time the nationalist regime had lost whatever support amongst the masses it originally possessed, and though it continued to enjoy the backing of the USA and the USSR, it had largely lost touch with the Chinese people themselves. It now relied heavily on the propertied classes such as landlords and bankers, apparently abandoning any hope of making China democratic and becoming instead ever more oppressive. Inflation raged unchecked, and embezzlement and corruption amongst senior officials became commonplace. Few ordinary people had much reason to be grateful to the Kuomintang.

Nevertheless, few people outside China understood the hollowness of Chiang's position, and most continued to look forward to the day when the nationalists would begin to reform and modernize China. Both the major powers in the area, the Russians and the Americans, showed little or no sympathy for Mao. Russia invaded Manchuria, seizing towns and cities, but gave very little aid to its fellow communists, signing instead a pact with the nationalists whereby Stalin promised to support Chiang and undertook not to interfere in China's internal affairs. The Americans for their part had a long-standing commitment to the nationalist side and deeply distrusted anything which might result in the extension of communism in the Far East; hence they airlifted Chiang's troops to whatever areas the Russians had liberated so as to forestall the communists there. Meanwhile they tried to avert civil war by bringing the two sides together and persuading them to negotiate. In September they arranged a meeting between Chiang and Mao in Chungking, but though the talks lasted for over a month no agreement resulted. President Truman sent General Marshall to China, but though he negotiated two cease-fires, both of them were short lived. He distrusted Mao, but he distrusted Chiang even more (for some odd reason he nicknamed him 'the peanut') and actively encouraged a third group known as the Democratic League, which had a certain amount of middle-class backing and campaigned for a democratically elected parliament and a style of government modelled on the West. Unfortunately, as soon as he got to know there was another contender in the field, Chiang moved against it, and eventually used his secret police to wipe it out and round up its supporters. By 1947 it was clear that a coalition government was out of the question. A decision had to be reached by force.

The prospects for the Kuomintang at first looked good. Chiang had considerable financial and material resources and enjoyed international backing. His armies were well supplied and well rested and outnumbered the communists by about ten to one. But the picture of strength was misleading. Many of Chiang's soldiers were half-trained and ignorant, with little idea what they were fighting for. The Generalissimo himself made gross military blunders. The whole regime was corrupt and incompetent. Inflation and chronic shortages made life impossible for everyone. The only way of getting things done seemed to be to have a bottomless purse and to be willing to grease palms all round. This was a solution which provoked the derision of the communists and the blind fury of the poverty-stricken masses.

1948 saw the start of large-scale military movements by the communists in the course of which city after city passed into Mao's control. There were massive desertions from the nationalist armies, sometimes entire divisions going over to the other side and taking their equipment with them. In the last months of 1948 the Kuomintang lost control of the Yangtse Valley. In January 1949 Peking surrendered to Mao; in April Nanking followed suit. Chiang's final desperate offers – a promise to allow a freely-elected parliament, and even an offer to resign in favour of a subordinate – failed to stop the rot. In September, he and his followers fled to Formosa (Taiwan), ninety miles off the coast of mainland China, and he set up his headquarters there in preparation for his intended comeback.

On 1 October 1949, Mao Tse-tung proclaimed in Peking the establishment of the People's Republic of China under communist control.

IDEAS AND PRINCIPLES

ANARCHY

This is a state of chaos resulting from a lack of government or a struggle between conflicting governments. It implies that a country is ungoverned, and sometimes that it is ungovernable.

EXTRA-TERRITORIAL RIGHTS

These are those granted by the government of a country to the nationals of another country in a given area, whereby they are governed in accordance with the laws of their home country instead of those of the country where they are residing. This concession, together with other privileges, is often used as an inducement to foreign nationals to establish residence there.

GUERRILLA TACTICS

These are the methods employed by combatants taking part in an informal war. Such people do not usually wear uniforms and their actions are not regulated by an accepted code of military behaviour; they are loosely organized and may even manufacture their own weapons. It was at the time of this guerrilla war in China that Mao developed his famous four principles of guerrilla warfare:

When the enemy advances, we retreat.

When the enemy halts and encamps, we harass them.

When the enemy seeks to avoid battle, we attack.

When the enemy retreats, we pursue.

'Guerrilla' is the diminutive form of the Spanish word 'la guerra', which means 'war'.

UNFAIR TREATIES

These were said by the Chinese to be those foisted on China by more powerful foreign states such as neighbouring Russia, Britain and France. Britain, for example, had secured Hong Kong as early as 1842, and had gone on to take more treaty ports and to force the Chinese to accept the commercial policy of the 'open door.' The Chinese often felt that the foreigners had made use of the country's political weakness to force humiliating terms on them and to deprive them of territories that were rightfully theirs. In the twentieth century, China often made efforts to recover these lost territories.

APPLIED MATERIALS

Texts and Atlases

Hugh Higgins, *From Warlords to Red Star*, Faber, 1968

Ping-chia Kuo, *China*, OUP, 1963

H. MacAleavy, *A Modern History of China*, Weidenfeld & Nicolson, 1967

John Robottom, *Modern China*, Longman, 1969

John Robottom, *Twentieth-Century China*, Wayland Pictorial, 1971

J.K.G. Taylor, *Asia and Australasia*, Arnold (History of the 20th-Century World), 1983; Chapter 1

N. Tarling, *Mao and the Transformation of China*, Heinemann Educational, 1977

Harriet Ward, *World Powers in the Twentieth Century*, Heinemann Educational, 1985; Part III

Documentary Books

Colin Bown and Tony Edwards, *Revolution in China, 1911–49*, Heinemann History Broadsheets, 1974

John Gittings (Ed.), *A Chinese View of China*, BBC Publications, 1973

Myra Roper, *China in Revolution, 1911–49*, Hill & Fell (Archive Series)

John Simkin, *The Long March*, Spartacus (Voices from the Past), 1986

EXAMINATION QUESTIONS

Candidates must answer Question 1 and Question 2.

You should spend about thirty minutes on each question.

QUESTION 1

Study the sources below and answer the questions at the end.

Source A

Name the following and explain in a few words the importance of each on the Long March.
   (i)   River A (1 mark)
   (ii) Province B (1 mark)
   (iii) Province C (1 mark)
   (iv) Town D (1 mark)
   (v)   Town E (1 mark)
   (vi) Mountain F (1 mark)
   (vii) Why did the leaders of the Red Army set out on the Long March when they knew (a) they would have to walk all the way with badly equipped troops and (b) they were likely to be attacked by both the Kuomintang and Chinese war-lords? (6 marks)

Now read these extracts and answer the questions after them.

Source B

'We swept across a distance of more than 6,500 miles on our own two feet, across 11 provinces....The Long March is a manifesto. It declares to the world that the Red Army is an army of heroes and that.....Chiang Kai-shek and the like are as nothing. It shows Chiang's complete failure. The Long March also tells the 200 million people in 11 provinces that only the road of the Red Army leads to their liberation....It has sown many seeds in 11 provinces, which will bear fruit and yield a crop in the future. To sum up, the Long March has ended in our victory and the enemy's defeat.'
   Mao Tse-tung

Source C

'In fact....the Long March was a great retreat. Only about one-tenth of those who started out survived it. And after it the communists were still on the point of being completely destroyed.'
   James Pinckney Harrison (historian)

Source D

'Heavy fog was all around us. There was a high wind and it began to rain. As we climbed higher there was a terrible hail storm. The air became so thin we could hardly breathe. It was impossible to speak. The cold was so dreadful that our breath froze and our hands and lips turned blue. Men and animals staggered and fell into chasms, disappearing forever. Those who sat down to rest or go to the toilet froze to death on the spot.'

    A Red Army Soldier

  (viii) What does Mao mean when he says that the Long March has 'sown many seeds' in eleven provinces? (2 marks)

   (ix) In what ways does Source C disagree with Source B? (2 marks)

    (x) Write down two questions you would ask about Sources B and C to check if they could be trusted. (2 marks)

   (xi) Why do you think the Red Army soldier wrote down Source D? Give two possible reasons. (2 marks)

  (xii) Write a paragraph saying whether you think the Long March changed the course of history. Give reasons for your answer. (5 marks)

(Total 25 marks)

QUESTION 2

Why did the communists defeat the nationalists in the civil war? (25 marks)

(NICCEA)

OUTLINE ANSWERS

ANSWER 1

Identifications are required, together with short explanations of the importance of selected features of the map, in the first six parts of Question 1. The answers are: Yangtse River, Kiangsi, Shensi, Shanghai, Yenan, Wild Tiger Mountain. The importance of most of these is to be seen in the context of the Long March of 1934. In part (vii), the answers explaining why Red Army leaders set out on such a perilous mission are required: it is not necessary to repeat those given for (a) in (b), since these are much the same, although for the full 6 marks the full reasons should be covered.

    Parts (viii)–(xi) then go on to evaluate the Sources B, C and D which are quoted in the remainder of this question. Part (viii) invites you to comment briefly on the consequences of the Long March – i.e. the 'seeds sown' which germinate later. Part (ix) is asking for something comparative: obviously Source C is much more pessimistic in its outlook than Source B. Part (x) is about reliability: the sort of question to be asked here could well be 'Who wrote them?', 'Why did they write them?', 'When did they write them?' and 'Are they primary accounts or written some time afterwards?' Part (xi) is asking you to speculate about the motives of the author: perhaps these remarks were recorded in his personal diary, or perhaps he was sending his impressions in a letter to a friend or relative. The final question, (xii), asks for an overall evaluation of the importance of the Long March. It is difficult to deny that it had a great impact both in history and mythology; you should offer reasons for thinking it important if you wish to score a good mark.

ANSWER 2

An essay-type answer is required for Question 2, focusing on the reasons for the defeat of the nationalists by the communists during the Chinese Civil War, 1946–49. Whilst narrative material may be admissible in this answer up to a point, its chief purpose should be to supplement the reasons offered. After a brief introduction it is desirable to devote a short paragraph to each of a number of different reasons, some dealing with the nationalist side and others with the communist side. On the side of the nationalists there should be some mention of loss of morale and support, corruption and incompetence, inflation and shortages, and shortcomings in the field, desertions, disloyalty of subordinates and so on. The communists, on the other hand, should be shown to be popular with the masses and especially with the peasantry, determined, disciplined and well-led. The conclusion of the answer should sum up the arguments in a concise verdict.

SUGGESTIONS FOR FURTHER WORK

1. Read the entry on China in a good encyclopedia, or in Chapter 1 of Ping-chia Kuo's book, and find out what you can about the geography of the country and its crops and products. Find out what you can about the Chinese calendar, about the language of the people and its pronunciation.
2. Read the accounts of some of those who took part in the Long March, and, imagining that you were one of their number, write an account to be handed on to your children when you grow older, so that the importance of the event may never forgotten. In the course of it, tell of your feelings towards Mao and the other leaders, the experiences you suffered at the hands of the nationalists and the adventures which befell you in the course of the Long March. The main purpose of what you write, however, should be to remind your children of the importance of Communist teachings for the people of China.
3. Construct a map of China and mark on it all the places you read about as being in the hands of the nationalists, the communists or the Japanese in the later 1930s and the first half of the 1940s. How are they grouped, and what does this grouping tell us about how they had come to be situated where they were in the course of these years?
4. Use your books on China, e.g. Nicholas Tarling's *Mao and the Transformation of China*, to write a biography of Mao Tse-tung up to 1949. How does his life story help to explain the high regard in which he was held as a Chinese leader?

STUDENT'S ANSWER – EXAMINER'S COMMENTS

Question
Describe the development of communism and the Communist Party under Mao Tse-tung up to 1937.

> **The first paragraph is irrelevant to the question set, and provides no more than a simple introductory narrative to 20th-century Chinese history.**

China, which was under the incompetent control of the Manchu Dynasty, was very weak in the early twentieth century. Foreign powers took over control of much of the country, and this created a movement for Chinese nationalism which revealed itself in the Boxer Rising of 1900, which was bloodily suppressed by the imperialists. Popular feeling grew, however, and in 1911 a revolution finally overthrew the Manchu and bought to an end two thousand years of imperial rule with the setting-up of a Republic. It was led by Sun Yat-sen, who founded a revolutionary party called the Kuomintang to give his country a modern government along western lines. His three famous principles were Nationalism, Democracy and Welfare.

In 1923 Dr. Sun's Nationalists received useful help from Soviet Russia in order to strengthen and modernize China.

A Russian Communist, Michael Borodin, was sent to train an army and to set up a communist government on the Russian pattern. In the meantime, a Chinese Communist Party had been set up in 1921 to introduce communist ideas into the country, and prominent amongst its members was Mao Tse-tung, the future Chairman of the Party, who at the time was working as a library assistant in Peking. In the early days the C.C.P. had few members, but nonetheless it made a big impact by taking up the cause of the working people, especially the peasantry who formed the greatest part of the Chinese population.

In 1927, when the Nationalist Army took Shanghai, Chiang Kai-shek, the Kuomintang leader, turned against the Communists and massacred them. In 1934 there took place the Long March. In the Southern provinces of Hunan and Kiangsi, Communist support had been growing amongst the peasantry and the communist armies under Chu Teh were rapidly growing in numbers. Eventually there were over 300,000 of them. Chiang responded to their threat by increasing his attacks on their positions. Eventually, the Reds felt sufficiently threatened to decide on a break-out from the areas which the Nationalists surrounded. Mao began the Long March by leading over 100,000 of his followers out of Kiangsi and across the Yangtse Kiang, on their way to the remote northern province of Shensi. On the way, his wife and many of his other followers died, perishing in the deserts, or in the snow of the high mountains which blocked his path. One of the most famous episodes was the crossing of the Tatu River which was on a bridge of chains with Nationalist machineguns mowing them all down. There were enormous casualties and very few of them succeeded in reaching their gaol. But later Mao founded universities there in caves and even grew tomatoes round the door. In this way the city of Yenan in the Shensi Province became the centre of Chinese Communism.

Quite a useful introductory statement about the growth of the Chinese Communist Party, but only a fleeting reference to the theory of communism itself.

Apart from a brief mention of events in Shanghai in 1927, there is little here about the growth of Chinese Communism to 1937. The answer concentrates too heavily on the Long March.

Overall, the writing and spelling are good. Unfortunately some of the main points were missed, or only briefly mentioned.

CHAPTER

11

CHINA
AFTER 1949

POLITICAL
    DEVELOPMENTS
ECONOMIC
    DEVELOPMENTS
GREAT LEAP FORWARD
SOCIAL
    DEVELOPMENTS
CHINA AFTER MAO
MAOISM AND
    STALINISM

GETTING STARTED

Mao's view of communism was rather different from that of his allies in the Soviet Union. But he was not dissimilar from them in his patriotism. He continued the long tradition of resistance to the 'foreign devils', seeking to rid the country of selfish and intrusive imperial interests and trying to recover the lands and rights that had been lost under the 'unjust treaties'. Nor were his fundamental aims very different from the Russian equivalent. He wanted to build a classless society, no longer dominated by the profit motive, and one in which the individual could find fulfilment.

The three strands of his policy – political, economic and social – were closely woven together to form the pattern of the new society he aimed for. In their way, these strands were similar to Sun's original three principles, but Mao, partly because he had more widespread backing than the early reformers, and partly because he did not hesitate to crush resistance when it showed itself, had far more success than his predecessors.

HISTORICAL DEVELOPMENTS

Before the final fall of the Kuomintang, a conference of about 650 communist delegates from all over China met in Peking to discuss the future form that the People's Republic should take. They, and other left-wing bodies, chose a central government council under Mao Zedong (Mao Tse-tung) as chairman and this body ruled the country for the next five years. In the interval they arranged for national and local elections of communist representatives to form the National People's Congress. In September 1954 this body finally came into being. Thereafter Congress deputies met regularly and it is the supreme governing body of the country. Deputies elect the chairman of the Republic and the members of the State Council, which is the equivalent of the cabinet and is presided over by the prime minister. The first president was Mao Zedong, and the first premier was Zhou Enlai (Chou En-lai). The constitution contains a statement of civil rights, including equality for women and the universal right of voting. The main difference between this system and the western democratic system is that in China, as in the Soviet Union, political power is in the hands of the all-powerful Communist Party, which controls the elections, supplies all the candidates for election and monopolizes all the membership of the various governing bodies. The party itself is organized on lines very similar to the state, with periodic congresses and a ruling Politburo most of whose personnel are the same people as those who occupy senior positions in the government. Opposition therefore finds it hard to express itself legally. The party, on the other hand, reaches right down to the roots of Chinese society. With over twenty million members, it forms a well-organized network of influence to control events and to carry out what it sees as its necessary work of education and propaganda amongst the people.

Because they wished to liberate the country from the grip of foreigners and from nationalist reactionaries at home, there was at the start little resistance to the rule of the new communist regime. In the rush to redistribute land and wealth in the first five years, few aristocrats and landlords were spared. People's courts imposed summary justice in which about two million perished. Opponents changed their views or fled; doubters learned to keep their mouths shut.

CAMPAIGN OF THE HUNDRED FLOWERS

> **You may be asked to develop any of these episodes in more detail.**

By 1957, however, it was time for some relaxation. Mao was of the opinion that the only way to achieve permanent socialism was to convince the people of its rightness; repression could not be substituted for persuasion for ever. Hence for a time restrictions were lifted in what became known as the Campaign of the Hundred Flowers. Ordinary people, together with bourgeois and intellectuals, were encouraged to find fault with the communist system. The leadership allowed this for a time, and then clamped down. Those who had spoken their minds were now silenced, and sometimes they were forced to publish humiliating retractions, headed by words such as 'I confess my guilt to the people.' Mao, having contrived to persuade his critics to reveal themselves, was now able to silence them.

CULTURAL REVOLUTION

In 1966 there followed the Cultural Revolution. For some time Mao had been concerned that the new leadership in China might fossilize into an unrepresentative clique more concerned with its own privileges than with the well-being of the people, just as had been the case in the bad old pre-revolutionary days. It was his view that there should be a 'continuous revolution': that is, when the ruling group lost their revolutionary momentum and the movement began to stagnate, they should be removed in favour of more radical people who would set the process in motion again. Mao seems to have made an exception in his own case, but none the less he seemed to be anxious to weed out any of his supporters who wanted to call a halt to the revolution and consolidate the gains made. Such people were called 'revisionists' and generally reviled. In 1966, with the active collaboration of a fanatical Red Guard, opposition such as this was purged. The country came to a complete halt as enemies, real and imagined, were hunted down. Schools and universities closed as committees met to reorganize the curriculum and purge it of bourgeois elements; the factories stopped as workers flocked to self-criticism meetings instead of to the work-bench, examining their prejudices and resolving to do better in future. Mass rallies brought the cities to a standstill and were gleefully attended by thousands of idle students who struck terror as much as they inspired hope in the hearts of the onlookers, the red plastic bound *Thoughts of Chairman Mao* brandished over their heads as licences for organized hysteria. By the end of the decade the Chinese people may have been purer in heart, but they were certainly slipping down the economic league tables.

By the late 1960s formerly moderate leaders, sporting new and more radical titles, were once again emerging. The army under Lin Piao came into conflict with the Red Guard and eventually overcame it. Even Zhou Enlai wanted to get back to normal and start the state's machinery once again. The struggle between the moderates (the 'rightists') and the radicals (the 'leftists') rumbled on until Mao's death in 1976, but the turbulence and chaos of the Cultural Revolution did not occur again.

2 ECONOMIC DEVELOPMENTS

AGRICULTURE

The first task facing the new government in China in 1949 was that of changing small-scale privately-owned farms to large-scale communally-owned farms. First the landlords' land was taken over and redistributed so that each peasant owned his own holding. The first stage was achieved by the land reform law of 1950, so fulfilling what had originally been one of Sun Yat-sen's objectives – the principle of 'the land to the tiller.' But though this ended the ancient abuse of landlordism it did not in itself bring about agricultural efficiency. Had things been left like this, there would have emerged a new class of conservative land-owning peasants with no use for the furthering of the aims of the revolution. Besides, with holdings of so small a size – the average was less than one acre – mechanization and new farming techniques would never have been developed, and the whole country would have remained poor and backward. The needs of the peasants for such things as seed and markets made it possible to go to the next stage and to start to organize co-operatives. The lands still remained in the peasants' ownership, but now about 100 families were working together and sharing out their produce. By 1954 it is calculated that almost 200 million people were members of such **collectives**. Mutual aid teams were built up, and cadres of selected communist leaders, giving guidance to the farmers, actually worked in the fields alongside the villagers. As second-stage collectives appeared it was not unusual for 300 or 400 families to work in organized teams, their back-up services now being much more thoroughly undertaken. By 1956 the drive to form larger collectives was intensified. In these, individual peasants were still entitled to hold a small portion of land as their own private property, but 95 per cent of the available land was now merged into large-scale **communes**. By 1958 there were about 26,000 of these throughout China, each one having 40,000 to 50,000 workers in it. As well as agriculture, these large new units undertook industrial developments too, embarking on ambitious drainage, irrigation and even hydroelectric schemes. Furthermore each one ran its own schools, clinics, libraries, theatres and shops, all of them collectively owned and operated. The aim of the large self-sufficient community seemed to have been realized. All the same, these things were often on so large a scale that life became extremely regimented and impersonal. For this reason in more recent years the average size of the commune has been brought down to something like 25,000.

> 〝Can you distinguish clearly between a collective and a commune?〞

INDUSTRY

Though the benefits for grain production were very obvious in the 1950s, the state of Chinese industry remained backward for some time. Early steps had done little more than restrain inflation and cut back on the massive unemployment left by the ending of the war. Much more remained to be done. Up to 85 per cent of heavy industry and about half of light industry came into public ownership within two or three years of the revolution. Then, in 1951, the State Planning Commission turned its attention to the further industrialization of the country, drawing up its first Five Year Plan, which came into operation in 1953. The initial emphasis, as in the Soviet Union, was on further industrialization, especially in the area of heavy industry. Coal, iron and steel, chemicals and machine tools were amongst the main targets and alongside these was the production of electricity for domestic and industrial purposes. Nevertheless the Chinese leadership hesitated to antagonize the people by too much compulsion. Small businesses were allowed to remain in private hands and were even permitted to take an agreed amount of profit until the 1960s. This sector of the economy remained more or less stationary during this period, but basic industries expanded enormously. Steel output rose from about 150,000 tons to over 5.25 million in 1957, and there were equally startling increases in coal, engineering and the allied trades. There was even a considerable growth in consumer manufacture.

3 ▶ GREAT LEAP FORWARD

In 1958 there came the Great Leap Forward. This was a spectacular attempt to step up both agriculture and industry, and so to achieve 'the work of twenty years in a single day'. The leadership encouraged the growth of small-scale industry throughout the countryside, beginning with 600,000 'backyard furnaces' to boost iron and steel output. They were manned by the peasants in the commune, aided by men from the local cadres with the necessary specialist skills. They made not only metals but machine tools, farm implements, spare parts and other things of day-to-day use in answering the commune's needs. The workers in their dungarees – the 'blue ants' as they were called, after their unceasing efforts – also constructed dams, reservoirs, irrigation channels, flood-control systems and other massive earthworks, often working only with the most primitive of tools. In terms of economic success, however, the Great Leap Forward was more of a stumble. The new furnaces produced steel of very poor quality, and the other products of their efforts were sadly inadequate. Some of their earthwork schemes were grandiose and were left half-finished. Worse still, they led to a neglect of agriculture, so that from 1957 there followed hard times. Food rationing had to be reintroduced in 1959 and it lasted until 1961. Some peasants were starving and the death-rate went up sharply, probably from malnutrition and its effects. China's industry recovered in the early 1960s, but the scars of their over-ambitious schemes lasted for many years.

❝ This is extremely important and still very much in the news. ❞

With the Cultural Revolution, bad times came again. Part of Mao's trouble was that he felt that the Soviet method of industrial modernization paid too much attention to economics and sacrificed everything in favour of manufacturing productivity, whereas he had the idea of shaping socialist man from the soul outwards; at the time the Red Guard was so busy stressing the importance of keeping the revolution moving that no one had time to put in a full day's work. Planning and output went by the board, and the numerous dislocations in every sector of Chinese society led to breakdowns and shortages once again. The Chinese people found that, far from accelerating their progress, ideology turned out to be a barrier to development. It was only after the fury had died down that education and production recovered once more. By 1970 the process of rebuilding began; scientific research was renewed and output began to revive.

Though China exploded its first atomic device at Lop Nor in 1964, the overall level of Chinese technology lagged far behind the west. This was partly due to factors such as the persistence in China of small-scale industrial enterprises, which the Chinese seemed to prefer to large automated plants; it was also partly due to the belief in Maoist China that 'socialism is a way of life rather than a way of industrial growth.' Hence China went on with the greater part of its industry operating on a small scattered basis, continuing to be dependent on purchases of plant and machinery from abroad, even though the dependence itself generated some resentment. Up to the death of Mao there were still masses of Chinese who were desperately poor, enjoying a standard of life well below that of those countries upon which they depended, and China's industrial base made it unlikely that it would ever be able to catch up.

4 ⟩ SOCIAL DEVELOPMENTS

Since the Chinese revolution there is no doubt that social conditions in China have been greatly changed. Modern buildings have been put up, the people are better housed and better fed, education has been improved, there are fewer beggars in the street and the whole atmosphere of the country has become more enlightened and progressive. This movement can be summarized under a number of headings.

THE POSITION OF WOMEN

In feudal China women were often regarded as the mere possessions of men. They were subject to barbaric practices such as the binding of the feet of baby girls, were married off in childhood and were actually sold in hard times by their husbands and fathers. In 1931 the Kuomintang had passed a law for the improvement of the treatment of women, but for the majority of women who lived in regions distant from the eastern coastal strip of the country this had had little effect and women had to wait until 1949 for any real improvement. In 1950 the marriage law grappled with this problem: it abolished child marriage, banned infanticide – the custom of murdering unwanted girl babies – and imposed heavy penalties for bigamy. In recent years women have been treated with more consideration. With the organization of public nurseries, laundries and restaurants, and in particular with strict limitations on the size of families, women have been freed from the more toilsome aspects of domestic work, whilst at the same time they have found new opportunities for education and employment in Chinese society.

PUBLIC HEALTH

At the time of the revolution, life expectancy in China was low and a large number of children died during infancy. Ordinary infectious diseases such as influenza and measles, frequently caused a high mortality, and deficiency diseases like rickets were common. The extension of medical services and the provision of hospitals and adequate number of qualified doctors were therefore high priorities in social policy. The result over forty years has been the creation of a hygiene-conscious people, with greatly improved conditions of health and cleanliness. New medical and surgical techniques have been pioneered. The ancient art of acupuncture has been extended and brought up to date. There have even been campaigns to stamp out the common house fly.

POPULATION

This is perhaps the most serious problem that has confronted the Chinese people this century. The reduction of infant mortality together with the conquest of disease has meant that an already large population has exploded massively in size, shooting up from about 450 million in 1950 to nearly 1000 million by the 1990s. In the 1960s, it was increasing at a rate of 20 million every year, or well over 50,000 every day. The government therefore publicized the need for effective measures of birth control, but quite suddenly the whole campaign was halted on the plea that the problem was not as serious as it was supposed to be – perhaps Mao was responding to political pressures so as to ensure that China would have a proper state of military preparedness. Chinese leaders evidently took the view that the overall density of the population was low; that the cultivated area was limited and could easily be increased to feed all the new mouths; and, more importantly, that China's population growth was below the level needed to sustain all the efforts that were reckoned to be necessary if the country was to be brought up to date. All the same, wiser counsels prevailed and the 1970s saw a return to population control. Recent years have seen the enormous increase of the single-child family, a development which not only makes possible much more intensive care for the family's offspring but also ensures that any massive increase in total population is a thing of the past. Control involves restraints which would be unacceptable in the West: there is an official marriage age of 25 for women and 27 for men and a 5 per cent pay rise given for the first-born, together with various other benefits such as health care and education, but these benefits are withdrawn if there is a second child and a third brings pay cuts of 5 per cent and the withdrawal of earlier benefits. There is also severe social disapproval from friends and neighbours for couples with large families.

EDUCATION

When the 1949 revolution took place, the main emphasis in Chinese schools was on simple literacy since the majority of the population at that time could not read or write. The early revolutionary governments, too, tried to extend the benefits of basic education to a larger number of children; between 1949 and 1959 numbers in schools rose from about 25 million to nearly 100 million. In the course of the 1950s, the existing patchwork of Chinese schools – private, state and mission schools – was merged into a truly national system. In lots of ways there was a heavy emphasis on politics; primary school children, for example, were taught arithmetic by getting them to calculate the number of American casualties in Vietnam. One major problem was the enormous number of characters in the written language. Efforts were made to simplify them and to reduce them in number, even to substitute a twenty-six-letter alphabet on the model of the Roman one. But the task has proved to be a long and difficult one. In 1966, with the Cultural Revolution, the whole educational system, furthermore, came to a halt, from the village primary schools at the bottom to the universities at the top. For nearly two years the system was totally disrupted. There were no classes, no examinations were set and new generations of school-leavers entered the labour market without qualifications. When schools were reopened, there was a new emphasis on combining theory with practice. The skills approach as well as the more traditional academic approach was now more welcome: practical subjects appeared on the curriculum; open-book examinations became more common; and stress came to be laid on social skills as well as on intellectual achievement. In the 1970s there was even a campaign against Confucianism, the philosophy most associated in the minds of the Chinese with ancient authority and scholarship. At the time of Mao's death, education was still a battleground between left and right, with both sides trying to influence the minds of the young through the content of their schooling; but the emphasis on the scientific and practical subjects survived, and eventually people tired of 'struggling and criticizing' as they had during the Cultural Revolution and schools were able to get back to the business of teaching.

WELFARE AND WORKING CONDITIONS

Hard work and poverty were the inheritance of most Chinese in 1949. With the introduction of trade unions at the time of the revolution, and the creation of a trade union federation in 1950 (though controlled by the state) conditions greatly improved. Conditions of work were reformed and leisure and holiday facilities were introduced. Retirement has been fixed in accordance with type of occupation at 45–55 for women and 55–65 for men. Smaller families have meant that more money is left for leisure pursuits, and though these do not compare with the range of those commonly available in the west, the Chinese are now better provided for than ever before.

❝ Details of Chinese treatment of national minorities is worth collecting. Tibet has been much in the news in recent times. ❞

NATIONAL MINORITIES

Getting on for one sixth of the Chinese population are not in fact Chinese. There are Mongolians, Tartars, Tibetans and many others, nearly all of whom have their own languages, customs and religions. Up to the launching of the Chinese constitution of 1954, the attitude of the leadership towards these peoples seemed to be a tolerant one, and the constitution itself promised that 'the national autonomous areas are inalienable parts of the People's Republic of China'. Mao's government, however, as time went on, came to lay increasing stress on the phrase 'inalienable parts' rather than the linked phrase 'national autonomous areas'. In the course of the 1950s, for example, Tibet, reoccupied as an ancient historic province of China in 1950, was shown less and less respect for its different ways until its people were driven into full-scale rebellion in 1959. Violent military action was taken against this distant country, its monasteries were closed and its religion extinguished; eventually its ruler, the Dalai Lama, was driven to take refuge in India and was briefly replaced by a pro-Chinese puppet, the Panchen Lama. After 1960, however, the conduct of the Chinese towards their subject peoples mellowed somewhat. Efforts were made to help them to preserve their own languages and culture, and they were linked in with the Chinese economic system instead of being subordinated to it. By the 1980s the Chinese seemed to be more sensitive than they had ever been before to the charge that they were in the habit of riding rough-shod over neighbouring nations.

<table>
<tr><td>**5 > CHINA AFTER MAO**</td></tr>
</table>

In January 1976 Zhou Enlai died and was replaced as premier by the almost unknown Hua Kuofeng, intended by Mao as a concession to strident voices on the left which had recently brought about the dismissal of the much more popular Deng Xaioping. Then in September 1976 Mao himself died. The right now felt itself strong enough to order the arrest of prominent leftists such as the 'Gang of Four', which included Madame Mao, Chiang Ching, herself. Hua Kuofeng slipped into Mao's job as chairman and brought back Deng Xiaoping as his premier. Later he and his other colleagues were replaced by other rightists such as Li Xiannian, Zhao Ziyang and Hu Yaobang. The political position became very confused, especially since all these different groups called themselves the rightful heirs of Mao. One Chinese commentator at the time observed that 'When the snow thaws, the road becomes very muddy'.

Those who had been silenced by the terror that followed the Cultural Revolution now had their revenge. The 'Gang of Four' were brought to trial by the rightists for a long catalogue of crimes, including the charges they themselves had brought against their enemies in the 1960s. After a protracted state trial a number were executed, though Chiang Ching's life was spared, presumably in anticipation of a recantation.

Mao's death made itself felt in a number of other ways. For a while, a little more criticism of Chinese Communist policies was allowed. In front of the 'Democracy Wall' in Peking – a stretch of wall set aside for political posters (or dazibao) – there was a sort of 'Speakers Corner' where greater freedom of expression showed itself in the open-air debates which took place.

There was also a greater liberalism in China's relations with the outside world. China patched up its relations with the USA after 1971, and in that year was admitted to the United Nations, with a permanent seat on the Security Council. Relations with Britain improved, and in 1987 Britain agreed to allow Hong Kong, the oldest of the alienated territories, to rejoin China in 1997. Relations with the USSR had their ups and downs, especially after the Chinese government was so hostile to the Soviet invasion of Afghanistan in 1979; but the accession of Gorbachev to power in Moscow in 1985 took some of the sting out of even this. China also patched up its differences with Japan after forty years of war, when it agreed to employ the latest in Japanese technology, especially in the newer industries. Agreements were also made with Britain and the USA for financial and other help. In China, vast new plants were being set up, like the Baoshan steelworks near Shanghai, and the government was once again trying to attract foreign investment by offering special conditions like low rents and taxes, and especially cheap labour to help to produce the goods. Some found such concessions distasteful, but the Chinese leadership swallowed their hurt pride in the interest of modernization.

At home, Deng was much less influenced by ideological theory than Mao had been – indeed, he was so little attached to political labels that he asked 'What does it matter whether a cat is black or white so long as it catches mice?' Deng allowed workers to return to the towns, where private enterprise began to reassert itself. Cash incentives reappeared in economic life. State concerns became more market conscious and turned out fewer goods of shoddy quality. In the market place a wider range of goods became available, and television sets and household appliances began finding their way into thousands of Chinese homes. By the later 1980s the Chinese government was even learning to smile on foreign tourists, not as 'foreign devils' but as valuable sources of foreign currency.

But liberalization went too fast for the older members of the Politburo. Freedom of speech, however reassuring to foreign observers, seemed very threatening to the leadership. Student demonstrations soon turned into riots, in which radical youngsters seemed to be undermining the whole basis of the Revolution. In 1989 there came a sharp clamp-down in Peking, when tanks appeared on Tiananmen Square in the city in a confrontation with thousands of unarmed opponents. For a time the opposition had things its own way and government forces seemed nonplussed by their reckless bravery. But brute force eventually prevailed: hundreds of rioters were killed and the rest dispersed as the rising was savagely put down. Thousands of arrests followed in a desperate effort to crush opposition, and the Chinese leadership, moved as much by panic as by harshness, aroused the hatred of most of the rest of the world, and especially that of its future nationals in Hong Kong.

The catastrophic collapse of Soviet communism in 1991 left the Chinese Politburo very much isolated as the sole remaining major communist power in the world. With its ideological foundations irreversably discredited, it faced a vexing dilemma: whether to persevere with the authoritarian course it had chosen for itself after Tiananmen Square and so continue to face the world in isolation, or whether to risk further liberalization, and possibly bring down on its own head the fate that has awaited the former Soviet Union. In the 1990s, with Deng partially retired from public life, the Chinese Politburo had not yet had the courage to make up its mind.

> **66 Up-to-date material is well worth collecting. 99**

IDEAS AND PRINCIPLES

AUTONOMOUS

An autonomous area is a politically independent self-governing area. The word is from *autonomy*, derived from the Greek word for self-rule.

CADRE

This is a nucleus of regular soldiers in a regiment who are the best trained, and therefore the most reliable. By extension, communists apply the word to the hard core of party supporters who can be trusted to educate and lead other members or persuade waverers to join. In China the word is also applied to anyone in a position of leadership or management.

CONFUCIUS

A Chinese thinker who lived from about 551 to 479 BC. He became minister of justice in Shantung Province, but his schemes for improving the lives of citizens were ignored by the local rulers, and he wandered round China in search of a wise ruler who would put his ideas into practice. When he returned home he set up a school in which his ideas were taught. He was widely respected as the founding father of Chinese scholarship.

POLITBURO

The ruling political committee of the Communist Party. The word is an abbreviation of the phrase 'political bureau.'

MAOISM AND STALINISM

They are similar in that they both seek to apply in practice the ideas set out by Karl Marx. But they have significant differences; not simply differences that are based on national variations, but more fundamental ones.

> **The two communisms have quite different flavours.**

(1) Stalinism was based on the urban proletariat – the railway workers, the factory workers and the town-dwellers; Maoism is peasant-based and is a rural communist movement originally independent of the towns. Mao believed that the cities were no more than 'the fish which swam in the sea of the peasantry'.

(2) Stalinism resulted from a small body of dedicated communist leaders who organized a *coup d'état* in the cities and largely ignored rural opinion; Maoism was a spontaneous peasant rising fighting a war of liberation under his leadership. This war was a guerrilla war. Mao observed that 'political power grows out of the barrel of a gun'.

(3) Stalinism was class-based and was perhaps closer to Marxist theory than Maoism. Mao hesitated to make enemies of the Chinese bourgeoisie; he saw that they had their own parts to play in modernizing and strengthening the country. It was only if they acted disloyally to the revolution that he treated them as class enemies.

(4) Stalinism made extensive and regrettable use of coercion and terror, e.g. with the show trials of the purges; Mao preferred to educate and to persuade rather than to terrorize. Hence the great emphasis on thought reform, mutual criticism sessions, and analysis and discussion amongst comrades seeking for the truth. Even opponents were sometimes persuaded of the error of their ways – it was the Chinese who first perfected the technique of what later became known as 'brain-washing'.

(5) Stalin set perhaps too high a store by the achievement of a high level of industrial output; Mao believed that 'economism' was the wrong road to follow. Maoism preferred to create 'new socialist man', a man who had the right attitude and beliefs; industrial production could come later, if it was really needed. To him, keeping up with capitalist Joneses and competing for the consumer market, as Mao believed Khrushchev was doing after Stalin, seemed almost to be treachery to the true socialist ideal.

(6) Stalin tolerated, even encouraged, a high level of Party bureaucracy, setting up a ruling clique which lost touch with its revolutionary roots. Mao saw this as ending in the same kind of tyranny as had existed under colonialism or landlordism – the rule of an unfeeling minority chiefly anxious to preserve its own powers and status. It was in order to prevent this from happening in China that Mao devised the Cultural Revolution.

APPLIED MATERIALS

See Applied Materials section for Chapter 10 and also the following:

Texts and Atlases

C. Bown, *China, 1949–75*, Heinemann, 1980
C. Chai and W. Chai, *The Changing Society of China*, New English Library, 1965
R.C. North, *Chinese Communism*, Weidenfeld & Nicolson, 1967
S. Schram, *Mao Tse-tung*, Pelican, 1966

Documentary books

Mao Tse-tung, *Thoughts of Chairman Mao*, Foreign Languages Press, Peking, 1966
F. Schurmann and O. Schell, *China Readings*, Penguin, 1969; 3 volumes

Tapes

Anthony Lawrence, *Watching the Chinese*, BBC; 4 tapes

EXAMINATION QUESTION

QUESTION 1

When Chinese people want to express their opinions publicly; they write in large letters on posters which are eventually put on walls. These dazibao and other buildings – 'big character' posters – became a major feature of the Cultural Revolution.

The Associated Press

(a)   Write a wall poster (in English) in which, in 1966, you support the ideas of the Cultural Revolution, and describe some of the actions you have taken.

(b)   Write a wall poster (in English) in which, by 1968, you suggest reasons why the Cultural Revolution should be ended.

(Total 30 marks) (SEG)

TUTOR'S ANSWER

ANSWER 1

(a) Attack the Top Dogs: Down with the Party Headquarters: We have to keep the spirit of the people moving: The Sixteen-Point Resolution is right. It sums up the energy and the drive of the people and the revolution against the faceless bureaucrats. We have three things to do.

We must struggle: against laziness, complacency, against party people in power who have lost their way and forgotten the revolution.

We must criticize: ourselves and each other, but most of all those who seek to propagate weakness and smugness, and throw away the revolution for the sake of continuance in office. Revisionism is an offence against the spirit which inspired the Long March and brought us safely through all our tribulations. Reactionary ideas, revisionist ideas, are the way of the capitalist roaders, but we are the true believers.

We must transform: all over China education, literature, art and spiritual accomplishment will transform our country. We will do away with formalism, the precious product of the arid intellect, and make way for that new creature socialist man, thinking not of himself and his ease but of his fellows and their service.

Comrade Mao is right: we must follow even where we do not fully understand. His spirit carried us so far; we must show ourselves worthy of him now.

We have stood in silence outside Party Headquarters to show our disapproval of those with vested interests making harvests of paper within; we have chased self-satisfied teachers from the classroom; we have made the chemistry professor clean the latrines and oil the students' bicycles. We have spoken with the fat get-rich-quick plant managers and put them into overalls for the good of their socialist souls; we have led work songs in the factory and in the paddy field whilst we bend our backs to the country's tasks.

Capitalist cobwebs are everywhere. Let us go forward to spring-clean socialism.

(b) The Cultural Revolution was needed and served its useful purpose. It kept our socialist thinking virile and stopped us from falling into slack and evil ways, patting ourselves on the back when we should have been urging further effort.

But what is it now? Who are these Red Guards? Idle workers whose factories are not in production because of all this moral stock-taking; teenage students escaping from classes and making trouble for the rest of us; numbskulls and troublemakers waving their little red books and hoarse with their senseless shouting. What they have done is gross intimidation. Telling shopkeepers what they should and what they should not sell: trousers instead of skirts for the girls; no lipstick and no decoration for the hair. If they see things they don't like, they pretend to themselves the things are counter-revolutionary and then they attack. Even our historic buildings, our museums are open to vandalism; they dictate what dances shall be performed, what music shall be played. This petty tyranny must cease.

And where does the Cultural Revolution leave our country? Our schools and universities are empty, our factories deserted. What shall we produce, what shall we sell, what shall we eat if we are all so busy shining up our souls and not getting our hands dirty? Our managers, our scientists, our technicians cannot remain unqualified, or we shall be left behind in the race and will once again become poor and hungry.

We have chosen between the capitalist road and the socialist road: let us now get back to the work in hand.

SUGGESTIONS FOR FURTHER WORK

1. Find out what figures you can for Chinese agricultural and industrial output and for Chinese trade. What do these tell us of China's recovery of its position in the world?
2. Build up a map of modern China, marking its provinces and its main cities. Mark in and colour its neighbouring lands, indicating which of them have been recovered for China over the past forty years.
3. As a 20- or 25-year old citizen of communist China, write to your relatives living abroad to tell them of the changes that have taken place in China over

the past ten years. Have these changes made you apprehensive or glad?

4. Part of the Cultural Revolution was the idea of giving students some say in how they were educated and in what subjects. Do you think this is a good thing?How would you like to see the same thing put into practice here?

5. Formulate the arguments for saying that contemporary China is (a) more democratic and (b) less democratic than countries in the west.

STUDENT'S ANSWER – EXAMINER'S COMMENT

Question

(a) Discuss the propoganda use of a photograph showing cheering masses at the time of the Cultural Revolution.

(b) What were the 'production brigades'?

(c) Write a detailed paragraph explaining why many thinking people accepted the Cultural Revolution.

(d) Write a detailed paragraph outlining the impact of the Cultural Revolution on the Chinese Communist Party.

> **The first sentence of the answer is good and would score well. The second sentence is not necessary.**

> **Note the misspelling of pamphlet and receive. The comment about brainwashing is also rather silly.**

> **The answer to (b) is good and makes intelligent use of the word cadre.**

> **The answer to (c) is a good one and uses some appropriate phrases, though the name <u>Khrushchev</u> is misspelt. (d), however, is short and rather sketchy; it will not score highly since it cannot qualify as a 'detailed paragraph.'**

(a) Its propaganda use would be to show to any Chinese who were in doubt that there were large numbers of other people who gave their full support to the Cultural Revolution. The Chinese made great use of political propaganda in broadcasts, newspapers, books, panflets etc., and they also invented brainwashing so that the Chinese should have clean brains ready to recieve communist teaching.

(b) The production brigades or production teams were groups of party members who supervised and took part in the activities of Chinese farms and factories at the time of the revolution. They were known as cadres and were amongst the keenest supporters of the party. Here it is suggested they needed gingering up for a new enthusiasm at the time of the Cultural Revolution.

(c) Those who accepted the idea of the Cultural Revolution believed that the communist movement had to be kept moving and could not be allowed to come to a stand-still. It was to be a continuous revolution. It would prevent the teachings of the communists from hardening into a rigid dogma and so would keep communist thinking flexible. It would prevent the growth of a group of people who were above the revolution and were privileged rulers of the new country. Mao Tse-tung hoped he would make the Chinese people relive their victories of the 1930s and so rekindle their revolutionary enthusiasm. It was also a way of avoiding the growth of revisionism as in Russia where Krusev was having a big shake-up in the party and the government.

(d) It purged many people in the Chinese Party and got them to read and practise Mao's ideas and beliefs as expressed in his Red Book. The Reds became the shock troops of revolutionary thinking.

USA:

THE
NEW DEAL

GETTING STARTED

In 1919 the USA seemed the strongest country in the world. In Europe both the winners and losers of the war had been exhausted by four years of relentless effort and sacrifice. The USA had suffered too, but relatively lightly in comparison: American goods were available to markets starved of consumer products during the war years, while European countries were struggling to switch from war-time to peace-time production. Henry Ford's car factories went into mass production, ship-yards went on overtime to replace war-time losses, everywhere production levels rose. Business-men looked to inexhaustible markets, rosy prospects inflated the value of companies and speculative dealings inflated the value of shares. Men borrowed to expand their companies, men borrowed to buy shares. All hoped to repay their loans out of profits. New consumer goods and rising profits gave a veneer of luxury to American society, but there was still plenty of poverty, especially among the unskilled labour, much of which was black, and in agriculture, where the world food shortages of 1919 had given way to the world plenty of the early 1920s with the catastrophic collapse of food prices. Farmers borrowed and remortgaged in order to survive; others abandoned the struggle against low prices and soil erosion, and moved into the towns to seek work.

HISTORICAL DEVELOPMENTS

1 THE ECONOMIC DISASTER

> **The Wall Street crash was a feature of the depression rather than its cause.**

The three republican presidents shared the general business optimism, proclaimed laissez-faire policies (i.e. policies of non-interference by the state in the economy) and could see no end to the tide of rising prosperity. They were soon to be undeceived. Already in the late 1920s problems in agriculture were turning into a crisis; in the factories goods in search of a market were stockpiling; heavy trade barriers kept foreign goods out of the USA, but deprived foreigners of the means of earning the currency with which to buy American goods. These signs of weakness were ignored by a stock market that soared to new heights in early 1929. But within a few months wary and experienced investors began selling shares and confidence was gradually undermined, until in October 1929 the Wall Street crash saw such a dramatic decline in share values that panic replaced the old unjustified optimism. Frantic selling occurred. Those who had borrowed to buy shares (i.e. bought on the margin) could not repay their debts. This had a knock-on effect. Creditors of those who could not pay, could not themselves pay their own debts. Bank assets often consisted of unrecoverable loans. The USA, which, unlike Britain, was a nation of small banks, saw the collapse of hundreds of local banks, taking with them the savings and current accounts of many small businessmen, themselves in difficulties because of the financial crisis.

President Hoover attempted to stem the crisis with words of confidence. But the republicans had been promising sustained prosperity since 1920, and Hoover's confidence was regarded with suspicion ('In Hoover we trusted, now we are busted'). He did, however make some positive efforts: he reduced taxes to increase the public's ability to buy goods, and he persuaded Congress to pass an Emergency Relief and Reconstruction Act in 1932 which provided employment on federal public works projects and loans to states with public works programmes of their own. These were valuable measures, but they were overtaken by events. By the beginning of 1933 there were nearly thirteen million unemployed – there had been one million in 1929 – and the banking system was on the verge of collapse as one bank after another closed its doors. Hoover's reputation and honest efforts were forgotten and the shanty towns of the unemployed, nicknamed 'Hoovervilles', gave him a more permanent and less welcome niche in history.

2 THE PRESIDENTIAL ELECTION OF 1932

> **Trace out the policy differences between the democrats and the republicans.**

Rightly or wrongly the American electorate blamed the economic disaster on the republicans in general and on Hoover in particular. There seemed little prospect of another republican victory in the forthcoming presidential election in November 1932, so the future seemed to depend on the democrats and their choice of candidate. Franklin D. Roosevelt had good political experience: he had served in the Wilson administration and had been Wilson's vice-presidential candidate in 1920. He had become governor of New York State in 1928, a tough post which was often a valuable stepping-stone for politicians with presidential ambitions. The fact that his legs were paralysed as a result of polio in 1921 was no political disability – on the contrary, it showed Roosevelt to be a fighter in his personal life as well as in his public life and ready to tackle any handicap. Yet Roosevelt had no clear-cut programme for getting the USA out of the depression. He promised a New Deal for the American people; he was to tell them they had 'nothing to fear but fear itself'; he promised a period of 'experimentation' and he intended to tackle the problems vigorously. But he was not an economist, and the American people had to take him on trust. The presidential election in November gave him a large electoral majority, but he had four months of waiting while the economic situation continued to worsen before the constitution allowed him to take over from Hoover.

3 THE HUNDRED DAYS

During the first 100 days of his government, it was necessary for Roosevelt to deal with the immediate crisis and to restore the nation's confidence. He waged psychological warfare on despair in his 'fireside chats' on radio: he was the first President to make direct and effective contact with the general public in this way. He could tell the public of his first vigorous measures. He ordered the temporary closure of all banks while their books were audited and balanced, and he imposed a ban on bullion exports. The Emergency Banking Act gave federal guarantees to the deposits of sound banks only, thus forcing the weaker banks out of business but restoring confidence in both the currency and the banking system. The Securities and Exchange Commission was established to regulate the activities of Wall Street in marketing shares and of companies in issuing them. The Home Owners Loan Corporation was created with wide powers of borrowing, in order to finance home owners in trouble with their mortgages. An Economy Act cut federal salaries and pensions by 15 per cent, helping to convince the public that the burden was being shared and that the government was making an effort to balance its budget. Prohibition, with its uncontrollable corruption and organized crime, was swept away: 'I think now would be a good time for beer', the president said.

> **An understanding of economic principles is useful here.**

4 ▶ THE FIRST NEW DEAL

Measures for the longer term had been initiated during the Hundred Days. They often took the form of organizations known by their initials and popularly referred to as the 'alphabet agencies'. The **Civilian Conservation Corps** was established in April 1933 to provide work for the young unemployed in reafforestation, flood control and soil conservation; by 1940 it had provided employment for 2.5 million young men. The **Federal Emergency Relief Administration**, soon to become the **Works Progress Administration**, was to provide relief in the form of work for the adult unemployed: four million in all benefited from this by 1939. The **Tennessee Valley Authority** was created to co-ordinate flood control in an area of severe agricultural depression, to turn thousands of square miles into fertile land and to provide much needed hydro-electric power through a series of dams. Needless to say, it also provided much employment. It was a vast undertaking, spreading across seven states. Smaller projects were the responsibility of the Works Progress Administration, which organized federal building programmes for schools and roads and built the Hoover Dam on the Colorado River. In agriculture the first of several **Agricultural Adjustment Acts** attempted to increase farmers' incomes partly by direct subsidy and partly by reducing output to raise prices. An attempt was made to help industry by the **National Recovery Administration**, which sought to control conditions in industry through joint committees of workers and employers. Trade unions were, for the first time, actively encouraged and the **Wagner Act** 1935 extended their powers and rights. Many industries adopted a minimum wage. Child labour was forbidden. Firms which co-operated with the NRA were awarded a blue eagle badge, and advertizing was called in to persuade the public to show preference for products bearing the blue eagle. A start was made on social reform with the **Social Security Act of 1935**, which began provision for old age pensions and unemployment insurance, although no attempt was made to extend the cover to health. All this activity told the Americans that *laissez-faire* had been abandoned and that the government was actually attempting to do something about economic and social problems. As unemployment figures began to fall and the country slowly began to claw its way out of the depression, the New Deal often got the credit for the improvement. It was not surprising that in the 1936 presidential election Roosevelt won the majority vote in all but two of the states. Even so the New Deal had many critics and opponents.

5 ▶ OPPOSITION TO THE NEW DEAL

Roosevelt had made the depression his personal responsibility, but not everyone was happy with his methods. The destruction of crops and livestock seemed scandalous when so many were poor and hungry. Businessmen feared the power of the trade unions, previously restricted by law and now unmuzzled. Moreover they thought the heavy clamp-down on monopolies and monopolistic practice an infringement of economic freedom. Although Roosevelt had been careful not to 'demoralize' the unemployed with an American equivalent of the 'dole', his public work schemes were often attacked for providing much relief and little work. Many regarded him as a socialist. Above all, the politicians felt that parts of his legislation were unconstitutional in that they undermined the powers of the individual states. The American Supreme Court, the watch-dog of the American constitution, declared eight major acts of the New Deal legislation unconstitutional, including the Agricultural Adjustment Act. Even the Tennessee Valley Authority looked for a time to be under threat. When Roosevelt attempted to change the court's membership in his own favour by creating six new judges, Congress threw out the necessary legislation. The Supreme Court took the hint, however. Its younger members were more favourable to Roosevelt; as the older ones retired he could appoint successors more sympathetic to the New Deal, and the Supreme Court softened its attitude. Even so a good deal of time was spent during the second New Deal in reviving or amending legislation rejected by the Supreme Court during the first New Deal.

6 ▷ THE SECOND NEW DEAL

There was not so crowded a legislative programme this time and there was more emphasis on social rather than economic problems. The **National Housing Act** provided money for homes and placed curbs on high rents. The **Fair Labour Standards Act** specified minimum wages and maximum hours. Another **Agricultural Adjustment Act** attempted to repair the damage to agricultural policy caused by the Supreme Court. Federal action against monopolies was co-ordinated and intensified. American attention was focused more firmly on domestic affairs as a series of **Neutrality Acts** confirmed the unwillingness of the USA to enter into any foreign commitments.

66 Does this show Roosevelt was a socialist? 99

The upturn in the economy of the mid-1930s was jolted by a four million increase in unemployment in 1938. Roosevelt attacked economic selfishness, claiming that while 'private enterprise nodded, one-third of the population remained ill-fed, ill-clothed and ill-housed'. The setback was temporary, and caused in part by a government fear of inflation which had caused federal aid to be restricted. The renewed recovery in 1939 and 1940 was probably as much the result of rearmament as of government policy. Roosevelt had a surprisingly tough fight against Wendell Wilkie in the 1940 presidential election. It might have been even tougher but for the European war, which persuaded Americans not to risk a change of government.

7 ▷ ASSESSMENT

Roosevelt's New Deal has been said to follow the policy and advice of the economist J.M. Keynes. Keynes wanted governments to spend their way out of the recession by initiating necessary public works, thus creating employment and spending power to stimulate demand for goods. He dismissed the need for balanced budgets (where government revenue in taxation is not exceeded by government spending), and wanted spending to be financed by borrowing rather than by higher taxation. Roosevelt's grasp of economics fell short of this. He was prepared to borrow in the short-term, but looked for balanced budgets in the long-term. He feared that 'priming the pump' (i.e. putting more money into circulation by government works programmes) might increase spending power to the point of causing inflation. Thus if Roosevelt's critics thought that he was doing too much, followers of Keynes felt that he was too cautious and doing too little. Hopes of a major boost to the construction industry from the Works Progress Administration were disappointing. The National Recovery Administration was already experiencing internal difficulties when it was declared unconstitutional in 1935. The Agricultural Adjustment Act had been a boon to farmers, but it too was declared unconstitutional in 1936. Production and trade improved in the late 1930s, but not to the levels of the 1920s until the USA joined the Second World War in 1941. Unemployment remained stubbornly high; 7,700,000 in 1937 was the lowest since 1930, but it was to return to over ten million in 1938 and was still over eight million in 1940.

66 The dates and the details of New Deal policies must be accurate. 99

It is easy therefore to see the New Deal as the coming of the new era and to exaggerate its achievements. But Roosevelt was the first American president to take upon himself the nation's battle and to fight it in the full glare of publicity from press and radio. To the Americans the depression was a terrifying and appalling experience. If Roosevelt could not defeat it, at least he could inspire his people to make a fight of it.

8 SUMMARY OF THE NEW DEAL PROGRAMME

The summary is arranged chronologically rather than alphabetically.

➤ *Emergency Banking Act* (1933) – to encourage successful banks and to eliminate weaker ones.

➤ *Securities and Exchange Commission* (1933) – to regulate share dealing and company share issues.

➤ *Economy Act* (1933) – to cut wages of federal employees by 15 per cent.

➤ *Abolition of Prohibition* (1933) – to allow the production, importation, sale and consumption of alcoholic drinks.

➤ *Home Owners Loan Corporation* (1933) – to help home owners in difficulties with their mortgages.

➤ *Civilian Conservation Corps* (1933) – to provide useful work for the young unemployed, especially in conservation.

➤ *Federal Emergency Relief Administration* (1933) which became in 1935 the Works Progress Administration.

➤ *Works Progress Administration* – to organize a federal works programme to provide work for the adult unemployed.

➤ *The Tennessee Valley Authority* (1933) – to develop and improve 40,000 square miles along the Tennessee River with drainage, hydro-electric power, afforestation, etc.

➤ *Agricultural Adjustment Acts* (1933 and 1937) – to reduce agricultural surpluses and to raise prices.

➤ *National Recovery Administration* (1933) – to develop co-operation in industry and to encourage quality products.

➤ *Social Security Act* (1935) – to establish insurance for pensions and unemployment.

➤ *Wagner Act* (1936) – to confirm and extend the rights of trade unions.

➤ *National Housing Act* (1937) – to provide money for home loans and to curb high rents.

➤ *Fair Labour Standards Act* (1938) – to regulate hours and conditions of work and to fix minimum wages.

IDEAS AND PRINCIPLES

THE US POLITICAL SYSTEM

The United States is a federation of fifty states, most of them on the North American mainland. There were originally thirteen British colonies, which united after the War of American Independence. Each state has its own capital, e.g. Richmond, Virginia, and its own political system; but there is a federal capital with over-arching powers in Washington, DC.

The constitution is the instrument under which the USA is governed. It is a written document which may be amended with the consent of the states. The twenty-two amendments are listed at the end of the document. The interpretation of the meaning of the constitution is in the hands of the Supreme Court.

Presidents are elected for a fixed term of four years every leap year; if they die or are incapacitated they are succeeded for the rest of their elected term by their vice-president. They are elected indirectly, i.e. by the votes of an electoral college in which each state elects as many electors as it has representatives in Congress. These are chosen in each state by the ordinary voters, but since they are all pledged to vote for a particular presidential candidate the electoral college results are usually known before it even meets.

Congress is made up of two houses: the House of Representatives and the Senate. Each state has two senators, irrespective of size, but the size of the body of congressmen going to the House of Representatives varies proportionately according to the size of the state's population. The House of Representatives is elected every two years, the elections in the intervening years between presidential elections being known as mid-term elections. The Senate is partially renewed in thirds every two years, so that it is entirely renewed every six years.

The Supreme Court has judges who are nominated by the president in office when a vacancy occurs. It is the most important court in the land, taking precedence over all other courts, and it has the special duty of interpreting the constitution.

Each state has its own state militia, just as it has its own police forces. In cases where the state militia is inadequate, federal troops may be used for the preservation of law and order.

APPLIED MATERIALS

Texts

S.E. Ayling, *Portraits of Power (Roosevelt), Harrap*, 1965
Josh Brooman, *A New Deal – America, 1932–45*, Longman, 1987
C.P. Hill, *Franklin Roosevelt and the New Deal*, Arnold, 1975
D.B. O'Callaghan, *Roosevelt and the United States*, Longman (Modern Times Series), 1966
John Simkin, *America in the Twenties*, Spartacus,1986
John Simkin, *Roosevelt and the New Deal*, Spartacus, 1986
H. Ward, *World Powers in the Twentieth Century*, Part I, Heinemann, 1985

Documentary

M. Yass, *The Great Depression*, Wayland Pictorial, 1970

Audio visual

Audio Learning, *The USA – Theodore to Franklin Roosevelt, 1898–1945*, PA/1267/24
Audio Learning, *The 1929 Financial Crisis*, LR/1241/21
Audio Learning, *The Wall Street Crash*, 1929, DM 04

EXAMINATION QUESTIONS

QUESTION 1

Give an account of
(a)   the effects on the USA of the Wall Street crash; and
(b)   the attempts of President F.D. Roosevelt during the 1930s to solve the problems which the crash had created.

(ULEAC)

QUESTION 2

It is 1936. At a public meeting in Nashville, Tennessee, there is a noisy debate and argument about the Tennessee Valley Authority. As a journalist write an account of the meeting for your local paper, trying to do justice to the arguments of both sides.

OUTLINE ANSWERS

ANSWER 1

The first question is a little deceiving: although it appears to be asking for a narrative it is in fact asking in the first part for an analysis of the effects of the Wall Street crash, and in the second part for an analysis of Roosevelt's work in the context of the problems he faced. In (a) the effects will be the immediate ones: the collapse of share prices and the bankruptcies that followed. Then there will be the effect on banks, the squeeze on industry, the slow-down in production and the massive growth of unemployment. Roosevelt's attempted solutions include attempts to restore confidence to the economy (banking policy, curbs on Wall Street, radio talks); then attempts to get people to work (the CCC and the WPA), attempts to revitalize industry (NRA) and attempts to prevent farming bankruptcies and evictions of farmers and home owners (AAA, Home Owners LC and National Housing Act). His mild attempts to deal with social evils (Social Security Act and Fair Labour Standards Act) can lead on to his pro-trade union policy culminating in the Wagner Act. Highest marks will be reserved for those who attempt to analyse the effectiveness of his policies.

ANSWER 2

The second question is empathetic. A noisy debate suggests feelings are running high and this should be reflected in your report. Supporters of the TVA will point to flood control, improvement in the quality and quantity of arable land, reafforestation schemes, employment in construction and farming, the bringing of electric power to backward areas and generally to the improved prosperity of a severely depressed area. Opponents will talk of the rights of individual farmers being ignored, of the powerlessness of individual states to exert a check on the TVA's powers, and of the flooding of certain districts to feed the dams and the hardship of those compelled to abandon their homes and farms. Some will suggest that most of the financial benefits have gone to outside construction companies and power companies rather than to local farmers. In the argument self-interest will come out much more clearly than national interest.

SUGGESTIONS FOR FURTHER WORK

1. Collect industrial and unemployment statistics for the USA in the 1930s, and assess the value of these statistics in helping you to understand the New Deal. Tip: useful statistics can be found in J. and G. Stokes, *Europe and the Modern World*, Longman, 1973, pages 222–3.
2. Why do you think the voters of Maine and Vermont cast the majority of their votes against Roosevelt in the 1936 presidential election?
3. If Roosevelt had fully accepted Keynes's ideas, what else would have been done to try to halt the depression?
4. Research in detail the work of two of the alphabet agencies.
5. Write, in the form of extracts from a diary, the experiences of an American farming family during the depression.

STUDENT'S ANSWER – EXAMINER'S COMMENT

Question

(a)   What event in 1929 had been a major cause of the depression in the USA?

(b)   Explain how this event led to a depression.

(c)   What was the 'Banking Crisis' of 1933 and how was it solved?

(d)   What was the problem of farm surpluses? How did the New Deal try to tackle this problem?

(e)   What were Hoovervilles? Why were they so called?

(f)   Explain why members of the 'upper classes' hated the President.

(g)   Explain the work of the New Deal alphabet agencies which tried to tackle unemployment. How successful were these agencies?

> **Unemployment was a symptom of the depression not a cause of it.**

> **So he does know about the Wall Street Crash.**

> **The answers to (d) and (e) are good .**

> **This is only partly right. Although taxes on the very rich were increased in 1935 most of the extra expenditure was financed by borrowing. If the upper classes hated him it was because they believed his measures were socialist, and the American upper classes had long been deeply afraid of socialism. Some also disliked the president's use of Federal power which they believed infringed state rights, but this criticism was not confined to the upper classes.**

(a) Unemployment.

(b) Many firms got into money problems and had to lay off workers.

(c) The banks of America, most of which were very small, lost heavily when businesses went bankrupt and could not pay their debts. So the banks themselves were unable to meet their customers demands for money, and a number were forced to close. The crisis was solved when the President ordered a 'bank holiday' and provided government money to help the banks when they reopened.

(d) Farmers were producing too much food so the prices they were getting were often below the cost of production. The new deal dealt with the problem by paying farmers to plough their crops back into the fields, thus reducing the surpluses and allowing prices to rise.

(e) Hoovervilles were shanty towns built by the unemployed, many of them war veterans, who flocked to the big cities, especially New York, looking for work. Living quarters were often huts made of wood and corrugated iron, and sanitation and other amenities were often lacking. They were named after President Hoover, whose policies were believed to be responsible for the depression.

(f) They hated him because he greatly increased government taxation in order to increase spending on social welfare.

(g) The New Deal Agencies tried to tackle unemployment by finding jobs for American youth and for the long-term unemployed by putting them to work on important social projects such as the Colorado and Tennessee dams and planting new forests. By 1938 they had been successful in helping to find work for over two million people.

> **This is a rather skimpy answer. Each of Agencies could have been given individual treatment, and the range of their activities needs better coverage than the few references given here.**

THE USA AFTER 1945

THE 1940s: VALOUR AND VICTORY

THE 1950s: AFFLUENCE AND APPREHENSION

THE 1960s: PROGRESS AND PARANOIA

THE 1970s: RECOVERY AND ASSURANCE

THE 1980s: DETERMINATION AND DOUBT

GETTING STARTED

After it finally abandoned its isolationism in 1941, the USA played a major part in the Second World War. Pitched headlong into the struggle when Japan attacked Pearl Harbor, US forces were strong enough by 1943 to start a counter-offensive, and by 1945 they re-occupied the Philippines, captured Okinawa and Iwojima, and stood poised for an invasion of Japan itself. Quite suddenly, in August of that year, the war came to an end with the dropping of two atomic bombs on the Japanese cities of Hiroshima and Nagasaki. The entire Pacific area had become a US sphere of influence.

In the western hemisphere, US forces also played their part. An Anglo-American landing in north Africa ('Operation Torch') under General Eisenhower in 1942 linked up with Montgomery's Eighth Army advancing from Egypt; together, these forces cornered the axis armies in Tunisia, forcing them to surrender in 1943. Allied troops conquered Sicily, and then fought their way up the length of the Italian peninsula. In 1944, US forces invaded southern France and poured through the Belfort Gap into Upper Alsace, where they contributed to the allied invasion of Germany across the Rhine. Meanwhile, other American troops had crossed on D-Day to the Normandy beaches and played their part in the liberation of northern France, recapturing Paris and pressing through the Ardennes towards the Rhineland in 1945.

US efforts at sea and in the air were also remarkable. The US Navy shared the burden of policing the Atlantic, whilst the US Army Air Force took part in the regular bombing of Germany in 1944 and 1945, organizing massive air strikes by day whilst the RAF bombed by night. Towards the end of the war Britain had become a vast aircraft carrier moored off the coast of Europe, groaning under the enormous tonnage of material that the Americans had stockpiled there.

HISTORICAL DEVELOPMENTS

Throughout the war a ceaseless flow of weapons, supplies and equipment flowed into Europe from the New World, the 'arsenal of democracy' as it was sometimes called. By the time the war ended, the Americans had built about 12,000 ships, 100,000 tanks and nearly 300,000 aircraft, many of them flown to Europe by young pilots who had just completed their training in Canada or the United States. During the war, dead American servicemen numbered about a half million. US government spending topped 400 billion dollars, a sum greater than that spent by the rest of the allies put together.

Though President Roosevelt died shortly before the end of the war, there was little prospect that at the end of it the USA would retire once more into isolation. The USA was clearly now one of the world's two great 'superpowers', with a great interest in preserving the European liberties which its soldiers had fought to restore. The USA was one of the chief founder-members of the United Nations Organization, set up at a conference in San Francisco in July 1945. US troops took part in the partitioning of Germany, and afterwards garrisoned their zone of that country. The USA lent a supporting hand to the tottering economies of western Europe with the Marshall Plan in 1947, and was the mainstay of the North Atlantic Treaty (establishing NATO) signed in 1949. By 1950, European powers had almost come to take the presence of the Americans in Europe for granted.

PRESIDENT TRUMAN

President Truman, who had been Roosevelt's vice-president, was scarcely known in Europe before his accession to the presidency. None the less, he served almost two full terms and achieved considerable success. His main concern, like that of Roosevelt before him, was with social policy in a country which, though rich, had great areas of submerged poverty in rural areas and in poor, non-white city precincts. Truman at first modestly confined himself to putting the finishing touches to the New Deal started by Roosevelt. In September 1945 he set out his programme of twenty-one points, aiming to build more working-class housing and to extend social security benefits. In 1946 he secured the passing of an Employment Act. But economic controls and planning and interference in American free enterprise stuck in American gullets, and he was steadily compelled to abandon his programmes. The Republicans gained control of Congress in 1946 at the mid-term elections and proceeded to put through the Taft-Hartley Act in 1947; US employers were freed by it from some industrial restrictions, but others equally damaging were imposed on the trade unions. Republicans also favoured tax cuts instead of extending social services.

Somewhat unexpectedly, Truman was returned for a second term in 1948 and continued with his social policies. In 1949 he brought in his Fair Deal, modelled on the New Deal of nearly twenty years earlier. Social security measures were extended, benefits were improved, working conditions and hours were further regulated, minimum wage levels were introduced, subsidies and other support for poorer rural areas were introduced and a new Housing Act extended the building of low-cost homes for those on lower incomes. He had ambitious proposals for more public works schemes, but unfortunately a number of his proposals did not gain congressional approval and had to be abandoned.

In 1950 Truman first came up against Senator Joseph McCarthy, Republican senator for Wisconsin, who claimed to have evidence of a widespread communist plot in the leading ranks of American society. There was little hard evidence of this but MacCarthy stirred deep fears in US society. Truman and the Democrats were opposed to what they saw as a 'witch-hunt', but dared not openly denounce MacCarthy for fear of becoming themselves the subjects of his accusations. It was not in fact until after Truman ceased to be President that the incoming Republicans pricked the McCarthy bubble.

Build up a table showing the domestic policies of each of the post-war presidents.

By 1950, the USA seemed to be developing into a new kind of state – one with a high level of consumer consumption and wealth, but one that was also nervous about the threat of communism. Individualism and consumerism seemed to dominate many Americans' thinking. Wages were generally high, as was the standard of living. Americans were developing advertising, hire purchase (by 1967 over 99 billion dollars were owed on hire purchase debts) and various other kinds of market device. Planned obsolescence was built into goods to prevent anything from lasting too long, so that there would soon be new demand for industrial products. Even buildings had a temporary look; put up one year, they might easily be torn down the next to make way for something even bigger. The USA was becoming a divided society too; successful whites began to move out into leafy suburbs, leaving the decaying city centres to the poor, the unemployed and the coloureds.

In 1951 the twenty-second amendment to the constitution was passed, limiting the president to two terms of office and preventing any future leader from doing what Roosevelt had done; get re-elected more than once. Supposedly a token of respect for George Washington, who had the good sense to withdraw from politics after eight years in the late eighteenth century, the measure actually concealed a deep-seated American fear of presidential dictatorship – a danger which became all too obvious in the days of Richard Nixon.

> **Some knowledge of the procedure for amendments is worthwhile.**

THE 1950s: AFFLUENCE AND APPREHENSION

PRESIDENT EISENHOWER

In 1952 Eisenhower gained a convincing majority at the election. He faced considerable tasks. He had to wind up the war in Korea which had been dragging on for two years, and he had to face the need for confronting the Russians in Europe. The details of the policy were left to J.F. Dulles, secretary of state during most of Eisenhower's two administrations. He squared up to the Russians wherever they showed themselves, following a policy often called one of 'brinkmanship'. Under him, a new regional alliance system, known as SEATO, was set up in south-east Asia; another, CENTO, for the Middle East, had US backing after 1959. Before this, in 1957, the president produced what is called the *Eisenhower doctrine*, promising aid to Middle Eastern states under threat from the USSR, including not only Israel but a number of other states such as Iran. Eisenhower even saw the danger of communism in the New World, where he came into political conflict with Castro, the Cuban leader who had seized power in a *coup d'état* in 1959. Throughout the decade the USA showed considerable apprehension over the expansion of communism in the world and sought to contain it.

In domestic matters, Eisenhower was a conservative. He had no wish to reverse any of the New Deal or the Fair Deal policies, but he was anxious not to be involved in too much government spending, and he generally fostered the interests of the prosperous middle classes on whom he depended for support. After 1956, when the Democrats recovered control of Congress, he vetoed several expensive attempts by reformers to push through housing and welfare schemes. In economic matters, too, he showed the same caution. Though there were recessions in 1953 and 1957, and a steel strike in 1959 which involved him in conflict with the trade unions, Eisenhower was able to preside at a time when the economy of the country was flourishing and when many Americans were enjoying a rising standard of living.

Eisenhower's skills were those of an efficient business manager; he liked to appoint the best men to the jobs and then leave them to get on with them. He liked to be on the golf links every afternoon. But for much of the time he was not in the best of health. He suffered a moderately severe stroke in 1957, and much more work fell on his ambitious vice-president, Richard Nixon. On the other hand, his supporters always said that Eisenhower worked very hard, but that he liked to give an impression of indolence to put his critics off their guard; certainly his mastery of language can be seen from the skilful and detailed changes he made to the drafts of his speeches – something which never ceased to impress Winston Churchill, for example.

One thing about which he felt strongly was race relations. Though he respected states' rights, Eisenhower was disgusted at the way many of the southern ones treated their negroes. His disgust was shared in the Supreme Court, where

Chief Justice Earl Warren, in *Brown v. Topeka Board of Education*, ruled against separate schools for negro children, saying that though theoretically these were 'equal' with white schools, in practice they were much inferior. The southern states tried to ignore the ruling, but Eisenhower insisted, and when the state militia refused to enforce the court's ruling he called on federal troops in Little Rock, Arkansas, to escort black students into school and protect them against the prejudices of white southerners. Even then other states persisted in their opposition. In 1955, in Montgomery, Alabama, there was a bus boycott on the part of negroes who objected to being segregated when they were travelling; and afterwards their protests spread to others who objected to whites-only cafés, hotels, libraries and drug-stores. By 1960 a civil rights movement dedicated to improving the lot of non-whites and other minorities had come into being.

In 1957 this movement was successful to the extent that Eisenhower agreed to the passing of a Civil Rights Act, attempting to prevent negro voters in the south from being deprived of their votes.

3 > THE 1960s: PROGRESS AND PARANOIA

PRESIDENT KENNEDY

In 1960, the Republican candidate for the presidency, Richard Nixon, was narrowly defeated by the Democratic candidate, J.F. Kennedy. As their TV confrontation had shown, Kennedy was the much more attractive figure: a Roman Catholic, a New Englander and, at the age of 43, the youngest candidate ever to become president. Youth and energy were the keynotes of his presidency.

In social policy he picked up where Truman had left off. He invoked the spirit of the old pioneer in his appeal for a *New Frontier* policy – directed not against the untamed wilderness of the western lands but against the twentieth-century evils of poverty, inequality and deprivation. He set as his goals a fairer, freer and more equal society, where the spirit of intellectual and scientific adventure should be free to press towards the realization of new endeavours such as the moon landing. His first efforts were directed against the recession which had overtaken the USA in 1959. He increased spending on public works projects, encouraged credit purchases to encourage demand and even embarked on a tentative wages and incomes policy to restrain inflation. His critics suggested that the inflation was of his own making and that sensible economies would be a more prudent course; but Kennedy thought it was more important to spend money on extending the existing social legislation. He increased welfare benefits, raised the level of minimum wages and took the first steps in the direction of a comprehensive social policy known as Medicare for the elderly, in the face of considerable opposition from those who disliked socialized medicine. He was also concerned with the issue of civil rights. Federal troops were again used to enforce desegregation in 1962, when they gave protection to black students entering the Universities of Mississippi and Alabama. He came out strongly against other forms of discrimination as well, as he made clear in a speech in 1963:

> We preach freedom around the world, and we mean it. And we cherish our freedom here at home. But are we to say to the world – and much more importantly to each other – that this is the land of the free, except for Negroes; that we have no second-class citizens, except Negroes; that we have no class or caste system, no ghettos, no master race, except with respect to Negroes? Now the time has come for this nation to fulfil its promise.

Some up-to-date knowledge of these bodies would be useful.

In foreign affairs he expressed his liberalism in the form of the Peace Corps, an organization founded in 1961 to allow skilled volunteers to give help to under-developed nations. He also put forward his Alliance for Progress with Latin America to increase co-operation with that area and raise the standards of these often desperately poor countries. In Europe, he suggested sweeping tariff cuts and encouraged the growth of trade with Europe. Though he was the heir of a rather unsound scheme to strike against Cuba at the Bay of Pigs – a plot originally hatched by the CIA under Eisenhower – his usual attitudes towards foreign countries were ones of broad understanding.

PRESIDENT JOHNSON

In 1963, Kennedy was assassinated at Dallas, Texas. He was succeeded by his Vice-President, L.B. Johnson. It was his job to translate into practice the often unfulfilled promises of his charismatic predecessor.

Johnson called his programme that of the **Great Society**, though in substance it was not much different from the New Frontier. He managed to get Kennedy's Civil Rights Act through Congress in 1964, outlawing discrimination in housing, jobs and education. A Public Voting Act in 1965 resulted in an increase in the numbers of registered black voters in the southern states, and led to a higher proportion of them actually using their votes. Another Civil Rights Act followed in 1968, attempting to end discrimination in the sale and leasing of domestic accommodation. In other areas, too, he was active. In 1965 he increased job opportunities for underprivileged young blacks through his Equal Opportunities Act. He also brought in the Job Corps to assist the unemployed to find work. In the realm of the social services he carried forward Kennedy's work in extending the provisions of Medicare for the old and Medicaid for the poor. In order to permit the restoration of decaying city centres he secured the Development Act in 1966; under it not only were new houses to be built, but the infrastructure of the city, such as its sewerage, was to be modernized. He gave attention, too, to the problems of industry. Additional proposals for wider trade union rights and for more liberal immigration policies failed because of the resistance of Congress.

Although the USA witnessed progress in domestic fields, its disastrous entanglement in Vietnam made a lasting scar on the conscience of the country. In the 1950s the country had drifted rather than been steered towards involvement in Vietnam's affairs. The first US technicians had been sent there under Eisenhower to give support services to the South Vietnamese government, but the tiny trickle had steadily increased under Kennedy and then under Johnson, until over a half million men were stationed in the country. In their desperate attempt to 'contain' communism the USA supported a number of ramshackle right-wing regimes, and by 1964 it was engaged in open war in South Vietnam against the communist Vietcong. The fighting was confused and bloody, but the war showed no signs of ending. Many of the Vietnamese had no love of the Vietcong, but regarded the Americans even more unfavourably as the foreigners destroyed their villages and napalmed their crops and forests. Fighting reached a new peak of intensity when the communists launched their Tet offensive early in 1968. Over half the country was in the hands of the Vietcong. Not even air strikes against North Vietnam and on the 'Ho Chi Minh Trail', through Laos and neighbouring Cambodia, used by the north to bring supplies to their adherents, seemed to have any permanent effect. By the time of the presidential election of 1968, US opinion was so nervy, domestic criticism so violent and L.B. Johnson so dispirited that he refused to run for a second term.

4 ▷ THE 1970s: RECOVERY AND REASSURANCE

PRESIDENT NIXON

The USA was in turmoil when Richard Nixon was elected to the White House in 1968. He won by a fairly narrow margin, having played up the previous government's inability to keep order in the country during the 'long hot summer' of 1968 and its apparent helplessness to bring about a solution to the Vietnam problem.

In foreign affairs he enjoyed a good deal of success. He embarked on a steady withdrawal of troops from Vietnam, doing his best to make the South Vietnamese government responsible for its own defence – a policy known as Vietnamization – and eventually negotiating a cease-fire in the country. He concluded a short-lived peace treaty between North and South Vietnam in 1973, under which the last Americans left the country. He also pulled off a number of agreements with Brezhnev, such as the Strategic Arms Limitation agreement known as SALT in 1969. He moved towards *détente* with China, encouraging the admission of communist China to UNO in 1971 and actually visiting that country in 1972 to cement the new-found friendship. He and his persuasive and ubiquitous secretary of state, Henry Kissinger, achieved names for themselves as trouble-shooters in a disturbed world. It was largely on the strength of this reputation that Nixon managed to get himself elected for a second term in 1972.

Nixon was less impressive in the realm of domestic affairs. He showed little enthusiasm for reform, and though he did not attempt to undo any of the reforms already made he showed some resentment towards critics, radicals and students, all of whom he was inclined to lump together under the general name of 'pinkos'. Though the troubles on the campuses and in the cities dwindled during his term of office, this was less because he had found a way of solving them than because of the thoroughness with which he clamped down on them. He made a number of positive moves in social policy, such as the appointment of a Council for Urban Affairs, but it was generally the US economy that occupied the centre of his attention. The massive amount of US overseas spending, not least on the defence of other nations, brought a big outflow of currency and weakened the dollar. The result was that the 1970s saw a curious new phenomenon – stagflation, in which economic recession and high unemployment (about four million in the early 1970s) combined with a steadily rising level of wages and prices. Nixon made strenuous efforts to live up to the Republican reputation, that it was the businessmen's party, and to bring things under control. He made efforts to freeze wages and prices; he introduced a surcharge on imports of 10 per cent to redress the adverse balance of payments; he cut back on government spending and thus on borrowing so as to reduce interest rates; and finally he devalued the dollar. This provided a temporary respite, but later in the 1970s trouble with the economy started again.

What America needed, he felt, was a steady spell of sound Republican government, especially with himself in charge, and so he embarked upon a process at the end of which he hoped to be able to repeal the twenty-second amendment so as to permit himself a third term. But it was the Watergate scandal that brought an abrupt and shameful end to his political career. A newspaper campaign, building on small and unsubstantiated rumours that he had been engaged in burglary, theft and misrepresentation at the time of the 1972 presidential election, eventually disgraced him. It came to light that in the course of pursuing his re-election – his Campaign for the Re-Election of the President was appropriately known as Creep – Nixon had not always stayed on the right side of the law. He did his best to excuse himself by trying to invent a new constitutional doctrine known as presidential prerogative, which more or less meant that the president could do as he liked; but the real quality of his presidency came to light when, after much wriggling, he agreed to produce certain tapes which showed that he so far trusted his intimate advisers that he recorded every word they spoke in the Oval Office. The tapes revealed to the American people that their president was foul-mouthed, mean-minded, opportunistic and petty, and not above breaking the law whenever it suited him. They reacted by threatening to impeach him for his misdeeds. Rather than face likely disgrace he resigned office, handing over power to his vice-president, Gerald Ford, who promptly pardoned him for whatever he had done, so closing the book on a rather unsavoury episode in US history.

> **Develop some detailed knowledge of this scandal.**

PRESIDENT CARTER

The presidential election of 1976, marking the two hundredth anniversary of the US Declaration of Independence, brought a Democrat rather than a Republican to the presidency. With a rather bucolic background (he was a peanut farmer from Georgia) Jimmy Carter presented an image different from the rather sleazy impression being projected at that time by smart Washington society. His modest, sincere manner came like a breath of fresh air to the jaded and dispirited capital. But though he promised well he achieved relatively little. At home he grappled without much success with the problems of a weakening dollar, an adverse balance of payments, high rates of interest and of domestic unemployment, and steadily advancing inflation. Perhaps his most serious problem was the energy crisis. The unpopularity of the USA in most parts of the Middle East generated retaliatory measures by OPEC (the Organization of Petroleum Exporting Countries) to raise the price of the oil which the Americans imported, and the resultant shortages brought efforts to deal with the problem. The USA decided that it ought to make better use of its natural oil and gas supplies; it made additional efforts to extract oil from coal and shale; it undertook engineering research to produce car engines which used fuel more efficiently; it imposed maximum speed limits; and there was even talk of rationing for a time. But many of the sensible measures which Carter put forward were not popular with Congress and in the end little came of them.

In foreign affairs he had some successes. He continued the work of improving relations with China, and encouraged China and Japan to make a peace treaty and resolve their differences after forty years of conflict in 1978; he promoted a reconciliation between Sadat of Egypt and Begin of Israel in a draft settlement for peace between the two countries to start in 1979; and he negotiated an agreement with Panama whereby the USA undertook to hand back the Panama Canal before the end of the century. But it was his deep concern for civil rights – very much evident at home too in his dealings with America's own ethnic minorities – which got him into trouble. He made the mistake of trying to lecture Brezhnev on the treatment of dissidents in the Soviet Union; and after the overthrow of the Shah of Iran, his ally in the Middle East, he protested against the brutalities of the regime of the Ayahtollah Khomeini. Relations with Iran were so bad that in 1979 Iranian students seized a large number of US hostages and held them for over a year. The Carter administration, in spite of its great world strength, seemed to be powerless to do anything about it. An attempt at a rescue by a hit squad of US helicopters was a disastrous failure, and it was only after the end of the Carter presidency that the problem was solved.

Though Carter had undoubtedly done something to restore American self-respect after the Nixon disasters, there were few people who were really sorry when he was replaced at the 1980 presidential election by the republican Ronald Reagan.

5 ▷ THE 1980s: DETERMINATION AND DOUBT

PRESIDENT REAGAN

Ronald Reagan came to office on a tide of right-wing sentiment. Anti-liberalism was in the air: ordinary people were tired of pandering to welfare spongers, black trouble-makers and militant feminists. Reagan preferred swingeing tax cuts in place of social welfare. When he promised to put the country back on its feet by encouraging once again the old virtue of self-reliance there were many who jumped at the chance.

He secured the enactment of a number of social reforms, such as the Energy Security Act, which had failed to reach the statute book under Carter, but his own record was not a distinguished one. He allowed an equal rights amendment to the constitution to be dropped in 1982, and in other ways showed little sympathy for the underprivileged. He put forward no remedies for unemployment, and whittled away the welfare entitlement of those out of work. In the early part of his presidency there were protests in American cities like Miami over such policies, but later these died down.

The president's dominating idea, previously tried out when he was Governor of California, was for large tax cuts combined with big reductions in government spending. The tax cuts duly made their appearance, but the economies somehow never materialized. Indeed, certain items of spending – especially defence and space research – were massively increased. Washington observers commented wryly on what they called 'Reaganomics': though welfare spending was cut by $110 billion a year the overall spending was going up, not down, and the deficit was increasing by $200 billion every year (the accumulated deficit by 1986 was over $2,000 billion). The effect of this, together with massive overseas spending, was that the dollar was under severe pressure and domestic interest rates moved upwards as the government was driven to increasing its borrowing.

In foreign affairs, Reagan took a firmly anti-communist line. He supported right-wing regimes in Latin America, Africa and the Middle East, and imposed trade sanctions on the USSR following a political crisis in Poland. The change in the Soviet leadership in November 1983 was followed by a steady deterioration in US–Soviet relations. Negotiations held in Geneva for the reduction of medium-range missiles were unsuccessful, and their failure led to an escalation of European missile deployment. Relations were badly strained in September 1983 following the destruction of a Korean passenger aircraft overflying Soviet airspace. In November there was considerable criticism of Reagan's foreign policy when the Americans occupied the Commonwealth island of Grenada in the West Indies. Reagan also attracted criticism in 1986 by launching an air blitz on Colonel Ghaddafi

❝Draw up a balance sheet for President Reagan: what light does it cast on the outcome of the presidential election of 1988?❞

of Libya and ordering more warships to patrol the Persian Gulf during the Iran–Iraq war. The transfer of power in the USSR to Mikhail Gorbachev in 1984 led, however, to increased diplomatic contacts between the USA and the Soviet Union, and disarmament talks were restarted. There were meetings in Geneva in 1985 and a summit meeting at Reykjavik in Iceland in 1986, but talks broke down over American unwillingness to negotiate their Strategic Defence Initiative (or SDI – sometimes called their 'Star Wars' policy in reference to a popular science-fiction film of the 1980s). Here he was pursuing a $26 billion research programme to determine the feasibility of a space-based defence system to give the USA immunity from nuclear attack. Prospects for more limited disarmament proposals in 1987, however, seemed likely to achieve greater success – even perhaps the total removal of missile weaponry from Europe.

Meanwhile, the society over which Reagan presided was becoming ever more divided into rich and poor. It had an air of sleaziness: drug-taking and drug-peddling were common; crime was rife in American cities; there were controversies over abortion clinics and surrogate motherhood; and after 1980 there was the rising danger – not only amongst the promiscuous – of AIDS. Yet, in spite of the 'Irangate' scandal in 1987, which seemed to connect the President's name with the sale of arms to Iran in order to give financial support to the Contra rebels in Nicaragua (which Congress had forbidden him to do) Reagan left the Presidency as popular as he was when he took it up, handing on the torch to his former Vice-President George Bush. Bush soon showed himself to have less of his predecessor's charm and professionalism, though he was something of a legend as the master of woolly hesitation. He experienced a brief blaze of glory as the conqueror of Saddam Hussein in the Gulf War (1991), but he was distinctly less successful in his home policies. He did not seriously address many of the country's most difficult social problems; he failed to balance the budget; and in spite of specific election promises, he was forced to increase taxes, much to the wrath of the Democrats in Congress. In the run-up to the presidential election of 1992 the fact that he seemed to be the strongest candidate was due less to his own merits than it was to the inability of the Democratic Party to field a credible candidate against him.

APPLIED MATERIALS

Texts and Atlases

B. Aspinwall, *The USA*, Blackie, 1987
B.W. Beacroft and M.A. Smale, *The Making of America*, Longman, 1987
A. B. Lancaster, *The Americas*, Arnold, 1985
D. B. O'Callaghan, *The United States Since 1945*, Longman, 1987
John O'Keefe, *America, 1870–1975*, Longman, 1987
John Simkin, *American Domestic Policy, 1945–80*, Spartacus, 1986
John Simkin, *American Foreign Policy, 1945–80*, Spartacus, 1986
Harriet Ward, *World Powers in the Twentieth Century, Part I*, Heinemann, 1985

Documentary Books

R.D. Heffner, (Ed.), *Documentary History of the United States*, Mentor, 1976
R.B. Morris, (Ed.) *Basic Documents in American History*, Anvil, 1965

Cassette/filmstrip programmes

Audio Learning, *The Cuban Missiles Crisis, 1962*, DM 09
Audio Learning, *The Kennedy Assassination, 1963*, DM 10
Audio Learning, *The First Moon Landing, 1969*, DM 11

EXAMINATION QUESTIONS

QUESTION 1
Write an essay to show how the USA was a power of world importance in your period. (NISEC)

QUESTION 2
(a) How great was the discrimination faced by blacks in the United States in the years immediately following the Second World War?
(b) Describe the tactics of and successes achieved by the Civil Rights Movement in the years up to 1970.
(c) Why have these successes been achieved? (SEG)

QUESTION 3
(a) It is 1951. Write a letter to a major American newspaper attacking the activities of Senator Joseph MacCarthy.
(b) In reply to the first letter write a second letter in which a supporter of Senator MacCarthy defends him against your attack.

(SEG)

OUTLINE ANSWERS

ANSWER 1
In your answer to Question 1 it is desirable to avoid too much in the way of description or narration; you should instead concentrate on the evaluation required in the question so that you can demonstrate effectively the higher skills that will secure greater credit. Of course a certain amount of description is unavoidable, but you ought to bear in mind that such work commands only a Level 1 mark, whereas relevant discussion of the matter of 'world importance' will get you to a higher level. The question can perhaps best be tackled by working out a number of paragraphs, each of which shows in a different way how the USA since 1945 (this being the period in question for this chapter) has been of world importance.

　　　Paragraph 1 might deal with the domestic situation in the USA, showing how from the point of view of population, resources, industrial and agricultural output, financial power and overseas spending the USA was of great world importance. It cultural influence is great: its films, TV programmes and music are played all over the world and its nationals overseas spread its influence day by day. Paragraph 2 might deal with its world role, showing how its participation in UNO and regional groupings like NATO and OAS give it a great say in world decisions; whilst its participation in international bodies aiming to relieve famine, protect health, foster economic development, etc., influences considerably the course of world events. Paragraph 3 might deal with the role of the USA in certain specific parts of the world, e.g. in Europe, where its missiles are stationed and where its influence on European defence policies can be seen: in the Middle East, where it plays an important part in Israel and the Persian Gulf; in the Far East, where it dominates the Pacific and has friendly relations with both China and Japan; and in Latin America, where its dominant economic position enables it in most cases to control its smaller and weaker neighbours. Paragraph 4 might deal with the question of armaments, illustrating America's original lead in the nuclear race and showing how important a part the USA played in the subsequent story, especially its critical role in the course of disarmament negotiations with the Soviet Union. In a concluding summary it could be pointed out that the USA is one of the two or three sides in the present world equation, and important on that account from the point of view of its underlying political philosophy; but it should be admitted that there are other factors in this equation too, and there are limits on the importance of the USA.

ANSWER 2

(a) Description of the types of discrimination faced by the US negroes will once again earn Level 1 marks in this question, but for higher marks there must be some evaluation of the question 'How great?' The best answers will show an element of comparative treatment; for instance, that the negroes were treated better after 1945 than they were, say, in the 1920s and 1930s, but still worse than whites expected to be treated in terms of education, accommodation, jobs, salaries and prospects.

(b) A description of the tactics employed by the Civil Rights Movement is called for in this part of the question, but for the higher range of marks it has to be linked with an estimation of 'success'. Successes can be seen at the social level in the inner cities, the factories and the more rural areas, even of the southern states, or in the quite impressive legislative record of the federal government in dealing with this problem; and at the political level, where an increasing number of negro persons have entered public life as magistrates, police officers, attorneys and even local mayors. But the rise of the Black Power movement revealed that by 1970 there were still many who thought that this degree of success was inadequate.

(c) Reasons here could include: the experience of the Second World War, when people of negro origin served with distinction and on terms of equality with whites; changing climate of opinion and rising expectations in American society and the rest of the world; the work of the Democrats, especially southern Democrats such as L.B. Johnson; the moderate and successful leadership of people such as Martin Luther King; and the changing attitude of US lawcourts in cases relating to race. Each of these reasons would need to be substantiated by one specific example.

ANSWER 3

This is an empathy question, and one that should be tackled in the first person and in the letter form required. You should not forget the style in which letters to the press are usually couched; if you are in doubt about this, you should look at the correspondence columns of the newspapers to see how it is done.

(a) You should in your letter deal with all the reasons such a correspondent might have for objection to MacCarthy's activities: misrepresentation, illiberality, 'guilt by association', character assassination, etc., showing how his activities may be said to be 'un-American' (the very charge he himself was bringing against those he denounced). It is permissible to cite the names and reputations of those Americans who take the same view as you do; it is even legitimate to question the political motives of MacCarthy during his 'witch-hunt'.

(b) As a supporter of MacCarthy you should show that you share some of his fears about communism, and seek to prove that a communist 'conspiracy' on the part of the disloyal, the misguided and the opportunistic in American society, if tolerated by the good-natured and easy-going majority, could have very serious consequences for the future. Some of the charges against leading public figures such as Dean Acheson and General Marshall could be repeated, and good use made of the case of Alger Hiss. You could conclude by suggesting that anyone wishing to suppress MacCarthy's enquiries had himself probably something to hide.

SUGGESTIONS FOR FURTHER WORK

1. Construct a table of post-war US presidents with their parties and the sizes of the votes they commanded in the electoral college. Who were their political opponents, and why were they defeated?
2. Find out what you can about the nature and purposes of education in US schools and colleges. What are the most obvious contrasts with this country?
3. Collect diagrams and photographs of US nuclear weaponry, and any other available performance data. Build up a file to show how nuclear weapons have developed since 1945.

STUDENT'S ANSWER – EXAMINER'S COMMENT

Question

Write an essay on the achievements and failures of Presidents of the U.S.A. between 1948 and 1968.

> **Factual knowledge here is quite good and material is presented in the right order.**

In 1945, President Truman tookover from Roosevelt when he died, and started his Fair Deal programme to finish Roosevelt's New Deal. He increased welfare services, protected the rights of trade unions and introduced more public works schemes to stop unemployment. Some Republicans thought he was too socialist, and accused him of being too soft on the Communists in China. There was a spy scare and Senator McCarthy, a Republican from Wisconsin, claimed he had uncovered nests of Communists high up in the U.S. government, and started a witch-hunt to unmask them. For a time there was sensational revelations and great public interest, but McCarthy fell into disgrace and the spy scandal blew over.

Truman withdrew from politics in 1952 and was succeeded by General Eisenhower who had made a great name for himself as a successful soldier during the Second World War. He was a Republican and went on with the work of halting communism both at home and abroad. The U.S.A. at this time was the richest country in the world, sending foreign aid to over sixty other governments, and at home there was a rising standard of living and great wealth and prosperity.

Eisenhower was followed in 1960 by the youngest President ever elected in the U.S.A., a Catholic from New England called J.F. Kennedy and only 43 years old. He brought energy and a new sense of purpose to U.S. affairs. With the 'New Frontier' policy he tried to start a new sense of direction towards greater social justice and fairer treatment of the blacks in American Society. He brought the same purpose to foreign affairs, where he successfully defended the U.S.A. at the time of the Cuban Missile Crisis. He also landed the first man on the Moon. But in 1963 he was assassinated in Dallas by Lee Harvey Oswald and power passed to his Vice-President, Lyndon B. Johnson.

Johnson carried out a big programme of reform called the 'Great Society' instead of the 'New Frontier'. The position

> **Missile is often misspelt in this way because of the American pronunciation of the word. It should in any case be the 'missiles crisis', since there was more than one missile.**

of Negro civil rights was improved during his years, but he
became more deeply and deeply involved in the fighting in
Vietnam until over half a million American soldiers were
there but he was not able to win the war. Eventually in 1968
he did not stand for election again, and the new Democratic
candidate was Hubert Humphrey.

This is broadly a narrative of successive Presidencies, with little or no explicit reference to achievements and failures. It would not score so highly as an answer which discusses the achievements and failures of each of the Presidents, as asked for in the question.

THE DEVELOPMENT OF THE COLD WAR

GETTING STARTED

Even at the time when they were allies in the war against Nazi Germany, the communist leaders of the Soviet Union and the leaders of the western nations never fully trusted each other. Relations between them were more formal than cordial. Though they shared common objectives in their fight, they did not do much to share their strategies, keeping most of their plans secret from each other. Western planes, for example, were usually denied the use of Russian landing grounds in the later stages of the war, even though this would have been a great convenience to them.

ORIGINS OF THE COLD WAR

POST-WAR EUROPE

POST-WAR GERMANY

THE KOREAN WAR

HISTORICAL DEVELOPMENTS

ORIGINS OF THE COLD WAR

After the war each side distrusted the intentions of the other. US leaders like Roosevelt and Truman gave generous names to their objectives, talking of peace, freedom and prosperity; but the Russians saw American aims as being imperialism and world economic domination. The USSR, on the other hand, claimed to be fighting for the ideals of communism and for world revolution, but the western allies suspected that this ideological camouflage disguised the underlying aim of expansion. By May 1945, the Red Army had poured into central and eastern Europe, and was now anxious to consolidate and defend its gains. The United Nations Organization, set up at the San Francisco Conference in April, seemed already to be an American-dominated body which could not be expected to offer genuine arbitration in the event of a struggle between East and West. They felt the only thing to do was to secure firm control of their bargaining counters in Europe if they were to prepare against the possibility of a Western take-over. Their former allies saw this as evidence of Russian arrogance and aggression; the Russians themselves, on the other hand, knew that the struggle with Nazi Germany had sapped their strength, and now they sought to prevent the West from finding out how overstretched their resources were.

The dropping of atomic bombs on Japan in early August sowed further mistrust. At their meeting in Potsdam only a week or two before, President Truman had deliberately concealed from Stalin the existence of the atomic bomb; now his secretary of state James Byrnes, felt able to suggest: 'The bomb might well put us in a position to dictate our own terms'. Byrnes seemed to think that the use of a weapon which the Russians did not possess would 'make Russia more manageable in Europe'. The exact opposite was the case. Russian leaders regarded the American action as evidence of their bad faith, and this reinforced their opinion that Truman was hatching some evil plot against the Soviet Union. Had they known of it, they would have found unwelcome confirmation of their view in the order issued to Montgomery by Churchill in the closing stages of the war to keep the German armies intact 'in case they had to be used against the Russians'.

Not only were relations bad in Europe, but soon the Russians found themselves eased out of Iran by the western allies, Soviet influence being replaced, as was said later , by the USA 'not with troops and revolution, but silently with dollars in support of the status quo'. The oil concessions promised to the Soviet Union failed to materialize and before long Iran was transformed into an American satellite. The USSR became all the more determined to resist in future further encroachments on their sphere of influence by what had by now become known in Moscow as 'the Iranian method'.

POST-WAR EUROPE

By May 1945, much of central and eastern Europe was under the occupation of the Red Army, the countries there having been liberated by the advance of Russian troops. Until the mistrust already described grew up between the former allies, it seems likely that the Soviet leadership had no intention of retaining its conquests permanently; but as suspicion deepened Stalin came to the conclusion that the only way to be safe was to establish undisputed Soviet control of the occupied territories through the establishment there of governments submissive to Russian wishes.

Such control was not difficult to bring about. The pre-war dictatorships had maintained themselves in power chiefly through ruthless police forces and a corrupt bureaucracy, which the democratic movements of the time were too weak to challenge. All that had to be done was to graft on to the existing system the supposed objectives of the 'revolution', nominally on behalf of the people. The Soviet leaders had an excuse for this in that during the war the former right-wing leaders had sided with the Nazis and now seemed ripe for destruction. Really, the only thing that was different was that in 1945 the Western powers had suddenly

> **If you refer to maps as you read this it will help you to trace out the fate of Europe in detail.**

developed an interest in the fates of these poor ignorant masses whereas in the inter-war years they had simply disregarded them.

In Poland, efforts were made in 1945 to merge the wartime government in exile under Stanislaw Mikolajczyk and the newly-formed Committee of National Liberation, operating under Russian sponsorship form Lublin; but this broke down and communists took control, forcing Mikolajczyk to flee to safety in London. Much the same thing happened in Hungary, where the prime minister phoned in his resignation whilst on holiday in Switzerland when communists ousted their colleagues in a government coup. In Bulgaria, on the other hand, Nikola Petkov, leader of the Agrarian Party, was arrested by the communists and actually hanged, and a people's democracy was established under communist leadership at the end of 1947. There was a similar coup in Czechoslovakia early in 1948: non-communists were not allowed to stand in the elections; Jan Masaryk, the son of one of the founding fathers of the country, was found dead in mysterious circumstances and President Beneš despairingly resigned.

The opposite was happening in Turkey and Greece. The Turkish government was not particularly popular, and the army was weak and in need of re-equipment; in addition it was under some pressure from the USSR to open the Straits to Soviet warships. At the same time in Greece, British forces were struggling to bring the country under British control. British-backed Premier Tsaldaris silenced the communist opposition and engineered an election victory under British supervision which made possible the return of the discredited monarchy. The result was a civil war in which the British lent every assistance to the right-wing government to crush the communist insurgents. Stalin looked on but, anxious to have a free hand himself in the countries his troops had occupied, decided not to intervene. When Britain, whose resources were exhausted by the Second World War, could no longer support the expense of the campaign, its government gave notice of its intention to pull out in 1947. The Americans then decided to act, the secretary of state Dean Acheson, saying : 'If the British are getting out of Greece and Turkey, and if we don't go in, the Russians will'. The result was the ***Truman Doctrine*** in March 1947 in which the president promised to support 'free peoples' against 'attempted subjugation by armed minorities or by outside pressures.' He did not name communism as the enemy, but no one had any doubt about what he meant.

3 ▷ POST-WAR GERMANY

In 1945 the allies had poured into Germany and occupied it. They agreed that Germany had to be demilitarized, denazified and democratized – for a time they wanted to deindustrialize it too, until it became obvious that such a policy was not very practical. They worked out a formula for reparations to be paid to the victors, and they set up a control council to decide matters affecting Germany as a whole.

Such agreements could not long mask the fundamental lack of trust between the powers. The idea of treating Germany as a whole, so that an agreed peace settlement would follow and the occupying forces then withdraw from the country and leave it to itself, soon faded into improbability; instead West and East used Germany to promote their own visions of the future.

The appalling physical destruction in Germany of both agriculture and industry leading to the threat of mass starvation, together with the breakdown of German civil and military discipline, forced the allies to take complete control of the country. Even after their partial restoration none of the occupation zones was very viable, and the allies had to go on importing large quantities of foodstuffs. At the same time the USA rebuffed Russian requests for assistance. In 1945 the Soviet government asked for a billion dollar loan partly to meet occupation costs. Unfortunately, the US government 'lost' the request. When it turned up months afterwards, Truman promised to 'discuss' the loan but attached such conditions to it that the Russians decided they would be better off without it. The US decision to cancel the wartime lend-lease arrangements was regarded by the Soviet Union as further pressure from America, and one which entitled the Russians to disregard their promise to their allies not to exceed certain limits in their reparations demands.

THE MARSHALL PLAN

Events then moved swiftly. At the end of 1946, the British and the Americans merged their zones into a single economic unit known as Bizonia. In June 1947 there followed the **Marshall Plan**, an ambitious programme of financial aid for Europe. Over the next few years about fifteen billion dollars was to be made available for post-war reconstruction. It was the work of the US secretary of state, George C. Marshall, and formed the financial counterpart to the Truman Doctrine. Theoretically the Plan was open to all states: 'Our policy is directed not against any country or doctrine, but against hunger, poverty, desperation and chaos; its purpose should be the revival of a working economy in the world.' Unfortunately the Russians claimed to discern behind the apparent generosity of the plan the dark hand of dollar imperialism and turned it down. Nevertheless in February 1948, the European recovery programme to dispense Marshall Aid was established, followed in March by a defence pact setting up the Brussels Treaty Organization. In March, too, Russia withdrew from the control council at work in Germany. In June the western powers introduced a new German currency intended for use in all the zones, but the Russians rejected the proposal when the US authorities refused them the right to print it as required. The Soviet authorities, who had already been harassing western communications with their zones in Berlin, now stepped up pressure to get their former allies out of the city, and in June cut off all road, rail and canal links entirely. Over two million citizens seemed likely to starve unless the allies could find some way to feed them. East and West stood suddenly on the brink of war.

THE BERLIN AIRLIFT

❝Detailed knowledge of this episode is important.❞

The answer was the Berlin airlift which for eleven months kept open the lines of communication between the west and the beleaguered Berliners. Round-the-clock flights took place, with planes landing at the two (later three) Berlin airfields every minute or so. Over two million tons of supplies were flown in, including foodstuffs, petrol and even coal. Eventually Stalin tired of his brinkmanship and gave up the struggle, raising the blockade in May 1949 even more abruptly than he had imposed it.

The Berlin blockade produced little other than a hardening of the hostility between East and West. Soon two new German states came into existence, each sponsored by its occupying power. In the west there was the Federal Republic of Germany, in the east the Democratic Republic of Germany. Since the Germans were not yet fully trusted, neither republic was fully independent at first, but by 1955 they had become sovereign states. Meanwhile, as the result of a joint Anglo–American initiative, the Brussels pact had been enlarged in April 1949 into the North Atlantic Treaty Organization, to which Canada, Iceland, Norway, Denmark, the Benelux countries, France, Portugal and Italy adhered, later to be joined by Greece, Turkey and Western Germany. The Soviet response was to develop the Cominform (already refounded in 1947) as an organ of communist planning and propaganda, and, in 1955, to launch the Warsaw Pact, comprising the Soviet Union and its smaller eastern European allies. In September 1949 the Russians exploded their first atomic bomb, from which developed a nuclear stand-off which has persisted to the present day. The two alliances continued to confront each other across the Iron Curtain after 1955, both hanging together remarkably well in the thirty years after their formation; but whether in future years the signs of stress developing within the two systems will eventually result in their collapse is a matter still very much open to question.

❝Some up-to-date knowledge of these bodies would be useful.❞

4 ▷ THE KOREAN WAR

The communist threat, however, was not confined to Europe. In the USA itself President Truman, after 1948, was under considerable pressure from Senator Joseph McCarthy and his supporters to clamp down on what was said to be a communist conspiracy within the United States comprising traitors, spies and even senior members of the State Department; they were suspected of sharing with an odd mixture of academics, movie actors and homosexuals the wish to overthrow freedom and democracy in favour of a Stalinist dictatorship. Beyond the USA

Chiang Kai-shek, the former leader of the Chinese Kuomintang, was overthrown in 1949 and compelled to flee to Formosa (Taiwan) when his forces were defeated by Mao Tse-tung, chairman of the Chinese Communist Party. In that country the People's Republic of China was set up in the autumn of 1949 at Peking. Somehow the McCarthyites contrived to suggest that the Chinese revolution was all America's fault, and that a little more diligence on the part of the US government could have prevented it from happening.

In April 1950 an American defence committee produced a document known as NSC 68 (National Security Council paper no. 68) advancing the view that the communists' recent victory in China and the recent Russian testing of the atom bomb were both part of the same threatening pattern – the rising tide of world communism. The committee recommended that the USA should 'strike out on a bold and massive program of rebuilding the West's defensive potential to surpass that of the Soviet world, and of meeting each fresh challenge promptly and unequivocally'. They went on to say: 'This new concept of the security needs of the nation calls for an annual appropriation of the order of 50 billion dollars, or not much below the former wartime levels'. So a new note of toughness crept into America's dealings with both Russia and China.

This toughness was particularly evident in Korea. This country, divided between the USSR and the USA in 1945, had been evacuated by their troops by 1950, though the separate political regimes they had sponsored there were both still in existence. Neither regime had much to recommend it. In the north, Kim Il Sung embarked on communist policies every bit as authoritarian as those of Stalin himself, whilst Syngman Rhee's corrupt police state in the south brutalized and terrorized its opponents to an extent which western news correspondents were forbidden to report. The only thing that both leaders agreed was that they could no longer accept a divided nation, though they were far from agreeing the form that their eventual reunion should take. Which of them started the train of events which led to the civil war between them it is difficult to say with certainty. The favourite Western version of events was that, acting on orders directly from stalin, the troops belonging to his Eastern puppet launched an unprovoked and quite unexpected attack on the south in June 1950. Stalin is supposed to have launched the attack in a bid to show that it was he, not Mao Zedong, who was the master of the communist world, his intention being to threaten Japan, his former enemy and now the chief base of US forces in the Pacific area.

In fact it is unlikely that Stalin would have been keen on such adventures. His forces were still very much feeling the effects of the Second World War, and in any case were too heavily committed in Europe to be easily redeployed in the Far East. At the same time, Russia's atomic weaponry was totally inadequate for an international confrontation. Furthermore, he had little faith in the long continuation of Syngman Rhee's government in South Korea, where it had fared badly in an election only about a month before the invasion. Above all, Russian representatives had recently walked out of the Security Council of UNO because of a quarrel arising out of communist China's exclusion from membership by the USA. If the Soviet leader knew that an invasion was about to be launched it seems unlikely that he would have absented himself deliberately from the only organization which could effectively prevent international intervention in Korea to protect the government of the south by vetoing any proposal to that effect. Nevertheless, this was the explanation of the affair which the Western powers chose to accept.

The war in Korea was a long-drawn-out affair, with fighting ranging from one end of the country to the other. In its initial attack, the North Koreans penetrated deep into South Korea, pinning back South Korean and UN (largely US) forces in the Pusan pocket. Then, with the assistance of a seaborne landing behind the North Korean lines at Inchon, the war swung the other way and the communist forces were thrust back against the Yalu River in the far north of the country. Chinese intervention followed and North Korea was cleared of UN troops, the campaign ending with an armistice in 1953 close to the 38th Parallel – the point at which it had first begun.

After the Korean War the alliance network was extended in further regional security pacts. The USA strengthened its military links with Japan and signed a defence agreement with Australia and New Zealand, and further alliances with the

66 This topic ought to be developed in some detail. See, for example, the applied materials section of this chapter. 99

Nationalists in Taiwan and with the governments of Thailand and the Philippines were made.

In 1954, these arrangements were unified in the form of SEATO – the South-East Asia Treaty Organization – incorporating, as well as all the countries above (with the exception of Japan), Britain, France and Pakistan. Alongside SEATO went CENTO – the Central Treaty Organization – formerly known as the Baghdad Pact, and comprising Turkey, Pakistan, Iran and Iraq (until 1959) in addition to Britain and the USA. Both SEATO and CENTO lasted until well into the 1970s.

By 1953, President Truman had been replaced by Eisenhower as president of the United States, and Stalin himself, the supposed originator of the Cold War, was dead. Whether his successors would be more peaceably inclined remained to be seen.

IDEAS AND PRINCIPLES

BRINKMANSHIP

The art of going as close to war as a leader dares without actually starting it. Thus a national leader may take his demands to the brink of conflict but then withdraw, or compel his opponent to withdraw. If it is a game of 'diplomatic chicken' in which the defeated party suffers considerable humiliation.

COLD WAR

A war stopping short of military action, but being conducted by both sides with economic and propaganda weapons and often making frequent use of the media. Thus the struggle between the USA and the USSR after 1945 was of long duration but never reached the point of open military conflict except occasionally and by accident.

CONFRONTATION

The situation of being face to face with an enemy and on the brink of conflict. The situation may be resolved by open conflict, as in the case of the civil war in Korea, or else by negotiation, as in the case of the Iran crisis of 1946, or by the withdrawal of one of the parties, as in the case of Stalin over the Berlin crisis of 1948–49.

CONTAINMENT

An action to enclose, or to set limits to the development of some opposing force, often by pacts or alliances. Thus the US government tried to confine communism to the areas in Europe where it already existed, and to resist its extension to other areas of Europe, seeing to achieve this through Marshall Aid, the Truman Doctrine and NATO.

COUP

From the French 'coup d'état': a sudden and illegal change of government; a forcible seizure of power. Thus the communists were attempting a coup in Greece in 1946, and successfully brought about one in Czechoslovakia in 1948.

DOLLAR IMPERIALISM

The strategy of enforcing the economic dependence of weaker countries on the USA through the granting of dollar aid. The US government could keep the smaller states of western Europe compliant to American wishes without actually having to go to the lengths of taking over their governments.

IRON CURTAIN

A frontier or boundary rigidly dividing one ideology from another, characterized by the lack of free movement of people or ideas between them. Thus the frontier in Europe dividing the pro-Russian communist states of eastern Europe from the remainder of western Europe is called the 'Iron Curtain'. In the case of China, a similar barrier is sometimes known as the 'Bamboo Curtain'.

SATELLITE

A smaller state under the influence of a larger neighbour, like a smaller planet in orbit round a bigger one. Thus eastern European states are sometimes accused of being satellites of the Soviet Union.

STAND-OFF

A situation of deadlock or stalemate where two powers stand apart from each other in mutual suspicion, and where their capacities are about equal. Thus a stand-off in the form of mutual nuclear deterrence was achieved by the 1960s with the concept of what became known as Mutual Assured Destruction (or MAD).

STATUS QUO

From the Latin *'status quo ante'*: the situation as it existed before. A state which is likely to lose by an alteration of the existing state of things will on this account object to changes in the status quo.

APPLIED MATERIALS

Texts and Atlases

C. Bown and P.J. Mooney, *Cold War to Detente*, Heinemann (Studies in Modern History), 1986

B. Catchpole, *Map History of the Modern World*, Heinemann, 1976

B. Catchpole, *Map History of Our Own Times*, Heinemann, 1983

H. Higgins, *The Cold War*, Heinemann, 1984

E.G. Rayner, *International Affairs*, (History of the 20th-Century World) Arnold, 1983

R.N. Rundle, *International Affairs, 1939–79*, Hodder & Stoughton, 1981

M. Simons, *Three Giant Powers*, OUP, 1976

H. Ward, *World Powers in the Twentieth Century*, BBC & Heinemann, 1985

J.B. Watson, *Success in Twentieth Century World Affairs*, Murray, 1984

Documentary books

R. Morgan, *The Unsettled Peace*, BBC, 1974

A.B. Lancaster, *From Containment to Coexistence*, Hill & Fell, (Archive Series), 1975

Video programme

Europe Since World War II, EAV

EXAMINATION QUESTIONS

QUESTION 1

Explain the reasons for the establishment and the significance of three of the following mutual defence alliances:

(a) NATO
(b) Warsaw Pact
(c) SEATO
(d) CENTO   (ULEAC)

QUESTION 2

Use the maps below showing Korea at different times in the 1950s to help answer the questions which follow.

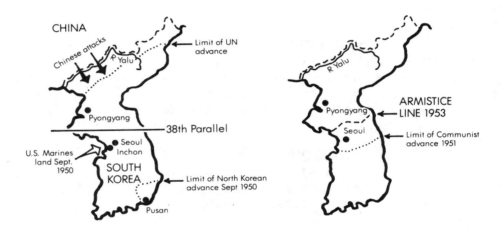

(a) (i) According to these maps, who fought whom in the Korean War? (2 marks)
     (ii) Briefly explain the significance of the '38th Parallel'. (2 marks)
(b) Why did so many countries become involved in the Korean War? (6 marks)
(c) 'The Korean War achieved nothing: by the end of it both sides were back where they started.' Explain fully whether or not you agree with this statement. (15 marks)

                                                   (Total 25 marks) (MEG)

QUESTION 3

Write two reasoned reports:

(a) One from a senior Soviet diplomat to the Moscow Politburo urging the imposition of a blockade on Berlin in the spring of 1948;
(b) The other from a senior US diplomat to the Ccuncil of NATO in the autumn of 1949 assessing western achievements in defeating the blockade.

                                                        (AEB/SEG)

OUTLINE ANSWERS

ANSWER 1

The first question is divided into (a), (b), (c), and (d), but only three of the four parts are required in your answer. There will be approximately equal credit for each of the three, say 7,7, and 6, if out of 20 marks. In each case, you will note, the question asks you to discuss reasons for the establishment and significance, so there should be a specific focus on each of these. Do not be tempted in the case of the former to go into too much detail about the historical circumstances surrounding the establishment of the alliance in question; it is easy to get carried away into a lengthy and undiscriminating narrative which wastes a lot of time and does not earn many marks. What you say should relate to reasons and should introduce only as much circumstantial detail as is needed to make the reasons convincing. It is not necessary, for example, in your answer to (a) to give a blow-by-blow account of the Berlin airlift in order to explain the establishment of NATO, though obviously some attention to the German situation is called for if you are to write a good answer. As far as significance is concerned, you should make some attempt to deal with the purposes which each alliance was meant to serve, and with the extent to which these purposes were in fact achieved. Significance could also be interpreted to include the general effects on world relations which the alliance produced. It would be legitimate to observe, for example, in (b), that the Russians have operated much stricter military and political controls over the Warsaw Pact countries than do the Americans over NATO; and that the efforts, for example, of the Hungarians to leave the pact in 1956, or of some of the Czechoslovakians in 1968, have produced a much more savage reaction from fellow pact members than would have been the case in the West.

ANSWER 2

There is a similar sectionalization in Question 2, but the mark tariffs attached show that equal treatment is not expected for its various components. The answers to (a), subdivided into (i) and (ii), do not amount to more than 4 marks altogether, whilst the answer to (c) is marked out of a total of 15 marks. In the case of the answer to (a) (i), a study of the maps provides some stimulus for the memory, since it reveals that China, the United States and the United Nations were involved in the war; but you will have to call on the resources of your memory to be able to say that the war started as a civil war between North and South Korea. The answer to (a) (ii) is even more of a memory item, though the map does make clear the minor point that the war ended in 1953 in much the same location as it had begun three years earlier. An accurate answer to (b) can be provided in one short sentence ('The Security Council called on members of the United Nations to send contingents of troops to Korea to repel the aggression of the North Koreans, and thirty-two of them did.'); but it should be noted that the tariff for this subquestion is 6 marks, and some elaboration will be called for if you are to get more than 1 or 2 marks. Such elaboration could properly deal with their motives, their relations with the United States, the general state of world opinion at the time or international apprehensions aroused by the success of Mao Zedong in the Chinese Revolution, since all these would indicate your good understanding of the subject matter; alternatively, your answer could point out that the contribution of many participating countries was only very nominal, and that in fact the war was largely an American affair from start to finish. Your answer to (c), however, should be given the fullest treatment as this part carries more than half the marks. Here it should be pointed out that to judge the effect of the Korean War solely in terms of the geographical locality in which it started and finished is a very superficial judgement; the war in fact achieved a good deal, but most of it was on the negative side. It was enormously expensive in terms of lives and property, not least of the Korean people themselves; it embittered their relations with the outside world for more than twenty years; it helped to keep Korea weak and divided from then until the present time; even as a limited exercise in international co-operation under the auspices of UNO it produced little effect and served only to deepen the reluctance of many states to become involved again in future. If you wish to point to something more positive than this, you could discuss the formation of SEATO and show how this emphasized US leadership in policies concerned to do with the Pacific area, perhaps even suggesting that the acceptance of the Colombo Plan in 1951 was a clear indication that the USA was determined to tackle those problems of poverty and misery which might force some Asian states into the hands of the communists; but even

Americans might think that policies which ultimately led them into the costly and fruitless Vietnamese War were not in the last analysis much of an achievement.

ANSWER 3

The third question calls for some empathetic identification with the Russians and with the Americans at the time of the Berlin blockade; the difficulty is in making the mental effort that makes it possible to empathize with both sides and not simply with one. The Russian would, of course, produce arguments in favour of the imposition of a blockade: to consolidate the Soviet position in East Germany, to remove a focus of disaffection for eastern European states with Russian policies, to end the irksome presence of the western allies in the former German capital and limit espionage and subversion in the Russian zone, and so forth. He might also mention current economic and financial problems, and offer comments on the reparations question and the question of the new German currency. He would see the whole matter through Russian, communist and east European eyes. The answer would be stronger if he were made to express views which such a person might have been expected to hold: that the western allies were seeking to use West Berlin as a 'capitalist shop-window' where they could display all the products which showed how far behind in material standards and industrial technology the Russians were; or that the West was determined to use its wealth to destabilize Russia's position in eastern Europe. The American, on the other hand, should be made to assess western achievements as the result of the blockade. He would represent this not only as a successful defence of the rights of Berliners, but as an effective demonstration of US power and authority in Europe, a confirmation of allied solidarity and a move towards the closer integration of the three western zones of Germany. He would almost certainly link it with the formation of the NATO alliance. Again the answer would be improved by expressions of opinion which were characteristic of US views at that time: that Russian interference in the lives of the German people was unacceptable to right thinking people; that America and the western allies had a moral commitment to freedom and democracy; and so on. Three other points are perhaps worthy of some attention: firstly that there is a gap of more than a year between the two reports; secondly that both the characters who are supposed to be involved are diplomats, and would on this account probably use vocabulary and terminology appropriate to such people; and thirdly that the audience to which they are addressing themselves – the Politburo and the council of NATO – are ones which will naturally colour the kind of comments that they both make. This is a question which calls for a more subtle degree of empathetic identification than many, but not one which directly requires the use of the word 'I'; nevertheless it does demand an accurate and detailed understanding of the international situation in Germany in 1948 and 1949. Credit will not only be given for factual accuracy in relation to the historical events that are described, but also for your understanding of the feelings of both sides at the time of the crisis.

SUGGESTIONS FOR FURTHER WORK

1. Compare the texts of President Truman's speech announcing the Truman Doctrine (12 March 1947) and Secretary of State George C. Marshall's speech announcing the Marshall Plan (5 June 1947). Tip: abbreviations of these speeches are reprinted in Harriet Ward, *World Powers in the Twentieth Century* (Study Topic 13). How true is it that these two speeches show the two sides of US policy at that time?

2. Imagine that you are a young person of about school-leaving age in Berlin in the winter of 1948–49, and that you are living in the British occupation zone of the city. Your father works for a transportation firm as a lorry driver

moving supplies, your mother works as an infant teacher and your elder sister works in a local government office dealing with cases of unemployment. Write a letter to relatives in Western Germany explaining your experiences during the Berlin airlift.

In attempting this exercise, you should make use of all the opportunities which the question provides. The reported experiences of your father, mother and elder sister can be made quite as interesting and important as your own impressions. How did people get about in a beleaguered city in winter-time? How were they affected by shortages of everyday supplies? What effects did the blockade produce on prices and wages? What were the effects on West Berlin's industrial production and on the lives of the men who worked in the city's factories? What were the relations between the Berliners and the troops of the occupying power? It is useful, too, to describe your feelings: only a little while earlier you have listened as a child to the threatening drone of allied planes overhead during one of the many dreadful raids on the city by the RAF or the USAAF; what do you now think of the allied airmen who are flying in the badly-needed supplies? Do you agree with the small group who laid flowers on the local grave of an air crew who were killed when they overshot the runway in dense fog? These are a few of the points which your letter might contain.

3. Collect further information about Berlin in the period after 1950 and show that the question of Berlin was an ongoing international problem for many years. Tip: you could begin with the information in Brian Catchpole's *Map History of the Modern World*, in the text of Section 54.

4. Look for photographs of the frontier dividing east from west (the 'Iron Curtain') such as those in B.J. Elliott, *Western Europe After Hitler*, Longman (Modern Times), page 30 or E.G. Rayner, *International Affairs*, page 82. What do photographs such as these tell us about East–West relations after 1945?

5. Compare the texts of the North Atlantic Treaty Organization and the Warsaw Pact. Identify the similarities and the differences between these treaties. Tip: abridged versions of the texts of these treaties are reprinted in Roger Morgan (Document 12 and Document 18).

6. Find out what you can about the political career of Senator Joseph McCarthy, and explain the effect which his views produced on American attitudes and policies during Truman's second administration. Tip: a textbook of American history might help you here.

7. Collect further information on the later history of Korea, in the years from 1953 to the present. Does this information show UN intervention in the period 1950–53 to have been useful and constructive, or the opposite?

STUDENT'S ANSWER – EXAMINER'S COMMENTS

Question

You are a member of one of the Allied occupation armies in Germany at the end of the Second World War. What were your feelings when the Berlin Blockade was introduced by Soviet Forces in 1948?

❝Provides useful biographical detail and sets later opinions in a clear perspective.❞

❝An imaginative and quite accurate account of actions and feelings at the end of the war.❞

❝An appropriate reference to the memories of the 1930s, and good use of the name Attlee.❞

❝This is a good example of differentiated empathy i.e. it shows that not everybody in 1945–48 thought alike.❞

❝An excellent answer on the whole. A very high standard of writing and expression, showing much imagination.❞

As a member of the Allied armies in Germany in 1948 I have strong feelings about the Soviet blockade of Berlin. I am a staff sergeant of the British Army of Occupation of the Rhine attached to the Motorized part of the British Ninth Army. Before the war I was a skilled lathe operator employed by Rolls Royce Motors of Derby.

We entered Germany in the spring of 1945 with deep feelings against the Nazis and under strict orders not to mix with the German people who had accepted their leaders' actions. We looked forward to a long period of co-operation with the Russians, who had a different political system which we did not entirely agree with, but they had fought well during the war. Some of my mates had told me enthusiastically of their reactions when in their eastwards advance they had met the Russians moving west. Though they had not been able to speak because they didn't know each other's language, they had danced together arm-in-arm, and had exchanged gifts and souvenirs. Now that the source of the evil in Germany had been blotted out they looked forward to a better world in future, with any disputes being peacefully settled by the United Nations.

Not many of us looked forward to the coming of an inevitable revolution against the capitalists like the Russians did, but the hardship and unemployment of the 1930s had left unpleasant memories in the minds of the older men and we were all agreed that a lot of changes in our system were overdue. Prime Minister Attlee in England thought much the same. So we didn't fully accept the early stories we heard about the Russians mistrusting us and grabbing hold of all they could lay their hands on in the eastern zone.

But the Russians turned out to be much less friendly than we had hoped, and the newspapers gave us almost daily examples of their failure to co-operate with us. Of course, there were soldiers amongst us who did not accept everything they read in the newspapers and who said that Churchill and other anti-communists in high positions were renewing old feuds and were determined to strike against the Soviets whilst they still had the atom bomb and all the advantages that gave them. They respected Stalin and admired the great efforts which the Russians had made during the war and the casualties they had suffered.

When the Russians imposed the Berlin Blockade there was deep disappointment that all our hopes for the future had been spoiled; those who supported the Russians were puzzled. We watched with dismay as they closed the roads and the railways and even the canals, and were excited though worried when the Allies started to fly supplies into Berlin during the Berlin airlift.

THE
COLD WAR
AND
DETENTE

EARLY REACTIONS
COEXISTENCE AND
CRISIS
THE SINO-SOVIET
SPLIT
THE ARMS RACE
CHINA COMES IN
FROM THE COLD

G E T T I N G   S T A R T E D

The death of Stalin removed from the scene one of the main figures in the Cold War. Soon after, the feeling began to grow in Russia that some sort of compromise with the western powers was possible. From early 1953 the Soviets seemed willing to negotiate. They withdrew their troops from their bases in Finland. In February they signed a peace treaty with Austria under which they recognized the independence of that country in return for a promise of its future neutrality. Khrushchev went to Belgrade, where, surprisingly, he told Marshal Tito that there was 'more than one road to socialism', abruptly reversing the policy of his predecessor in isolating Yugoslavia. In July the Russians accepted an armistice in Korea after months of fruitless negotiation.

HISTORICAL DEVELOPMENTS

EARLY REACTIONS

At first the US government was not impressed with Russian changes after 1953 The republicans, back in power under Eisenhower, were not prepared to renounce their hostility. Eisenhower chose as his secretary of state John Foster Dulles, who until his death was unrelentingly anti-Russian. In his very first speech he declared 'To all those suffering under Communist slavery let us say: " You can count on us".' His assurances, however, did little for the workers who rebelled in East Germany in June 1953; their government used tanks to crush the revolt, and Khrushchev's policy turned out to be every bit as harsh as Stalin's before him. Dulles began a build-up of nuclear weapons, including the new and much more powerful H-bomb, in an effort to 'place more reliance on deterrent power'; but in August the USSR it-self tested an H-bomb and the USA lost its advantage over its rival. Events in the east also upset Dulles. Tension between the Chinese communists on the mainland and the exiled nationalists on Taiwan had steadily been increasing, and Dulles, firmly convinced that Mao Zedong was little more than a Soviet puppet, firmly up-held Chiang Kai-shek. Early in 1955 the communists began bombarding the off-shore islands of Quemoy and Matsu. The USA called in its Pacific fleet and even threatened the use of nuclear weapons against the mainland. Further south, in Indo-China, there was a similar story. Here there was a war between the French, seeking to re-establish their colonial rule in the country after the war, and an Indo-Chinese guerrilla force led by Ho Chi Minh, which was equally anxious to get rid of them. At first the US government had no desire to be seen propping up an out-of-date colonial government; but the French were clever enough to play on American fears of creeping communism, and eventually secured their help. In April 1954 Eisenhower began to worry about the future of south-east Asia, fearing that a communist victory in one country might send them all tumbling like a row of dominoes into enemy hands. This **'domino theory'** seemed all the more plausible when the French were finally beaten at Dien Bien Phu in May and began to withdraw from the country.

> **There is something to be said for making this a special study topic.**

In July agreement was reached at Geneva to neutralize Laos and Cambodia, and to divide Vietnam into two along the 17th Parallel, leaving the north in the hands of the communists and the south in the hands of Bao Dai, the French puppet emperor. The idea was that the two halves would shortly hold elections and would be reunited under a commonly accepted government. Unfortunately by the time the elections were due in 1955, the south had passed into the control of Ngo Dinh Diem, who refused to take part in them and set about increasing his armed forces in order to prolong his control of the country.

All the same, in the course of 1955, the prospects for international harmony seemed to brighten. The Russians seemed pleased to have the Americans treat them as equals and adopted a less strident tone. In Moscow, Izvestia produced the headline 'A New Era in International Relations Has Begun'. In the USA, even Secretary of State Dulles seemed less hawkish.

CO-EXISTENCE AND CRISIS

In February 1956, Khrushchev used the occasion of the twentieth party congress of the Soviet Communist Party to announce basic changes in Russian thinking. He made a dramatic and unexpected attack on Stalin, accusing him of tyranny and self-glorification. He also tried to update the rather musty ideological line, which had for some time lagged behind the realities of Soviet strategical thinking. To the eastern European countries he seemed to be offering greater tolerance by his emphasis on 'different roads to socialism'; to the developing world he seemed to offer the chance of peaceful socialist development instead of inevitable revolution; very importantly, too, he offered an olive branch to the West by announcing his idea of peaceful co-existence.

The debunking of Stalin, whose reputation rested on his supposed infallibility, naturally undermined the authority of his eastern European puppets, whose authoritarian behaviour was closely modelled on his own. In East Berlin, industrial workers called a general strike and full-scale military intervention by Soviet tanks was necessary to crush it; the party leader, Walter Ulbricht, got a very nasty shock before he was back in the saddle. In Poland, too, economic and political grievances led to revolt, and the popular communist leader, Gomulka, previously deposed by Stalin for the crime of 'Titoism' – the unforgivable sin of thinking for himself – came back to power. In Hungary, Gerö, first secretary of the Communist Party after Rakosi, was forced by popular pressure to restore Imre Nagy as prime minister. Nagy introduced liberalizing measures, freed the media from public control, did away with the one-party system and called fresh elections. More seriously, he proposed to leave the Warsaw Pact. To communists his political reforms were shocking enough, but his intention to break ranks with his allies seemed to threaten the whole cohesion of eastern Europe and in particular the security of the USSR. The West welcomed these developments exultantly. But whilst the world's attention was diverted by the Suez crisis, the Soviets moved in tanks and troops and brutally restored order, carrying off Nagy and unceremoniously executing him in favour of a 'safer' leader in the person of Janos Kadar.

This topic deserves special attention.

SUEZ

What were the connections between the Hungarian crisis and the Suez crisis?

The Suez crisis heightened tension in a different way. Here the USA refused to give its backing to the Anglo–French invasion of Egypt, designed to overthrow the Egyptian leader, Colonel Nasser, and stem the rising tide of Arab nationalism. In the UN Security Council the world witnessed the unusual sight of the USA and the USSR voting together against Anglo–French imperialism. The two countries got their wrists publicly slapped and had to withdraw their troops, whilst President Nasser's reputation soared high in the Arab world. Britain and France both lost a lot of face, and it was a long time before some of their leaders forgave either the United States or the United Nations.

1958, however, saw a more usual alignment of the powers reassert itself. In this year, Britain intervened in Jordan to support its right-wing, English-educated King, Hussein, this time with US approval. Simultaneously they landed their own troops in the Lebanon in response to a left-wing coup in Iraq which threatened to turn the Middle East into a Soviet sphere of influence. In the same year, Khrushchev provoked a new Berlin crisis by declaring that he intended to hand back East Berlin to the East German government. The East Germans, anxious to stem an increasing flow of refugees through the city to the west, threatened to cut off Berlin from contact with the rest of Germany, so stirring uneasy memories of the 1948 blockade. The Soviet leader went further: he demanded a final settlement of the whole German question, a decision on which would almost certainly force western troops out of Berlin. This put the Western allies on the spot – was Berlin worth the outbreak of a nuclear third world war?

But at the last minute Khrushchev held out an olive branch to his opponents. During the summer of 1959 he took up a suggestion previously made by the British prime minister, Harold Macmillan, to hold a foreign ministers' conference, and they met twice that summer. Khrushchev went on to meet the US president, Eisenhower, at his Pennsylvania retreat of Camp David, where the two men agreed to hold another summit in Paris the following year. During 1959, too, Dulles retired and died. His death increased the chances of a negotiated settlement.

THE U2 INCIDENT

Make a table of all the summit meetings you can trace and summarize their decisions.

Unfortunately the Paris summit meeting in 1960 came to nothing. Shortly before the leaders met the Russians shot down an American U2 spy-plane which had been taking reconnaissance photographs from 80,000 ft, and produced its pilot, Gary Powers, an agent of the Central Intelligence Agency, whom they were holding prisoner. Khrushchev was furious and rounded on Eisenhower accusing him of deceit. The president at first denied the accusations. Khrushchev found it hard to decide whether Eisenhower was so incompetent that he did not enquire what was going on behind his back, or whether he was so dishonest that he intended to brazen out his lie even after he had been caught in the act. Shortly afterwards the president admitted his responsibility but went on to say that it was the United States' right if necessary to spy on the Soviet Union. That pleased Khrushchev no better. Instead of pursuing detente, he said threateningly: 'On the ruins of destroyed imperialism the victorious peoples will create with tremendous speed a civilization a thousand times higher than the capitalist system, and will rebuild their bright future.'

BERLIN AGAIN

1961 began in equally ill humour. The new US president, J.F. Kennedy, got off to an aggressive start by reaffirming the Truman Doctrine and promising 'to defend liberty wherever it is threatened'. He and Khrushchev promised to talk at a new summit to be arranged in Vienna that summer, once more over the Berlin question. By this time, the flow of refugees had become a tide, reaching about 2,000 a day by June. Khrushchev wisely decided to separate the question of East German recognition from that of the refugees. On his orders a wall was built dividing East Berlin from West Berlin. It was built practically overnight out of rough concrete blocks and was patrolled by uniformed guards armed with machine guns. The wall cut off the flow of refugees immediately. It also provided the west with a cheap propaganda victory – this was the socialist paradise where you had to build a wall to stop the grateful workers getting out. Later that autumn the East German government, still seeking diplomatic recognition, started to create difficulties at crossing points in the city. For a time American and Russian tanks faced each other at Checkpoint Charlie in the Friedrichstrasse, their guns muzzle to muzzle. Some time after, President Kennedy visited the city and drew great cheers from the citizens when he said: 'Today in the world of freedom the proudest boast is "Ich bin ein Berliner"'.

CUBA

This crisis was followed by another one over Cuba. When Kennedy inherited the presidency he inherited also a rather half-baked CIA plot to send in a band of volunteers trained in Florida and backed by American hardware to overthrow the communist government of Fidel Castro, a radical and a patriot who had recently ousted the right-wing dictator Batista from power and was now busily engaged in taking over American assets in the island. Kennedy decided to let the enterprise go ahead, but the CIA had badly miscalculated. In a few days the 1,500-strong invading force had been rounded up. The whole 'Bay of Pigs' fiasco turned out to be a sort of Suez crisis, ill-starred in its outcome and roundly condemned by world opinion. Castro (like Nasser) was driven further into the arms of the Russians.

During 1962, as a result, Castro began to install intermediate-range ballistic missiles (or IRBMs) at launch sites scattered throughout Cuba. These were supplied by Russia and could be fitted with nuclear warheads. They were capable of destroying every US city within 4,000 kilometres, including New York and Washington. Kennedy reacted toughly by ordering a blockade of Cuba to prevent further missiles being put ashore, further threatening unlimited nuclear retaliation against the USSR as well as Cuba if any US city were attacked. Khrushchev tried to bargain, offering to remove his rockets from Cuba if the USA would remove theirs from Turkey, where there were US bases: 'Your rockets are in Turkey. You are worried by Cuba. You say it worries you because it is 144 kilometres from the American coast. But Turkey is right next to us.' Kennedy, however, would not yield an inch – publicly, that is, for fear of upsetting the Turks, his NATO allies; privately, he had already agreed to withdraw his rockets, (this was accomplished stealthily shortly afterwards), so that this was not much of a concession. Unaware of these developments, the UN Secretary-General, U Thant, attempted to intervene, but his efforts were of no avail. In the end, Khrushchev had to back down, removing his missiles in return for an American promise not to invade Cuba.

The Cuban missiles crisis, when for a few days the world stood on the brink of nuclear destruction, produced significant results. A 'hot-line' telephone and telex link was set up between Washington and Moscow to prevent a future crisis and to avoid the frightening possibility that nuclear war might break out by accident. On the Soviet side, Khrushchev, condemned by Soviet 'hard-liners' for his so-called 'adventurism' in diplomacy, was overthrown and was succeeded by the ageing Brezhnev, who followed a much more cautious path. But, most important, a

❝This topic deserves special attention.❞

quarrel between the USSR and China, which had been simmering below the surface for some time, broke out into a public dispute.

3 ▷ THE SINO-SOLVIET SPLIT

> **Make notes on the causes of the quarrel between Mao and Khrushchev.**

Originally not very keen on an alliance with the Chinese communists and seeming to prefer to ally himself with Chiang Kai-shek, Stalin became after 1950 one of Mao Zedong's staunchest supporters, signing a 30-year treaty of friendship and alliance with him in 1950, and afterwards lending him military and technical expertise in the task of building up Red China. But Communist China was much less docile than the Soviet satellites in eastern Europe, and Mao was far from being a puppet. Often it was Stalin who had to fall in with Chinese wishes, as when he agreed to withdraw from Port Arthur in the Far East. Strangely, it was only after Khrushchev debunked his predecessor in 1956 that Mao came into the open as one of Stalin's champions.

Khrushchev had listed a variety of criticisms of Stalin. He denounced him as authoritarian, egotistic and brutal, and guilty of glorifying himself by a 'cult of the personality'. He thought his thinking was rigid and old-fashioned, and that he was too much concerned with conflict and linked to the idea of the inevitable revolution. Khrushchev himself rejected the inevitability of war. He thought that co-existence was possible, that there was more than one road to socialism and that the Soviet Union in a fair fight could beat the West at its own game. All this was unwelcome in China. Mao was of the same generation as Stalin and cast in much the same kind of mould. Hence he accused Khrushchev of the same kind of 'deviationism' from the true teaching as Stalin had accused his opponents of. Furthermore, he thought that by hobnobbing with western leaders and pandering to consumerism in the USSR, he was behaving altogether too like the people whom it should have been his business to denounce. Mao even complained that 'Khrushchev is altering the character of Soviet state power and changing the state back into an instrument whereby a handful of privileged bourgeois elements exercise dictatorship over the mass of Soviet workers and peasants'.

On the surface there was little disagreement, but behind the scenes Mao's criticisms of Khrushchev mounted. When Khrushchev was crushing resistance movements in satellite countries in the mid-1950s, Mao told him that his actions smacked more of imperialist than of communist motives. In particular Mao was doubtful about the idea of co-existence; he feared that the only practical way to come to terms with capitalism was to sell out to it, and this is what he thought Khrushchev was doing. He fumed when Khrushchev in his earthy peasant style made fun of him; he believed that Khrushchev stood condemned out of his own mouth when he criticized the simple notion of equality with the words: 'If a people walks in rope sandals and eats watery soup out of a common bowl, that is Communism, but if a working man lives well and wants to live even better tomorrow that's almost as much as restoring Capitalism'. Khrushchev vigorously defended co-existence, too, pointing out the need to avoid a 'doomsday' conflict and observing: 'As for US imperialism being a "paper tiger", those who employ the phrase know quite well that the tiger is equipped with atomic teeth.'

The problem came to a head at a conference in Bucharest in 1960, when Khrushchev laid great stress on the changing nature of the East–West problem, but the Chinese delegates emphasized the continuing danger of capitalist imperialism. They said they believed that 'the competition between the United States and the Soviet Union had subsided because of the intrusion of China'. As a result, the Chinese generally welcomed the fall of Khrushchev in 1964, but this did not change things much. Under Brezhnev the USSR moved slowly closer to **détente** with the west. Irritation in China mounted. Tension along the border between the two countries in central Asia increased. The most serious was in Manchuria, where fighting developed along the Yussuri River, particularly over the scattered islands in it whose ownership had never been agreed. By 1970, Sino–Soviet relations had deteriorated to the point of open conflict.

The war in Vietnam revealed much the same kind of picture. After the division of Indo-China into communist and non-communist areas at Geneva in 1954, Vietnam had become a country whose southern part had received American support first from Kennedy and then from Johnson, whilst the northern part, under

Ho Chi Minh, fought to free the country from foreign control. The Americans fought a long battle and lost. Failing to agree conditions for a cease-fire, President Nixon attempted to hand over the war to the South Vietnamese to fight for themselves. The death of Ho Chi Minh in 1970 did not make the communists any more inclined towards peace, and Nixon had to renew his offensive, launching massive air-strikes in North Vietnam and even in Cambodia, where there was a good deal of support for the Vietcong. His idea was 'to bomb the Vietnamese to the conference table', and it was a failure. Only after it had been dropped was a cease-fire agreement arranged in 1973, under which US troops were withdrawn. By 1975 the whole of Vietnam had fallen into communist hands.

Throughout this time the North Vietnamese communists had sought the support of China and the USSR. The Russians had contributed a supply of armaments, trucks, tanks and aircraft parts, hampered more by the distances involved than by any lack of enthusiasm for the cause. China was less enthusiastic. They had to overcome a long history of suspicion between China and Vietnam, and they were less than pleased with the promptness of the Russian response – they even denied Soviet air transports the use of Chinese air-strips whilst they were flying in supplies. After their victory in 1975, the Vietnamese continued to be the object of Chinese mistrust. Vietnamese forces spilled over into supposedly neutral Laos and Cambodia (Kampuchea) and China was so upset by the behaviour of its former protégé that there was a short frontier war between China and Vietnam from which it was the Chinese who had to retire first. Worse still, in 1978 Vietnam signed a treaty of friendship with the Soviet Union, and thus became a Soviet 'pawn' in south-east Asia as irritating to the Chinese as the Soviet 'pawn' Cuba in the Caribbean was to the Americans.

In 1980, communist China condemned the Soviet occupation of Afghanistan, regarding it as an imperialist adventure, and relations between the USSR and China cooled further. By this time, Deng Xaioping was distancing himself from the earlier principles of Mao Zedong, and the political system of the country bore increasingly little resemblance to that in Russia of Brezhnev, Andropov and Chernenko. What had been a world split by a simple division between Washington and Moscow had now become a more unstable three-way division between Washington, Moscow and Peking.

4 ▷ THE ARMS RACE

The nuclear arms race began in 1945, when the USA used the A-bomb against Japan. At that stage they did not intend to share their secrets with the Russians. When Stalin heard of President Truman's doubts about him, his suspicions of the western powers hardened, and the relations between them gradually developed into a Cold War. In 1949, however, the Russians developed and tested their own A-bomb, and the initial advantage of the West was lost. Things grew worse in 1953, when both the USA and the USSR tested the H-bomb, many times more destructive than its predecessor. But the USA, which had been stockpiling nuclear devices for some time, still had a long lead over the Soviet Union. On balance, considering that the USSR had the advantage in conventional weapons – troops, tanks and aircraft – there was a kind of parity between them.

There was some relaxation of tension on the death of Stalin, but this did not last for long. Soviet repression in Hungary in 1956 aroused fresh fears, and in the following year the USSR scored two notable triumphs. The first was the testing of an intercontinental rocket (ICBM) designed to carry a warhead several thousand miles, thus threatening the Americans for the first time with direct attack; the other was the launching of Sputnik I in October, a move which put the Soviet Union ahead in the space race. Under pressure, the Americans began to develop intermediate-range ballistic missiles (IRBMs), and by 1958 a number of NATO allies had agreed to have such weapons stationed on their soil. They also began to consider the use of 'second-strike' weapons so as to be able to retaliate against a Soviet attack. Retaliatory missiles were hidden in massive concrete 'silos', and were even sent to sea in Polaris submarines, in order that the West should be able to strike back.

The vulnerability of the USA to Soviet attack continued to be a matter of public concern in Kennedy's presidency. This was heightened by the Cuban Missiles crisis in 1962, when Kennedy and Khrushchev clashed in a perilous global confrontation. The latter had the good sense to back away from all-out conflict and both turned to negotiation instead of annihilation. The result was the **Nuclear Test Ban Treaty** in 1963, ending all forms of testing except those carried out underground, where there was less risk of damaging 'fall-out'. This was followed in 1968 by a **Non-Proliferation Treaty** designed to prevent nuclear weapons falling into the hands of the smaller powers. Later in fact Israel, India, South Africa and a number of others 'joined the nuclear club', thus increasing the possibility of a war unleashed by some bloodthirsty and irresponsible national leader. So it was in 1969 that Johnson and Brezhnev renewed their negotiations, embarking at Helsinki on **Strategic Arms Limitation Talks** (or SALT), eventually initialling an agreement on the subject.

Agreements between the communist and non-communist worlds were taken further by later Presidents: Nixon extended the scope of the SALT talks in an agreement signed in Moscow in 1972; Ford reduced the numbers allowed in Vladivostok in 1975; and in 1979 in Vienna, Carter and Brezhnev came up with a more comprehensive treaty in the form of SALT 2.

When the Russians invaded Afghanistan in 1980, however, co-operation came to a halt. The new Republican President of the USA, Reagan, rejected the new treaty, and the two sides began to square up to each other again. All the same, the increasingly heavy cost of their armament programmes and the urgent problems which both governments faced compelled the USSR and the USA to resume their talks in 1982, this time under the name of the **Strategic Arms Reduction Talks** (or (START). The results of the first talks, in Geneva, were small, but the new leader of the Soviet Union, Mikhail Gorbachev, put forward much bolder proposals in the second round, at Reykjavik in 1986; indeed, these were so radical that Reagan found them impossible to accept. In 1987, in Washington, some real progress was made, but the cuts agreed still fell considerably short of those demanded by Gorbachev. Only the world-shattering political developments which took place in eastern Europe and in the USSR at the beginning of the 1990s brought any really better prospect of reducing East-West tension.

5 ▷ CHINA COMES IN FROM THE COLD

> **❝ Maps would be useful in studying the topic of Chinese expansion. ❞**

Chinese communism after 1949 projected a very unfriendly image, based equally on its distrust of foreigners and on its harsh new political philosophy. In the early 50s China intervened decisively in the Korean War. Over the next decade, it absorbed Tibet, nibbled at Burma, Assam and Nepal, and in 1962 went to war with India over the distant province of Ladakh. China also supported Chinese communities in Indonesia, Malaya and elsewhere in their struggle for freedom.

To the outside world this looked like aggression. Few were aware of the 'unfair treaties' under which China had been robbed of its lands in the previous century; opponents such as Dulles saw the situation as a well-orchestrated conspiracy between Mao and Stalin to impose communism on the world.

In 1960, however, the first rumblings of discord between the USSR and China became audible, and gradually their quarrels became more public. Khrushchev thought that Mao was a lunatic extremist, willing to plunge the world into destruction in the hope that some of his nation might survive the holocaust. Mao for his part accused Khrushchev of disloyalty to communist doctrine, freely comparing the Bolsheviks to the Tsarists and referring to 'the anti-Chinese atrocities of the new Tsars; their Fascist heel tramples the Motherland.'

What was even more surprising was the *détente* which took place between China and the USA. In 1971 the US government agreed to admit Communist China to the United Nations, with a permanent seat on the Security Council; at the same time Taiwan (or 'Nationalist China') was removed. In 1972 Henry Kissinger, the US Secretary of State, and later President Nixon, visited Peking and began the slow and painful repair of relations between the two countries.

Mao had always insisted that US support must be withdrawn from the Nationalists if relations between the USA and China were to improve permanently. In

1975 Chiang Kai-shek died, followed in 1976 by Mao himself. Quite suddenly in 1978 the two powers reached agreement, and full diplomatic relations were resumed. Deng Xiaoping visited Washington in 1979, and American businessmen set off at once for China in search of new markets.

Reagan maintained American cordiality towards China during his presidency. At the same time, China came to an agreement with Britain over the future of Hong Kong, and in 1986 the Queen visited China to cement this new friendship. By the mid-80s, earlier Cold War attitudes had mellowed and the threatening confrontations of earlier years seemed less likely to recur. Tiananmen Square created ripples for a time, but did not permanently sour relations between China and the rest of the world.

6 ▷ THE END OF THE COLD WAR

Change came in a breath-taking rush at the end of the 1980s. It began in eastern Europe, where discontent had simmered under the surface for many years, showing itself from time to time, but generally finding itself ruthlessly suppressed by the police and security authorities. Communist leaders like Erich Honeker of East Germany reacted to opposition in the only way they knew, by clamping down on it. Gorbachev's attitude, when he visited these countries was one of mild encouragement for the reform process. Two results followed: the eastern European peoples were encouraged to become bolder in their demands, and their leadership began to feel that the Soviet leader had pulled the rug from under them and was denying them the backing they deserved.

Cracks soon appeared in the eastern European monolith, and discontent bubbled up through them. Poland moved towards democratic elections and the communist leadership was replaced by popular figures like Lech Walesa. Restrictions between East and West Germany were relaxed; the Berlin Wall was breached and finally dismantled altogether. Popular governments replaced the old rulers of Czechoslovakia and Hungary. In Romania, one of the most repressive communist regimes was overthrown, and the dictator Ceausescu and his wife were tried and summarily executed, their bodies exultantly displayed on TV. Even in Albania the forces of change were seen at work. As the fog of communism lifted, a new eastern Europe began to emerge, the forces of nationalism now suddenly were more power-ful, and to some observers seeming almost as threatening as the old communist order.

The Soviet Union was not immune to the nationalist virus. Outlying states like the Baltic Republics and Moldova, never happy with their shotgun marriage with the USSR, clamoured for freedom, soon to be followed by others such as Belorussia and the Ukraine. Half-hearted efforts were made by Gorbachev to allay discontent, but in the main he, seeing the need for radical change, was already more than half-way to recognizing the justice of their claims. The KGB, the Soviet Army and the conservatives in the Kremlin were alarmed, and threatened the breakaway states with violence and repression. In August 1991 there was an attempted political coup against Gorbachev. This failed, not so much because of his strength as because of the stout resistance put up by his rival Boris Yeltsin, now the elected President of the Russian Republic. In the wake of the coup the Soviet Union faded away altogether; the Hammer-and-Sickle flag was hauled down for the last time; and the constituent republics went on to try to work out new relationships between them in the Commonwealth of Independent States.

❝Up-to-date information would be very useful here.❞

IDEAS AND PRINCIPLES

CO-EXISTENCE
The possibility that, instead of conflicting together, two opposing forces, ideas or sets of people can come to a compromise together and learn to live in relative harmony side by side; a way of accommodating differences without going to the lengths of war.

DEVIATIONISM
A deviationist is a person whose idea of a policy or a political doctrine (usually communism) varies from the normally accepted teaching. In a society where strict adherence to every detail of political teaching is important, deviationism is often presented as a most serious crime.

DOMINO THEORY
The view that the knocking over of one domino (e.g. by the communists) would lead to the fall of a country to its (communist) neighbours and that this domino would in its turn knock down the next one, so that in the end a whole area would be lost, is called 'domino theory'. Resistance to such possibilities in the 1960s and 1970s was a favourite way of 'containing' the growth of communism. Domino theorists believed that it was extremely important to prevent the first domino from being knocked over, as in the case of Vietnam.

HARDLINERS AND REVISIONISTS
Those who interpret a policy or a political doctrine strictly and do not permit the smallest deviation from it are said to be 'hardliners'; those who adopt a more flexible approach, and permit such things to be revised, updated and adjusted are said to be 'revisionists'. The word 'conservative' is also often applied to those reluctant to see change, whilst the word 'radical' may be applied to those willing to come to terms with it.

HAWKS AND DOVES
See immediately above. 'Hawks' are usually regarded as fierce birds of prey showing little inclination to release their prey; 'doves' are more placid and peaceful and prefer a quiet life.

MULTILATERAL/UNILATERAL
For a policy (such as disarmament) to be carried out multilaterally, it is carried out in accordance with the terms of an agreement between a number of powers; for it to be carried out unilaterally, it is carried out according to the wishes of the single power deciding it, and without any reference to the other powers. Unilateralism is sometimes said to deprive the negotiating power of the bargaining counters that enable a multilateralist treaty to be reached.

APPLIED MATERIALS

See previous chapter.

EXAMINATION QUESTIONS

QUESTION 1

As an official spokesman of the government of either the USA or the USSR in 1964, explain the attitude of your government towards the Cold War in the period 1953–64.

You may include any of the following or other material in your answer:

  your ideological convictions;

  your attitude towards your diplomatic allies;

  your attitude towards your diplomatic opponents;

  your country's defence requirements;

  your thoughts on conventional arms and nuclear weapons.

(AEB/SEG)

QUESTION 2

In 1960 the following cartoon appeared in *Crocodile*, a Soviet magazine:

(a) (i) To which country did the aircraft in the cartoon belong? Explain how the cartoon enables you to work your answer out. (2 marks)

  (ii) Briefly explain why this aircraft was particularly in the news in May 1960. (2 marks)

(b) Why, in the 1960s, did American and Soviet leaders pursue a policy of détente? (6 marks)

(c) 'The only real reason for the continuing hostility between the USA and the USSR since 1945 has been their different political beliefs: democracy against communism.' Explain fully whether or not you agree with this statement.

(15 marks) (MEG)

OUTLINE ANSWERS

ANSWER 1

The first question provides a list of guidelines, but the instruction indicates that you may use some or all of them, or you may include other material not on the list. It is difficult to see how you could write a good answer and still ignore all the suggested guidelines, but if you were to leave out some of them and include instead useful additional material, this would get credit. The marking scheme in such a question needs to be extremely flexible. Candidates who confined themselves to the guidelines suggested could get full marks if they elaborated the themes satisfactorily; what they must not do is simply to express in different words the substance of the themes without contributing any ideas or knowledge of their own. The question, of course, calls for empathetic awareness of the standpoint either of US or of Soviet spokesmen during the years on offer; a factual historical account will not alone suffice to get high marks. Let us suppose that you have chosen the Soviet alternative in the question. Your ideological, i.e. communist, convictions will govern your whole outlook: you will see the Cold War in terms of a struggle between the correct principles of communism and the erroneous capitalist principles, and you will be expected to have some familiarity with what the correct Marxist–Leninist principles are. It will not be enough to reel them off as you have learnt them from your notebook; you must also show some understanding of them and sympathy with them. As a spokesman, too, you must take good care that you express them correctly, since conformity with the true principles is an essential requirement in your official position. Similarly, the attitudes you show towards your diplomatic allies must be correct, and the criticisms you express of your opponents must be those that have the stamp of current official approval. You should also be able to rehearse with knowledge and conviction the Soviet position at the time on the arms race. If you deal with your country's defence requirements you will need to know the arguments in favour of the Warsaw Pact, and the particular situations inside the various satellite countries involving the Soviet Union in their defence. Pertinent comments on the Berlin question will contribute towards your answer. If you make any observations on the US side of the problem, your attitude towards the USA must be consistent with the Soviet attitude at the time: the inclusion of the standard Soviet criticisms of the USA, and even the repetition of the current clichés will help your answer to carry conviction. Remember, too, in your answer, that the Soviet stance of 1964 was in a number of ways different from that which was usual in 1953.

ANSWER 2

You should not fail to note in respect of the second question the very heavy weighting of marks on the last component of the question. This carries 15 marks, whereas all the other parts put together carry only 10. Your response to the final part of the question should therefore be much the most full and detailed. In (a) (i) a correct identification of the country (the USA) will suffice for 1 mark; for the other mark a short statement based on knowledge of the U2 spy-plane incident or based on visual recognition of President Eisenhower should be made. In (a) (ii) a mention of the shooting-down of the U2 over the Soviet Union will score 1 mark; the other mark will be gained from a statement about the impact which the incident had on the holding of the Paris Summit in 1960. Part (b) of the question concerns the reasoning which lay behind the American and Soviet pursuit of *détente* in the 1960s. Note that the question relates to causes rather than to results: it would be less important, for example, to explain the consequences of the Nuclear Test-Ban Treaty of 1963 than it would to trace the crisis atmosphere of the Cuban missiles affair which led to the signature of that treaty. But the general picture relating to the rapid growth of nuclear weaponry, the 'balance of terror' and the misgivings which these things inspired in the US and the Soviet leadership are also relevant here. Part (c) of the question, however, aims to elicit a 'mini-essay' – anything up to fifteen or twenty lines – with a clear focus on the introductory quotation. You will have to show that you realize what the quotation means and be prepared to discuss it, though the question does not suggest that you ought to agree with the quotation. If you accept the quotation, the evidence for your acceptance ought to be set out; if you reject it, you ought again to produce evidence for your rejection. Best of all, you ought to produce a balanced judgement, weighing ideological considerations, such as the communist dread of the capitalist system or the American fear of the dangers of militant communism, against the more practical realities of superpower politics in terms of spheres of economic, commercial and military influence. You may incline to the view that ideas override material interests, or that the basic realities of power cloak themselves in ideological garb, but your argument should seek out telling examples of each in an effort to establish that there are two sides to the case. A certain proportion of the credit will be awarded for the selection and use of suitable examples.

SUGGESTIONS FOR FURTHER WORK

1. Find out more about the Cuban missiles crisis of 1962. Tip: you might use the book by Robert Kennedy, *Thirteen Days: the Cuban Missiles Crisis*, Macmillan.
2. Mao Zedong described the west's atom bomb as a 'paper tiger' in the 1950s, and later applied the same description to US imperialism generally. What do you suppose he meant by this? Do you think he was right?
3. Collect information about the later history of Indo-China (Vietnam, Laos and Kampuchea) since 1975, with photographs and other illustrations if possible. What new light does your information cast on the 'domino theory'?
4. Build up a file on each of the following: a) the changes being proposed by Deng Xaioping in China, and b) those being proposed by Mikhail Gorbachev in the Soviet Union. What does your information tell you about the changing character of Chinese and Soviet society in the later 1980s?

STUDENT'S ANSWER – EXAMINER'S COMMENTS

Question

(a) Explain the involvement of the USA and the USSR in the Angolan conflict of the 1970's.
(b) What was the attitude of the USA to Russian involvement in Afghanistan and Poland in the late 1970's and early 1980's?

> **A few good-sounding phrases but this response contains many errors of both fact and analysis. Can you list the most obvious errors in the answer?**

(a) Both the USA and the USSR helped to start a war in Angola. When the Portuguese granted independence to the country in 1975, the USA showed the main interest because it feared the extension of communism there and wanted the oil found in the country, so the USSR became involved because it did not want the Americans to steal a march on them so it vetoed their proposals in the Security Council of U.N.O. It was clear that both powers regarded the country as an arena for international skirmishing. There was some minor trouble from Cuban troops and a mild interest was shown for a short time by South Africa. There was also some trouble from the new leader of the country, Colonel Ghaddafi, who concentrated

troops around the Angolan capital, Tripoli. But it was
the Americans and the Russians who were chiefly to blame.
   (b) Russia invaded Afghanistan and Poland at the end of
the 1970s and the Americans didn't like it, and the U.S.
Senate refused to ratify S.A.L.T. II. During the Reagan
Presidency the situation didn't get much better.

**❝ Whilst not without merit, this answer is too
short and undeveloped. Russia did not invade
Poland at the end of the 1970s though there
were fears of such an invasion especially in the
early 1980s. ❞**

GETTING STARTED

The collapse of Turkey during the First World War left confusion in the Middle East, much of which had previously been under Turkish government. During the war, Britain had offered to help the Arab countries of the area to free themselves and set up a state of their own. T.E. Lawrence (Lawrence of Arabia) helped to organize the Arab revolt, and their forces, together with British armies under General Allenby, defeated the Turks and liberated Syria and Palestine.

About the same time, however, the British government gave its backing to a Zionist scheme to create a 'Jewish national home' in Palestine, which was the historic promised land of the Jews. This promise took the form of the Balfour Declaration, sent by the British foreign secretary, Earl Balfour, in the form of a letter to Lord Rothschild, the leader of the Jewish community in Britain.

> His Majesty's government view with favour the establishment of a national home for the Jewish people, and will use their best endeavours to facilitate the achievement of this object, it being clearly understood that nothing will be done which may prejudice the civil or religious rights of the existing non-Jewish communities in Palestine.

In fact, neither of these solutions was put into effect at the end of the war: In 1916 British and French diplomats made an agreement – the Sykes–Picot Agreement – to carve up the area between them, apportioning Syria and the Lebanon to France, and Iraq, Jordan and Palestine to Britain, as mandated territories. Though the affairs of the other areas were fairly speedily settled, Palestine remained a thorn in the side of Britain throughout the whole inter-war period.

HISTORICAL DEVELOPMENTS

PALESTINE UNDER THE BRITISH MANDATE

❝Analysis questions on the causes of the Arab-Israel quarrel are common.❞

The main problem was the increasing conflict between the Arab inhabitants of Palestine and the increasing flow of Jewish immigrants. The earliest Jewish settlements had been farm colonies conducted along communal lines and known as - *kibbutzim*. The first had been set up in 1879 in the area of what is today Tel Aviv. By 1914 there were over 40 kibbutzim, and a sizeable Jewish minority in Jerusalem and other towns. The Arabs, whose customs, language and religion were quite different, resented this influx, and in particular resented the money which the Jews used to buy up the farmlands which the Palestinian Arabs considered to be rightfully theirs. It became increasingly clear that Britain's aims of permitting the creation of an Arab state and of simultaneously providing a Jewish 'national home' were contradictory. There were riots in Jaffa in 1921, and British forces in trying to maintain order were obviously fighting a losing battle. The British colonial secretary, Winston Churchill, in a government White Paper, tried to reassure Palestinian opinion by declaring that a 'national home' for the Jews did not necessarily mean a 'national state'; but these were rather empty words, and Britain took no serious steps towards limiting Jewish immigration, which by 1925 was running at over 10,000 a year, mainly from Bolshevik Russia and Poland.

Renewed rioting took place in 1929, sparked off when a Jewish boy kicked his football on to an Arab's land; before they were quelled there had been about fifty Jewish and over a hundred Arab deaths. The British government issued a second White Paper, reaffirming British promises to the Palestinians; but this document aroused such bitter criticisms from the Jewish community that Ramsay MacDonald back-tracked in the face of their accusations of anti-Semitism, and issued instead what the Arabs called a 'black paper' in which he declared he had no intention of either checking Jewish immigration into the country or of limiting land purchases. The situation got worse after 1933, when anti-Semitic policies began to be introduced into Hitler's Germany. Immigration went up from 4,000 in 1931 to 30,000 in 1933 and over 60,000 in 1935. By 1936 there were about 400,000 Jewish inhabitants of Palestine, as against 850,000 Arabs.

It was in 1936 that communal trouble broke out again. The Palestinians organized a general strike, and armed bands of Palestinian volunteers roamed the hills, attacking Jewish farms and terrorizing their workers. Britain increased its garrison of the country to about 20,000, but failed to quell the disturbances. In 1937 a Royal Commission under Lord Peel was set up to find a solution. The plan it put forward, to create three small states, one for the Arabs, one for the Jews and the third (including Jaffa and Jerusalem) as an international zone under the authority of the League of Nations, pleased nobody, and was quietly dropped. Demonstrations and violence continued. In 1939 the British government produced yet another solution: Jewish immigration was to be strictly limited and was to stop altogether after five years, and further transfers of Palestinian land to the Jews were to be strictly controlled. Later in 1939, however, the Second World War broke out, and the whole question was put on ice.

❝The impact of the war on the problem could usefully be studied.❞

By 1945 the situation seemed to have gone on too long for any compromise solution to work. The Arabs were bitterly hostile to the continuation of the British mandate, and formed an Arab League of twenty states to resist it, demonstrating in towns and blowing up oil pipelines in the desert to harass the British as much as they could. The Jews too found themselves pushed in the direction of extremism. Some formed terrorist groups such as the Irgun Zwei Leumi and the Stern Gang (so-called after Abraham Stern, who had left the Irgun in 1942 to form a terrorist group of his own but had been captured by the British and shot), not only to revenge themselves on their Palestinian opponents, but also to demonstrate to the British that they meant business. The official Jewish defence force (the Haganah) was largely officered by men who had volunteered to fight against Hitler's Germany during the war, and in many cases they were British trained and used British equipment. All this inclined the Palestinians to the view that Britain favoured the Jewish cause, an impression reinforced by the so-called ***Biltmore Programme,*** issued by Zionists in New York, in which the Jewish community in the

USA pressed for the relaxation of immigration restrictions in Palestine in favour of the masses of refugees there after 1945. The Attlee government in Britain, however, refused to do this, and was inclined to resist the pressure of the US government under the new president, H.S. Truman, to change its mind. Ben Gurion, the Jewish leader in Palestine, therefore came out in open opposition to the British. Jewish extremists launched a terrorist war, blowing up roads and bridges, and finally planting a bomb in the King David Hotel in Jerusalem in 1946, killing over ninety British personnel. Meanwhile, illegal Jewish immigration, on jam-packed ships like the *Smyrna*, the *San Dimitrio* and the *Holgana* continued, and masses of Jews, weary but happy, came to make their new homes in the land of their dreams.

In 1947 the British foreign secretary, Ernest Bevin, announced that his government was going to hand over the whole Palestine question to the newly established United Nations Organization. The UN General Assembly sent a Special Commission on Palestine (UNSCOP) to Tel Aviv, and they eventually reported in favour of a plan for the partition of the country very similar to the one previously outlined by the British in 1937. The scheme, somewhat more generous to the Jews than the British plan since it gave them most of the Negev down to the Red Sea, was adopted by the United Nations, but it was furiously rejected by the Palestinians, who saw themselves becoming foreigners in their own land. Nevertheless, the British government made it clear that they intended to withdraw from Palestine whether there had been a settlement or not, and they began to make preparations for their departure. On the day the British left, 14 May 1948, Ben-Gurion proclaimed the independence of his country, which was recognized with remarkable alacrity within hours by the Truman administration. On the following day the infant Israel was invaded from all sides by its Arab neighbours.

2 ▶ THE FIRST ARAB-ISRAELI WAR, 1948-9

Neighbouring Arab states in 1948 welcomed the opportunity of wiping Israel off the map. Egyptian forces moved along the coast of the Mediterranean towards Gaza and from there struck northwards in the direction of the Israeli capital, Tel Aviv; from the opposite direction Syrian troops pushed across the Jordan and into northern Palestine; from the east Jordan's crack Arab Legion – soldiers trained and equipped by the British – occupied the West Bank and seized Jerusalem. At this stage, in June 1948, the UN succeeded in imposing a truce, with about one-third of Israel's partition territory in Arab hands. But fighting broke out again in July and after a tough campaign the Israelis succeeded in driving their Egyptian enemies out of the Negev in October as far as Eilat on the Red Sea, and clearing the whole of Galilee of Syrian forces. They also negotiated a settlement with Jordan whereby they partitioned the West Bank, and even the city of Jerusalem, between them. The result of these victories was that Israel had not only survived the invasion but had actually increased its share of Palestine. There followed another UN truce, and the remaining Arab states followed Egypt's example in signing cease-fires with their Jewish neighbour. Unfortunately the first UN mediator, the Swedish Count Bernadotte, was murdered by Jewish extremists, his job being taken over by his deputy, Ralph Bunche. By February 1949 the war was over, but the Arab states did not accept the finality of the situation and indicated their intention of eliminating the Jewish threat at the first opportunity.

The UN Truce Supervisory Commission in the meantime established the frontiers of the new state, and in 1950 Britain, France and the USA joined together to make a tripartite declaration that they would protect Israel against any possible renewal of hostilities. About a million Palestinian refugees fled from the country to nearby states: about 25 per cent northwards to Lebanon and Syria, about 35 per cent into the Gaza Strip – still held by Egypt – and about 40 per cent into the West Bank territory and into Jordan. The very large number of displaced persons only intensified Arab resentment and hardened their determination for revenge.

> 66 It will help your study of this topic if you make a table showing the effect of **each** Arab-Israeli war on the neighbours of Israel. 99

> 66 Maps would be useful in studying all these wars. 99

3 ▶ THE SECOND ARAB-ISRAELI WAR, 1956

Colonel Nasser of Egypt, coming to power in 1954 after the overthrow of King Farouk, was bent on pursuing his schemes not only for strengthening and modernizing his country, but for assuming the leadership of the whole Arab world and spearheading its drive to exterminate Israel. He denounced western interference in Middle Eastern affairs, in particular the US-supported Baghdad Pact, set up in 1955 ostensibly to check the expansion of communism in that area. In 1955 he began to import arms from Czechoslovakia, and in July 1956 he nationalized the Suez Canal, a move guaranteed to infuriate Britain and France, its previous proprietors. At the same time he mounted a propaganda offensive against Israel, signalling clearly his hostility towards them. The irregular frontier war, the endless raiding and counter-raiding and the closing both of the Suez Canal and the Gulf of Aqaba to Israeli shipping, combined to produce something like a siege mentality in Tel Aviv, and the Israeli government decided to act.

> **The Suez crisis is important at this point.**

At the end of October 1956 the Israelis, having earlier taken the precaution of concluding a secret agreement with Britain and France that if they attacked Egypt they would not be left to face them alone, suddenly seized the Gaza Strip and invaded Sinai, reaching the east bank of the canal within hours of launching their attack. The USA proposed a resolution in the Security Council demanding a cease-fire, but Britain and France vetoed it. Declaring that their sole intention was to prevent possible damage to the canal, they sent both sides an ultimatum demanding immediate withdrawal from the vicinity of the canal, and moved swiftly to the support of their ally, Israel. An Anglo–French force, after a rather leisurely journey form their base in Cyprus, landed at Port Said on 5 November, occupied it after devastating attacks on Egyptian air force machines on the ground, and began to advance along the canal in the direction of Suez on the Red Sea. Nasser appealed to the UN to intervene, and meanwhile-blocked the canal by sinking ships in it. With the USA and the USSR for once acting together, and with overwhelming support from most Third World countries, the UN stepped in. Israel was ordered to leave the Sinai Peninsula, and reluctantly did so. Britain and France, neither of them willing to continue to defy such a clear expression of world opinion, agreed to withdraw their forces, and the last troops left Egypt by the end of November.

As far as Israel was concerned, it was difficult to represent the war as having been a great success: the country had gained no territory, was still exposed to the danger of Egyptian attack and was branded together with Britain and France as an aggressor. But at least for a time Israel had a respite from Egyptian frontier raids, and the Gulf of Aqaba – though not the Suez Canal – was opened to Israeli ships once again. Furthermore Israel had shown that it could defend itself very effectively, and that it was determined not to be caught napping. On the other hand, the Egyptians came out of the war in a stronger, more confident, mood, with Arab ambitions unabated and Nasser's prestige strengthened. But the permanent issues remained unsettled. A solution to the question of the Palestinian refugees was as far off as ever, and Arab states still stubbornly refused even to acknowledge Israel's existence. By 1960 border incidents had started up again with raids into Israeli territory by Arab guerrillas and reprisal raids by Israeli forces. It was only a question of time before another spark set fire to the powder-barrel.

4 ⟩ THE THIRD ARAB-ISRAELI WAR, 1967

In the course of the 1960s, Arab states adopted an ever more threatening tone towards Israel. In 1964 Nasser said: 'Future prospects are for war against Israel, for which we shall set the time and the place'.

In 1966, the Syrian defence minister, Hafiz Hasad, took up the theme:

> We say: we shall never call for nor accept peace. We shall only accept war and the restoration of the usurped land. We have resolved to drench this land with your blood; to oust you, aggressors, and throw you into the sea for good. We must meet as soon as possible and fight a single liberation war on the level of the whole area against Israel, imperialism and all the enemies of the people.

Syria became more closely linked with Egypt in what was rather grandly called a 'United Arab Republic' in 1963, and a Palestine liberation movement, known as Al Fatah, came into being. The PLM began guerrilla raids into less securely defended places in Israel, wrecking buildings and killing the inhabitants; the Israelis retaliated by striking into Lebanon and Syria to destroy PLM bases and attacking Syrian positions in the Golan Heights from which artillery had been intermittently shelling Israeli targets. Nasser persuaded UN Secretary-General U Thant to withdraw peace-keeping forces from Sinai and began moving his troops into forward positions there. Once again he sealed off the Gulf of Aqaba and moved artillery and troops to Sharm-el-Sheikh at the tip of the Sinai Peninsula. Soon he had over 100,000 men in the Sinai Peninsula, with 1300 tanks and 500 aircraft ready for action; on the West Bank Jordanian troops were moving on station, accompanied by the Iraqi forces in alliance with them.

Once again the Arabs had made the mistake of giving Israel advance notice of their intentions. In fact, since 1956 the Israelis had prepared themselves well. They had reduced the numbers of their men in infantry detachments, and had given greater importance to armoured tank divisions and the air force. Israelis realized that when the time came there would not be a minute to lose if the country was to survive. Hence the government decided on speed, mobility and attack. On 5 June 1967, Moshe Dayan, the tough Israeli minister of defence, decided on a pre-emptive strike. In the early hours, Israeli troops poured into the Sinai Desert, and within two hours Israeli fighter-bombers had wiped out the Egyptian air force on the ground. With their air superiority immediately established, the Israelis had little difficulty in harassing and destroying Egyptian forces wherever they encountered them. Advancing along the Mediterranean coastline, the Israelis reached El Arish within a day, within two days Sharm-el-Sheikh on the Red Sea, and within three days the Suez Canal once more, in several places. The main Egyptian body at El Nakhl, more or less cut off in the middle of the Sinai Peninsula, was swiftly surrounded and pounded into submission.

Meanwhile, in the first few hours of the war the Israelis occupied Jerusalem and overran the entire West Bank of the Jordan. Within three days the king of Jordan, Hussein, swallowed his pride and asked for an armistice. Against Syria, Israeli armour advanced into the Golan Heights, a hazardous undertaking that could have cost them dearly considering that it was the very strongest points of the Syrian defence system that they were attacking; but though the Syrian forces fought tooth and nail they were no match for the opposing heavy armour, and the Israelis broke through to within twenty miles of Damascus. By 10 June the Syrians too had asked for a cease-fire. In the course of what came to be known as the Six Days War, Israel had doubled itself in size, and was left in secure possession of the Golan Heights, the West Bank and the whole vast area of the Sinai Peninsula as far as the Suez Canal, now their frontier with Egypt. The Egyptians once more blocked the Suez Canal, imprisoning a number of ships in it, most of which had virtually rotted away by the time the canal was re-opened over ten years later.

The UN once again sent a mission to determine and protect the frontiers, but the peace was an uneasy one, constantly interrupted by conflict between the sides. A new truce had to be arranged in 1970, but both the Arab and the Jewish side looked askance at the UN proposal for both parties to withdraw from the territories they had occupied (the US-sponsored Rogers Plan, UN Resolution 272 and all the diplomacy of the UN emissary Dr Gunnar Jarring failed to persuade them to do this); eventually Israel's prime minister, Mrs Golda Meir, rejected it altogether, flatly refusing to budge an inch from the position that had been won until Israel should have some kind of guarantee for its future security. In desperation the Arabs turned to terrorism instead of negotiation, and the Arab governments started to turn the screw of increased oil prices through OPEC in order to blackmail the western powers into softening their anti-Arab line.

5 ▷ THE FOURTH ARAB-ISRAELI WAR, 1973

The early 1970s saw a number of extremist Arab terrorist organizations spring into being to secure the acceptance of Palestinian demands. One, the Popular Front for the Liberation of Palestine (the PFLP) was responsible for an outrage at Lydda airport in June 1972, where there were about 100 casualties in a running battle between an Arab guerrilla suicide squad and airport security; another, Black September (so-called because of the violent crushing of an earlier Palestinian movement, this time by Jordanians in this month in 1970), attacked Israeli athletes later in the same year after they had competed in the Munich Olympics, murdering 11 of them before being gunned down themselves. The Israelis, following an 'eye-for-an-eye' policy, retaliated savagely in each case.

Then suddenly in 1973, and this time without any preliminary warning, Egyptian and Syrian forces once more attacked Israel. Though unsupported by Jordan, whose king had recently quarrelled with the Palestinian Liberation Organization (the PLO), the leader of which had brought thousands of his fellow Palestinians to Jordan and at one point seemed to be about to overturn Hussein's government, the Egyptian and Syrian invaders at first had good success. They enjoyed the diplomatic approval of the communist bloc and they were well equipped with Soviet arms. Furthermore the day chosen for the Arab attack was Yom Kippur, the Jewish Day of Atonement, when many Jews were in their synagogues. Nearly 1,200 Syrian tanks set about the reconquest of the Golan Heights, and Egyptian troops thrust across the Suez Canal and hurled themselves against the Israeli defence line there – the Bar Lev Line. Numbers of Israeli aircraft were shot down by heat-seeking Russian-built SAM missiles. But Israel itself was well supplied with US weapons and expertise, and within a fortnight was able to turn the tide.

The Israeli air force began to recover the initiative, and was eventually able to knock out over 1,000 Syrian tanks. Israeli ground forces went over to the offensive in Sinai, expelled the Egyptians, crossed the canal and swung in behind Suez from the west, cutting off the entire Egyptian Third Army in a huge pocket on the west side of the Canal. The USA and the USSR joined to arrange a cease-fire, expressing the hope that this time a permanent settlement could be reached; but the position continued to be one of deadlock, with the Israelis refusing to give up anything they had won and the Arabs stubbornly rejecting any agreement that meant accepting the existence of an Israeli state.

6 PEACE-MAKING, 1978

As long as President Nasser lived, Egyptian hostility towards Israel was as strong as ever, but when he died in 1970 and was succeeded by Anwar Sadat, Egyptian policies began to moderate. Nixon, as part of his 'shuttle diplomacy', had visited the Middle East, and his visit was returned by Sadat in 1975. Two years later he took a further bold step towards resolving the dispute with Israel. He visited Jerusalem, and in a speech to the Knesset (the Israeli parliament) made a personal appeal for a better understanding between the two countries. Though he exposed himself to the possibility of a rebuff at the hands of Israeli extremists, in fact he was given a cautious welcome by Menachem Begin, who was now prime minister of Israel, his Likud Party having recently ousted the Labour Party from office. Some time afterwards, Begin visited Cairo and indicated his country's willingness to pursue terms of settlement. Events in Lebanon caused these negotiations to falter in 1978, but President Carter breathed new life into them by inviting both men to Camp David where they closeted themselves together and hammered out a framework for a settlement. Agreement was eventually signed in March 1979.

❝Detailed knowledge of the settlement would help in answering questions on this topic.❞

For his part, Sadat offered to end what had developed into a thirty-year war with Israel, by offering them a peace treaty and final diplomatic recognition. In return, Begin agreed to withdraw from Sinai in three stages, restoring the whole area to Egypt in spite of there being numerous Jewish settlements planted there in the interval; simultaneously he promised he would set about the task of providing full autonomy for the Arab communities living under Israeli rule in the Gaza Strip and on the West Bank, though both sides agreed that this final step would take some little time to accomplish. It was, however, visualized that the peace process would be complete by the early 1980s.

The conclusion of this agreement created a sensation, not least in the USA and the western nations. But extremist Arabs regarded Sadat's actions in breaking ranks with his allies as a gross betrayal, and the headquarters of the Arab League were abruptly moved from Cairo to Tunis, with Moammur Ghaddafi of Libya beginning to emerge as the new leader of the Arab national movement instead of the Egyptian leader.

Yet it was the Jews whose actions seemed most likely to wreck the agreement. Israel, after much heart-searching and many protests from right wingers, eventually completed the handing back of Sinai, but failed conspicuously to halt the planting of new Jewish settlements on the West Bank. It went on in 1980 to pass the Jerusalem Law, which transferred the capital from Tel Aviv to the Holy City, declaring it 'entire and united'. Then in 1981 Israel formally annexed the Golan Heights from Syria. Arab nationalists and religious leaders grew ever more disenchanted with developments.

Sadat did not increase his popularity with Arab radicals when he offered sanctuary to the deposed Shah of Iran, toppled in a coup by the Ayahtollah Khomeini in 1979. The malcontents vented their displeasure in 1981 when they shot down their president bloodily in a hail of small arms fire at a military parade in Cairo. His successor was his vice-president, Hosni Mubarak, but in practice he was a moderate also, and he made no effort to renew the war. The middle 1980s, therefore, saw peace on at least one Israeli frontier, but in other areas the old quarrel went rumbling on.

7 ▶ THE WAR IN LEBANON, 1978-85

During the 1970s the condition of the Lebanon became ever more disturbed. There was an increasing number of Palestinian refugees in the country, and these frequently came into collision with the Lebanese authorities. Superimposed on this was another struggle, between a national movement of left-wing Muslims and conservative Christian groups supported by the Phalangist militia. Trouble flared up in 1975, and in spite of more than fifty attempts to impose cease-fires the struggle dragged on until October 1976.

Syrian intervention played an important part in the conflict. In 1976, in their efforts to restore order in the country, the Syrians came into conflict with the Palestinians, and the intervention of a more widely based Arab peace-keeping force failed to stop the fighting. As the result of the final cease-fire in October 1976, a more effective 30,000-strong Arab Deterrent Force (ADF), composed largely of Syrians, took its place. All this was very alarming to Israel, which looked upon Lebanon as a hotbed of Palestinian unrest and greatly feared the extension of Syrian influence there. Guerrilla raids across the border by Palestinian bands had already produced numerous Israeli incursions into Lebanon, but on a fairly small scale. But in March 1978 Al Fatah staged more serious raids and provoked full-scale Israeli retaliation. Israeli forces advanced into southern Lebanon, occupying it as far as the Litani River, including Sidon. The UN Security Council intervened to send a UN Interim Force in Lebanon (UNIFIL), initially of 4,000 men; they eventually persuaded Israel into handing over to the right-wing, mainly Christian, militia who maintained their links with the Israelis.

Unfortunately it proved impossible to bring back peace to Lebanon. In 1979, Israel encouraged a right-wing Lebanese army officer to set up an 'Independent Free Lebanon' in the south next to their frontier, policing it with his South Lebanon Army (SLA), but when the Syrians retaliated by taking over much of the northeast of the country, including the Baka'a Valley, Israeli forces once again moved into Lebanon in June 1982. The limited objectives of this invasion soon escalated into a war to crush the PLO. By August the Palestinians were in a desperate position, with more than 6,000 of them trapped in the capital, Beirut. US intervention enabled a cease-fire to be agreed, under which a multinational peace force from France, Italy, Britain and the USA was sent to Beirut to bring about the withdrawal of foreign troops from Lebanese soil. Israel embarked on talks with Lebanon and, though the Syrians refused to co-operate, came to an agreement under which they were to withdraw from the vicinity of Beirut. By September 30,000 of them were redeployed in the south where, with the support of the SLA, they continued to police the country. Thus, by the end of 1983 the multinational force was able to arrange the withdrawal from Beirut of Yasser Arafat and the PLO, under which he went to Tunis and they were dispersed amongst a number of Middle Eastern countries.

Throughout 1984 and 1985 a bitter and confused struggle took place in Beirut to create a stable government, but all endeavours met with limited success. Fighting continued across the 'green line' separating the two parts of the city – the Christians in East Beirut and the Muslims in West Beirut. Sometimes there was fighting between the rival militias of the Shi'ite and the Sunni Muslims. By the time the multinational force withdrew in 1985, Lebanon was effectively divided

❝Up-to-date information would be valuable here.❞

into three: the north and east of the country, largely controlled by the Syrians; the area around Beirut, barely under the very shaky control of a creaking Lebanese government and its army; and the southern part of the country, which was still occupied by Israel. The Israelis embarked on a slow and cautious withdrawal, but from time to time fighting spluttered into action along the frontier. PLO forces, too, began to trickle back into the country. So there was every reason for Israel to regard Lebanon as one of the many unfinished items of business on its agenda.

IDEAS AND PRINCIPLES

DISPLACED PERSONS

These are often the victims of war or civil unrest. Moved from their homes, they may lose all their belongings and often become refugees. If they have no papers they may lose their rights, and if they are unable to find a country willing to accept their entry they may become stateless.

THIRD WORLD

The first and second worlds are those of the East and West, sometimes known as the 'communist bloc' and the 'free world', i.e. the states supporting the former Soviet Union or those supporting the USA. The Third World comprises the politically non-aligned countries, many of them the developing countries of the Afro-Asian bloc, e.g. India.

WHITE PAPER

A government publication dealing with a particular problem and often advancing a solution to it recommended by the experts who have been investigating it; similar to the reports of royal commissions, which are produced as Command Papers, or Blue Books (so called because of the colour of their covers).

ZIONISM

This was a movement for the return of the Jews to Palestine, a reaction against the policies of anti-Semitism commonly practised in Europe in the nineteenth and twentieth centuries. Launched by Theodore Herzl, under whose inspiration the first Zionist Congress was held in Basle in 1897. During the First World War one of its leaders, Chaim Weizmann, won British support for the movement at the time of the Balfour Declaration.

APPLIED MATERIALS

Texts and Atlases

G.B. Regan, *Israel and the Arabs*, Cambridge, 1987

R.N. Rundle, *International Affairs, 1939–79*, Hodder & Stoughton, 1981 Chapter 15.

John Simkin, *The Arab-Israeli Conflict*, Spartacus, 1985

M. Scott-Baumann, *Conflict in the Middle East: Israel and the Arabs*, Arnold, 1987

J.K.G. Taylor and J.A. Kohler, *Africa and the Middle East*, Arnold, 1984

Evidence and source-based

H. Browne, *Suez and Sinai*, Longman, 1971

Bill Mandle, *Conflict in the Promised Land*, Heinemann, 1976

Cassette/filmstrip programmes

Audio Learning, *The Arab–Israel Conflict, 1948-80*, PA/1270/18
Audio Learning, *Birth of Israel*, DM 12
Audio Learning, *The Middle East, 1900–1945*, PA/1268/18

EXAMINATION QUESTION

Study Sources A, B and C and then answer Questions (a) to (g) which follow.

Source A (1967)

line 1   'We are now ready to confront Israel. The Israelis have claimed many things about the 1956 war, but none of these are believed now that the secrets of the 1956 collusion have been uncovered – that means collusion in which Israel took part. Now we are ready for the confrontation. We are now ready to deal with the entire Palestine
line 5   question.'

Source B (1972)

'My name is Ghazi David and I am twenty-four years old. I was born in Nazareth, but today I am stateless. In May 1948 when I was nine months old my family was forced to leave our beloved land.

'The aggressive war of June 1967 was the second decisive landmark in my
line 10   life. The new expansion of Israel and the new waves of refugees multiplied the tragedy many times. The two most cherished ideals of my people are to remain Palestinians and not be refugees. I am left with no alternative but to fight our oppressor. That is why I have joined the Palestine National Liberation Movement.'

Source C

Interviewer: Is there any possible way that Israel could absorb the large number of
line 15   Arabs whose territory it has gained control of now?
Moshe Dayan: Economically we can. But I think that is not in accord with our aims for the future....We want to have a Jewish state. We can absorb them, but then it won't be the same country.
Interviewer: And it is necessary to maintain this as a Jewish state and purely a
line 20   Jewish state?
Moshe Dayan: Absolutely, absolutely. We want a Jewish state.

(a)   Describe in your own words the attitude of the speaker in Source A towards ***the 1956 war*** (line 2).(2 marks)

(b)   What were the secrets referred to in line 2?(2 marks)

(c)   The speaker in Source A says that Israel has claimed many things about ***the 1956 war*** (line 2). Describe two of the things which Israel might have claimed.(2 marks)

(d)   (i) Is the person who spoke the words from which Source B is taken pro-Israel or anti-Israel?(1 mark)
    (ii) Give one piece of evidence from Source B which supports your answer to (d)(i). (1 mark)

(e)   By reference to both the causes and the events of the 1967 war, show to what extent the speaker was correct in describing the war as ***aggressive*** (line 9). (4 marks)

(f)   (i) What position did Moshe Dayan hold at the time of the interview given in Source C?(1 mark)
    (ii) Why was Dayan so determined to establish ***a Jewish state*** (line 17)? (2 marks)

(g)   Sources A and B take one view of events in the Middle East; Source C takes another view.
    (i) Quote an example from each source to show the different viewpoints; and
    (ii) indicate the value to the historian of these different viewpoints.

(5 marks)
(ULEAC)

TUTOR'S ANSWER

(a)   He is militantly hostile to Israel, asserts that there was collusion with the western powers (which was denied at the time) and that the uncovering of this secret discredits anything which Israel may have said.

(b)   This refers to the secret pact made at Sèvres in October 1956 under which Britain and France assured Israel of their solidarity with the Israeli cause, and promised to assist them and thus recover the control of the Suez Canal Zone and of the canal itself.

(c)   That Israel was under constant threat from large numbers of refugees (about 200,000 altogether) encamped in the Gaza Strip, many of them armed and desperate; that there had been a propaganda offensive by Nasser against Israel and a state of undeclared war for two years; and that Israel was merely acting in self-defence.

(d)   (i)   Anti-Israeli.

     (ii) 'I am left with no alternative but to fight our oppressor.'

(e)   ***Causes***: The war appeared to be an aggressive one on the part of Israel, since it was designed as a 'pre-emptive strike' against neighbouring Arab states; but the Israelis would have claimed that it was provoked by anti-Israeli attitudes on the parts of the Arab states, and that fundamentally it was they who bore the grudges.

    Events: The war itself showed ample evidence of Israeli aggressiveness. The Egyptian air force was destroyed on the ground at the start of the war, and fast-moving Israeli columns soon reached El Arish and Sharm-el-Sheikh. Defeating the Egyptians at Abu Aweigila, the Israelis closed in on El Nakhl, smashing the Egyptian forces as they tried to escape through the Mitla Pass. At the same time, Israeli troops occupied the West Bank and seized the whole of Jerusalem; meanwhile Israeli armoured forces in the north advanced from Galilee into the Golan Heights and pushed the Syrians back to within twenty miles of their capital, Damascus.

(f)   (i)   He was the Israeli minister of defence.

     (ii) He preferred a purely Jewish state to one that had under its control a large number of non-Jewish people. Although he believed that Israel was capable economically of absorbing non-Jews, this was not 'in accord with our aims for the future', and he preferred a purely Jewish solution. He does not give reasons for this; but it may be inferred from the context that since the Jews themselves had in the past often been a down-trodden minority people, they wanted to avoid inflicting the same on others.

(g)   (i)   Sources A and B are pro-Arab, whilst Source C is pro-Israeli. Source A: 'we are now ready to confront Israel'. Source B: 'I have joined the Palestine National Liberation Movement'. Source C: 'Absolutely. We want a Jewish state.'

     (ii) They are important because they illustrate the two sides of the case: Source A shows the militancy of the pro-Arab movement, whilst Source B explains the underlying reasons for the feelings of hostility. On the other hand, Source C shows the determination of the Zionist Israeli adherents, and illustrates their purely nationalist objectives.

SUGGESTIONS FOR FURTHER WORK

1. Construct a detailed map of Israel as it is at present, and within its boundaries mark out the territories originally allotted to the new state by the UN in 1947. Make a table to show how Israel secured control over the other territories: Why? How? When?

2. Collect photographs of modern Jerusalem and, if possible, a street-plan of the city. How do you explain its very special status for both the Muslim and Jewish communities? Tip: start with E.G. Rayner, International Affairs, Arnold, page 181.

3. The plight of the displaced Palestinian refugees has produced an Arab terrorist movement, with numerous terrorist societies, each with slightly different aims. Find out what you can about these and write notes on:

    Lydda Airport battle, 1972
    Munich Olympics killings, 1972
    Entebbe raid, 1976
    Beirut massacres, 1982.

4. Find out what you can about the plight of the Ethiopian Falasha in 1984 leading to **Operation Moses**. Why did the operation produce the results that it did in Israel and amongst the Arab countries?

STUDENT'S ANSWER – EXAMINER'S COMMENTS

Question

It is late in 1972 and there is to be an international conference. This conference will discuss events of recent years to do with the Middle East. These events are the high-jacking of aircraft to Jordan in 1970, the shootings at Tel Aviv airport, and the attack on Israeli athletes at the Munich Olympic Games.

(a) Write a draft of a speech to be made by a representative of the Palestine Liberation Organization. The speech will justify these actions.

(b) Write a draft of a speech to be made by a representative of the Knesset (the Israeli Parliament). The speech will attempt to persuade the conference to condemn these actions.

(30 marks) (SEG)

❝Not without appropriate feeling, but rather long as an introduction to this very specific question.❞

(a) The Jews have no right in morals or in law to be in Palestine and they ought to be thrown out immediately and by force if necessary. If a man comes into your house and steals your silver spoons you don't sit down with him at the table in order to consider how many of them to give back to you and how many he ought to be allowed to keep as a reward for his work; you send for a policeman and have him locked up. It is the same with our country, Palestine. The country belongs to us. We have been here for hundreds of years, and the Jews are newcomers who we should never have allowed to enter in the first place. Our brothers and our relatives have been turned out of their lands which have been theirs for ages and the Jews have cheated us and abused us and now they have turned us out of the homes we live in. We hold the view that Palestine should be for the Palestinians!

❝The tone of this paragraph seems quite different from the first paragraph. It is a straightforward narrative account and has no empathy; i.e. the writer is unlikely to mention 'indignation' and the 'alarming' nature of hi-jacks.❞

❝This is transparently thin and contains almost no information. It is an effort to make bricks without straw.❞

❝This is the best effort in the answer to combine the facts with empathy; otherwise the answer seems to keep the history and the empathy in different compartments. Overall, the answer is well written.❞

Aircraft high-jackings became common around 1970. In 1970 an aircraft flying over the Middle East was high-jacked by high-jackers and was forced to fly away from the course it was then flying, in spite of what its captain and crew wished and to fly to Jordan, where it landed. The incident caused great indignation, especially amongst the people of the country from which the plane originally came. It proved to be not the last of a number of high-jack attempts, all of which at the time seemed very alarming.

In 1972 the Popular Front for the Liberation of Palestine claimed responsibility for the killing of 26 people and the wounding of over 70 others at Lydda Airport in Israel. Our heroes in 'Black September' struck again later that summer when they executed eleven Israeli athletes at the Olympic Games in Munich. The outside world may have considered them to be innocent, as many of our expelled Palestinian brethren are innocent, but this act of retribution brought to the world's notice the plight of our countrymen and was a necessary act. Sadly five of our men were shot. The three other Palestinians arrested after the demonstration were later released by the West German authorities, and this is a triumphant vindication of the justice of our national cause. How can the world fail to see how our country calls out for deliverance and justice?

(b) Ran out of time.

❝This is inexcusable. An over-extended answer in one part, followed by such a lame confession will limit you to about half the marks available. You must take care to distribute your time properly between answers.❞

INDEX